Praise for *I Wish I Knew This Years Ago*

"Why didn't anyone tell me this stuff before?"
—Wade A.

"Now I know that I know."
—Brian S.

"I wish I had this information earlier."
—Danny W.

"Every entrepreneur needs Firmstride to achieve financial
well-roundedness."
—Lori W.

"As a business owner, I had always heard there were tax advantages.
I had just not known the details. Firmstride explained and helped us
navigate them."
—Tanis J.

"Firmstride helped us get control of our cash flow with a straightforward
cash management system that has given us a sense of security and level
of freedom. The budget stress in our marriage morphed into enjoyable
spending with peace."
—Keith W.

I Wish I Knew This Years Ago

How Small Business Owners Can Save Money on Taxes, Buy Passive Income, and Gain Unshakeable Confidence in the Future

NICK WARREN

Dock Media
Albuquerque, NM

I Wish I Knew This Years Ago copyright © 2025 by Nick Warren

Dock Media
Albuquerque, New Mexico

Publisher's Cataloging-in-Publication

    Names: Warren, Nick (Nicholas John), author.
    Title: I wish I knew this years ago : how small business owners can save money on taxes, buy passive income, and gain unshakeable confidence in the future / Nick Warren.
    Description: Albuquerque, NM : Dock Media, [2025] | Includes bibliographical references.
    Identifiers: ISBN: 9798998673528 (hardcover) | 9798998673511 (softcover) | 9798998673504 (ebook) | 9798998673535 (audiobook)
    Subjects: LCSH: Small business--Taxation--United States. | Small business--Finance--United States. | Business enterprises--Taxation--Law and legislation--United States. | Deferred credit. | Success in business.
    Classification: LCC: HD2346.U5 W37 2025 | DDC: 336.2070973--dc23

This book is dedicated to my wife, Monica, my best friend and the love of my life.

Contents

Tell Me What You Think

Let other readers know what you thought of *I Wish I Knew This Years Ago*. Please write an honest review for this book on your favorite online bookshop.

★ ★ ★ ★ ★

What's Next?

Wealthy business owners understand that various tax codes exist and that they can legally choose which one to use so they pay the least in taxes. You may not have known you have that choice. This is why you feel like you've been fighting with one hand tied behind your back and are over-paying your taxes. In this book, you'll discover how to select the right tax code to reduce your taxes—and how to build the systems to do it.

CHAPTER 1

"HOW COME NO ONE TOLD ME THIS BEFORE?"

When Cory and Anya got married and started a business, they had no idea that they had set themselves up for failure.

Cory grew up in California in a family barely scraping by; Dad framed houses for a living. Anya had immigrated to the United States at age ten. And while they both had hardscrabble backgrounds, they were also the first in their respective families to attend college, own their home, and now, to own a business. And early success upgraded this power couple into serial entrepreneurs—they got *one* business off the ground and agreed they shared an intuitive "feel" for how to market and grow anything from scratch. Anything!

They were not about to forget their humble beginnings, however. At the outset of their marriage, they didn't earn a lot of money, even with two incomes, and debt weighed them both down. Fortunately, the church where they were active helped them create a realistic budget, pay off their debt, and learn financial self-control, aka "delayed gratification."

So when Cory and Anya went all "build it and they will come" with a car wash, and lo and behold they, the customers, did, they jumped on the chance to acquire a nearby dry cleaning company. The owner wanted to retire, Cory and Anya wanted serial entrepreneurship. Win-win. And so the couple expected that the straightforward business and startup skills that served them so well in clearing their debts would help them manage businesses one and two simultaneously.

Things started to pick up with the businesses. Cory and Anya paid themselves a salary from the two businesses that was just enough to pay bills and eat out nice once in a while while paying down their debt. They used the technique their church was promoting—placing literal, actual cash into different envelopes: gas, groceries, phone bill, rent, etc.

As their income—and savings—started to grow, Cory and Anya exchanged physical envelopes for virtual ones, opening different checking accounts instead. But that soon ballooned out of proportion.

Eventually, they were dealing with forty-three (!) separate checking accounts to handle all the different categories of expenses they would cover. Anya had to monitor all the bank accounts all the time, and sometimes, the balance would drop dangerously close to zero. Even when they later consolidated into one checking account and multiple credit cards to simplify, they still felt out-of-control—and overwhelmed.

Let's zoom out from budgeting for a moment. You see, Cory and Anya had always paid themselves through their paychecks, that is, paychecks issued by their businesses and made out to each of them personally. Their accountant, whom they'd found through a local referral, had not explained how to "take a draw," what that even meant, or how to figure out how much they could in the first place (or second or third). While Cory and Anya could read their profit and loss (P&L) report from their books, they never learned about a "balance sheet" or "statement of cash flows." They saw no need for learning about those because the P&L each month showed that they were making money. Good enough, right?

Wrong.

So wrong.

Big mistake, even.

Because then the unexpected happened. As it always does. In March of one particular year, Cory and Anya's accountant sent them their draft tax return. They skimmed down to the "amount owed"—and they were shocked. And unprepared. And shocked.

Cory and Anya owed $165,000 in federal taxes and $35,000 more in state taxes. This tax bill was bigger than they had paid themselves on their paychecks for the entire prior year. Their checking account's full balance would not even cover the state tax due.

How was this even possible? What could they do to get their tax bill down? Anything? Or was it too late?

Cory and Anya knew something was wrong, obviously, if this could have happened without any warning or updates or . . . anything. They were frustrated and confused, and money was now a big issue—not something they could ignore. It was not just a business problem it was a stress-in-our-marriage problem. This is **not** what they were supposed to see from owning their own business. So what changed?

Well, something had to change, for sure. The couple started holding back money they would have used for experiences with their two young kids, and they stopped donating money to their church. They considered selling one of the businesses, with also, perhaps, Cory getting a W-2 job at a local company so they could get a regular and routine paycheck and make this money issue go away, but they both knew that would be the wrong solution. Cory and Anya loved running a small business, and they wanted to figure it out.

In the end—or should I say the beginning?—Cory and Anya found a guide who taught them that wealthy business owners understand that various tax codes exist and that they can legally choose which one to use so they pay the least in taxes. They had no idea they had such a choice and they had been fighting all along with one hand tied behind their back. They needed the proven systems and strategies to use the tax codes that would be best for their situation. Those systems supported a better way to spend, earn, save, and live. **Cory and Anya** . . .

- **Learned to correctly read and interpret their profit and loss, balance sheet, and statement of cash flows to understand what was going on with their business.**
- Learned how their paychecks affect their taxes and reduced their wages immediately to mitigate taxes. They made up the difference with a draw and realized they could have been taking more money out of the business for *many* years prior. This is

an example of how they shifted income from one tax code to another that was more favorable.

- **Discovered (and implemented) other ways to *legally* reduce their taxes.**
- Began planning for and setting aside cash to cover their upcoming big cash needs. They also got better at predicting those needs, including quarterly estimated tax payments and the April true-up payment. No more tax surprises.
- **Contacted their financial advisor and set up a SIMPLE 401(k), which helped them attract and retain employees while providing them a way to save for their future.**
- Learned how to manage the income from their businesses and channel it towards building passive income through a brokerage account managed by their financial advisor while also donating money through a Donor Advised Fund (DAF) so they could support their church and local charities.

Everything changed for Cory and Anya. It started with the desire to solve a problematic tax bill. But in the end, it was much more than that. It was about how to manage family cash, how to understand—and thus manage—taxes, how to pay themselves better, and how to make their business work for the family and not the other way around. Cory and Anya *almost* learned all this too late after financial disaster hit.

But they didn't. They found their guide just in time.

That guide was **Firmstride**.

And I'm its founder.

Hello.

So Who Am I?

My name is Nick Warren. I am founder of Firmstride. I've spent nineteen years climbing the corporate ladder of a Fortune 500 technology company after I earned an electrical engineering degree. From the outside, I was a successful mid-level manager with a good salary, RSUs, job stability, good health insurance and a number of good professional wins under my belt.

But something inside me was restless. I wanted to help improve marriages by helping people with finances and more freedom for myself and my family. Deep down, I knew the only way to get what I wanted was to **own a business**.

I caught the entrepreneur bug, and I couldn't be cured. So I took the leap. I left the comfortable world of corporate America to pursue my dreams of being an entrepreneur. I wanted all the things entrepreneurs dream of—bigger impact, higher income, freedom of time, and the thrill of seeing the direct impact of my own effort on my own success.

It was both difficult and exhilarating. In my first business, I expected to find all the answers I needed from the team of advisors I had assembled. These were people I either knew or was connected to via my personal network—my accountant, attorney, banker, and financial advisor. These were the experts, the people who were supposed to guide me through the financial and legal mazes of business ownership so I could come out the other side with my dreams come true.

I asked them all a simple but crucial question: *How could I save money on taxes and generate wealth beyond what I could have achieved in corporate America?* After all, that was one of the main reasons I jumped ship. I had made the leap of faith hoping that these people would be able to point me in the right direction.

But to my surprise, not *one* of them had a good answer. Not even one. The best advice I got? "Donate more to charity. Tax write-off." Yep, that was it. Where were all the tax savings I had heard about from owning a business? How were wealthy families paying so much less in taxes? It wasn't that these professionals weren't knowledgeable. In fact, they were each great in their own domains.

Somehow I intuitively felt that wealthy people knew something I did not. It wasn't until later that I discovered the difference was in knowing how to play the tax game. And not just knowing how to play the game but **to choose the right rules to play by**.

You mean you can select the rules? Yes.

And I learned that if you're going to select the rules to play by, why not select the rules that work to your advantage?

Your accountant and lawyer may know that you can select which rules to play by to maximize your advantage. But can they help you get it done? Your accountant, attorney and financial advisor are each trained, certified and incentivized (paid) to stay in their lane (provide laser-focused advice exclusively from their one own profession based on the tax code that pertains to their work). I discovered that it didn't occur to my advisor team that the answer to my desire for tax savings actually lies in changing the rules by which I was playing. Just acknowledging that there are multiple tax codes from which you legally choose never came up.

And then I went to work in the family office industry. This is a small boutique industry that takes care of all the financial challenges faced by an uber-wealthy family. I worked in a firm that catered to multiple families on the smaller side of the range that still operated their business day-to-day. I learned that the whole time I had been trying to build my family wealth I had been playing by a set of tax rules that were **optional**. I was actually free to play by whichever rules resulted in the smallest tax bill. And it was 100 percent legal. Wealthy people know this and they use that knowledge to make the decisions that result in them keeping more of their money.

I developed the **Family Wealth System**. This system to manage wealth covers everything-from managing your advisors to protecting your assets to the fullest extent of the law, to minimizing tax risks to generating sustainable passive income streams. Wow—that's a lot. And it's all not just ideas—it's a system of tools, processes and tasks that integrate all the different elements of wealth for a business-owning family into something that consistently delivers real results. Covering the whole Family Wealth System is beyond the scope of this book.

So we'll focus on those last two items, which take top priority: tax law (pain avoidance) and passive income (pleasure seeking). I'll show you how to protect yourself from situations like Cory and Anya had to face. I'll show you how to keep making money even after you've retired, whatever that looks like for you. This holistic, systematic, process-driven approach is what no one advisor—or team of advisors—could offer me, and it's what I wish I had when I first started out as an entrepreneur making money.

So let's do that. Let's make more money—and save more money. And to get into that, I have a question for you.

Where Do You Hurt?

OK, I lied. I have *several* questions for you. In no particular order:

- Do you feel like you are paying more than your fair share of taxes?
- Do you get surprised by your tax bill in April?
- Do you want to be more confident about making proper estimated quarterly tax payments so you have more control over your final tax bill in April?
- Do you want to get just enough understanding so that you can know that you are taking the right steps to build and protect the wealth you're generating in your business?
- Do you have a plan for what will happen when you no longer want to operate your business?
- Do you have a great advisor team (accountant, attorney, financial advisor, banker, and insurance agents)?

If two or more of your answers to those questions felt uncomfortable, there may be a problem. Or at least a concern. Maybe a "to-do" for the list. For "someday."

Well, I'll tell you this: A lot of business owners don't know they have a problem until something really bad happens. Here's a few real examples of *really bad*:

- You get your tax bill in April and it is more money than you paid yourself last year in total. This problem may destroy your personal finances and you could have seen it coming and handled it smoothly without any stress.

Where in the world did these astronomical numbers come from?

- You are busting your ass in your business and crushing it according to your Profit and Loss statement. But your personal bank account just isn't going up. Your wife is asking you if keeping the business is worth it and she's starting to secretly open credit cards on the side to make ends meet. And then one month, you don't have enough to pay your mortgage, and it's painfully obvious to the ones that you love that you do not have it together.

Why isn't all that money you think you're generating making it into your personal bank account?

- Your business is generating $100,000 per month in profit, and your family is living comfortably at $55,000 per month covering living expenses, taxes, and philanthropy. This leaves about $45,000 at the end of the month. You don't know what to do with it and are afraid of making the wrong move. So to be safe, you've been just stockpiling the cash in your business operating account. You know you shouldn't do that but . . . the fear of making a huge costly mistake with the money is preventing you from taking action. After years and years of this approach, you realize all that saved money has earned next to no interest, it's lost purchasing power thanks to inflation, and it's too late to work the magic of compound interest all those idle years.

Why didn't anyone tell you how to channel all that cash into some kind of investment that actually gave you a return that you could live off so you had more options with your business?

- A customer comes into your business, falls because a chair broke she was sitting on, hits her head and gets seriously hurt, and decides to sue your business. Your attorney informs you that you could lose the business and the building if you lose the case and are liable. You realize you should have set up your business entities differently and now it's too late.

How can you protect yourself from these kinds of risks and liabilities?

- Someone tells you about a tax-saving tip that could have saved you $150,000 off your taxes last year. You research it on the internet and it looks like it might have worked. But then your CPA tells you that you missed the opportunity.

Whose job was it to identify that tax tip before? Should you be mad at someone about it?

How to Solve These Problems Before They Become Problems

Remember I said I sought out to solve my own problem? I did—and solved a whole lot more in the process.

I'm an engineer that likes to solve the root cause of problems. Over time I learned approaches and methods to solve the problems I was facing myself as an entrepreneur, a husband and father. I was fortunate to have a wife who was supportive and patient since learning these by trial and error took many years. It's likely she's become a saint in the process.

My Family Wealth System came about as I collected and integrated the methods, concepts and processes created by others; I figured out what actually worked for my family running a successful business. It took me many years and shouldn't have to take you that long.

While I learned through trial and error, you don't have to. I learned from my mistakes, so that you can learn from my mistakes when it comes to taxes and passive income.

Where did I learn these techniques and models from?

I studied the basics of business management as a mid-level manager in corporate America. I learned business operating models such as Balanced

Scorecard (created by Dr. Robert Kaplan and Dr. David Norton) and the Entrepreneurial Operating System®, or EOS (created by Gino Wickman). I crave systems and processes that are repeatable and work for real families - like mine - that aren't perfect.

But I also learned from others. Evan, my first financial advisor, who we worked with from 2000 when my wife and I were two W-2 employees at a growing tech company in Austin, Texas, to 2017 when he retired, taught us to manage our cash and how to implement a financial system (i.e. cash management, giving, and channeling money to passive income). We saw and experienced how Evan's simple system yielded a better outcome than simply trying to achieve our "number" or some other financial goal each month. I also joined a firm in the family office industry that had developed their own system for managing the wealth of the firm's clients. I got to see how high net worth families (the term used in the industry) integrate different parts of a financial ecosystem to achieve outcomes not otherwise obvious in any one specific domain.

I saw how simple choices—like which tax code to use for your income—could make a huge difference over time.

And of course I figured it out as I was going. I started my first business from "ground up" in October 2016 with a great partner, and I learned all about running a small business and the complexity that comes from trade-offs made with family finances. This is when I started to experience frustration working with my advisors on my finances. We got lucky to get (and follow) good advice and I experienced how personal finances within the context of a business family are different from what the typical family experiences.

I have been on "both sides of the fence." I've been the advisor and the advised. But now? I've decided to articulate the system I have personally experienced and found to work because I want to help families that own and operate a business to thrive.

Who Is This Book For?

Maybe you've picked this up wanting to start a side hustle. Maybe you're looking to just make a few bucks here and there. This book isn't for that, it's for serious entrepreneurs that earn $200,000 to $2 million dollars per year in total taxable income from their business. Most of the systems in this book won't be useful to anyone outside that range or who doesn't operate a business.

If you fit that bill, congratulations! This book is going to help you . . .

- Save money on taxes so that every April isn't as painful.
- Control cash flows from your business to your personal accounts, so that you have what you need when you need it.
- Create sustainable passive income, so that when you decide you want to do something different you can step away from your business.
- Manage risk of loss of the hard-earned money from your business.
- And all of this will contribute to peace of mind, moving from a feeling of not knowing what you are doing to a feeling of confidence that you do indeed know that you know and have the team in place to make it happen. You'll have less fear about the future, since you'll know that you have what you need for your family's future. And with the knowledge of what is actually going on, you'll have increased confidence in your advisor team.

And while before I'd offer these as part of my Family Wealth System coaching, now we're opening up these outcomes to more people, through the book you hold in your hands!

But Why This Book?

So, why is this book worth reading when it's not the first (and won't be the last) book on small business money management?

I've seen a pattern play out all too often—business owners are good at their business and they are not good at knowing enough about how to handle the wealth their business generates. Why is this the case? I have some ideas.

- Business owners aren't *taught* this stuff. No school teaches these basic concepts in an integrated fashion in business-owner speak. Families with massive amounts of wealth pay hefty sums to specialized advisors who know this kind of stuff. But it doesn't have to be that way. I believe business owners at all levels can get just enough understanding (I like the English word *sufficient*) to effectively protect their own family interests.
- Many advisors do not work effectively across disciplines because they don't have the knowledge and often can't take the time to develop it. Certifications and licenses held by those advisory professionals typically do not encourage or even allow working across the diverse disciplines that impact a typical business owner's family, much as those professionals may want to.
- A lot of business owners think their advisors are responsible for the big decisions that directly impact their and their family's financial success. *Isn't your accountant responsible for making sure your taxes are right?* No! They just make sure the form is filled out correctly based on what you tell them. Whose fault is it if you forget to tell them something? *You're responsible for your own financial well-being.*

But there's another reason business owners often fail at managing their own wealth. They try to learn on their own using the internet and they give up. So many articles about personal finance are using information to sell a professional service, and they overcomplicate it. "This is so important but so complicated, you have no chance of understanding how to do this complicated thing that you absolutely must do! Did we mention it's really complicated? You should just hire us to do it for you!"

Here's an example. Go find an article about the importance of a will and odds are good that the article makes it feel so difficult to parse out on your own. So just "Click the link at the bottom to schedule a free 30-minute consultation with one of our experts!" The sale is made by telling you, "It's tricky, but you know it's important, so we can help you navigate this."

The complexity holds you back from making progress. Did you know many states accept holographic wills? What's that? It means hand-written. If you knew that your state accepted handwritten wills, you could decide for yourself and you would know that you know the answer. You might decide to just find an online template for a will, write it out by hand in ten minutes, and get'r done—then come back to a more advanced estate plan later with all the bells and whistles. Do you think there's a law firm website out there that suggests such an approach since it doesn't cost you a penny?[1]

Now imagine having sufficient understanding of your business financial statements, taxes, business entities and passive income so that you know that you know and you have the right team of advisors in place to get the work done. You *get* it. There are no surprises. And no anxiety over potential surprises. You can plan. And the plans are not guesses or goals. You work a system. And the system works.

That said, there's going to be a lot for us to cover in order to get you up the learning curve on the Family Wealth System. At many points in this book, you will probably wish this was a two-way conversation. Ask questions, get feedback for your situation, go deeper into new topics, make sure you're doing it right, etc. Well, it can be! You may want to get training or coaching from Firmstride, my training coaching firm, which you can learn more about at firmstride.us.

But before we delve into what to do differently, let's start with identifying (and avoiding) what *not* to do. How do we make our tax liability small? Here's how to get there. And we're going to get there by *thinking big*. Perhaps bigger than you have ever thought about taxes before.

---

1 - One of the frameworks I love and use is the **Four Stages of Competency**. This framework helps us feel good about knowing we don't know. At Firmstride, we move all clients from unconscious incompetence (we didn't even know we didn't know) to conscious competence (we know just enough to be "dangerous"). And along the way, we'll make sure you have the right *who's* to execute and keep you on the tracks towards managed taxes and channeled passive income.

CHAPTER 2

WHAT EVERY SMALL BUSINESSOWNERWANTS (NO, NOT THAT)

S am and Teresa own a business-to-business (B2B) business that offers short- and long-term commercial equipment rentals. In early 2023, they had ten employees for whom they did their best to make their company a great place to work with health insurance and a 401(k), which their financial advisor helped them set up. That same year, Sam and Teresa got a big, unexpected break when a competitor in the area shut down. Sam jumped at the opportunity and bought most of their equipment inventory. It was a huge gamble but likely to pay off since their potential customer base had effectively just doubled.

Leading up to that calculated risk, Sam and Teresa's business had made money each year. But with the equipment investment in 2023 and its depreciation, the year was barely profitable from a cash perspective—and a big loss from a tax perspective.

They leaned heavily into sales late in 2023, which bore first fruit in early 2024 when they won a number of substantial rental contracts because of their expanded offering. They had never made this kind of money before and so much of it was going right back into the business. Half way into this record year, Sam started to worry about the taxes he knew they would owe. So he and his wife started to look for help because they were investing all their spare cash back into the business.

The couple asked their tax preparer what they could do to lower their tax bill before they got it. "Give more to charity." Really? OK. So then they asked their financial advisor what they should do. He introduced them to a financial coach who specialized in helping business owners with their taxes.

The coach interviewed Sam and Teresa, and during the initial call, Sam shared that his biggest concern was to reduce the current-year tax bill. After a few questions from the coach about the business, Sam admitted that he wasn't sure he had everything set up properly and that he often felt out of control. Sam kept coming back to the issue looming on the horizon—taxes. The business was growing so fast they had never faced these kinds of issues before.

After a few meetings, and after reviewing the family's situation, the coach discovered the truth of the matter. The family would indeed owe a lot in taxes; the solution was not going to be a simple checkbox on their tax return. The save-money-on-taxes solution needed to have been implemented years prior. The family had never selected the right tax code or implemented any of the strategies that would reduce their taxes. As a result of not making those decisions they had always overpaid and the pain hadn't become real until their business had grown. Because the family had not carefully selected which tax code they wanted to use they didn't make the next decision correctly—their business entities. The entities were not selected properly to take full advantage of the tax code for the nature of the business they were operating. In addition to not being tax efficient, the business entity was not providing thorough legal protection to the family or isolating the risks between the businesses.

The family also didn't have a method for controlling cash flow from the business into the family accounts. Like many entrepreneurial families, they had a lot of chaos, and they assumed someone else would eventually "sort it all out." The business was paying for many of the family's living expenses. While they knew they should separate their business and personal finances, Sam and Teresa didn't understand the tax rules they were playing by and *to what extent* they needed to separate expenses, or what steps they should take to do that. So they had decided to simplify everything and just run as many expenses as possible through the business. They didn't know if this was good or bad and they didn't know what strategies might work or not for saving money on taxes. But the fact that they didn't know, they knew for sure was bad.

The couple had other issues controlling the cash from the business. They did know they had to run payroll (their tax preparer had told Sam to do that) and so had been paying themselves as much as possible to cover their family living expenses. Neither understood how their wage or their draw affected their total tax bill. In short, they didn't understand how to select the tax codes that would be best for their situation.

It gets worse. Sam and Teresa also didn't know how to estimate current and future tax payments. They had never earned a significant profit in years prior beyond what their payroll withholding would cover, so they didn't know whether they needed to make quarterly estimated tax payments (and they did).

They regularly reviewed their profit and loss and the business was earning profit. They wondered if they were really making any progress overall. Because they didn't understand their balance sheet they had no way to know or track their progress.

"A successful and growing business can hide a lot of underlying problems."
— Ash Razdan, Global M&A Consultant

Saving money on taxes is not about some trick on the tax return. Paying as little as possible in taxes is the outcome from

1. understanding that there are different tax codes from which you can choose to have your income taxed,
2. selecting the tax code that will minimize how much you owe and
3. maxing out the strategies that are allowable within that tax code while staying compliant.

For 2024, the family was able to use a few end-of-year strategies to save money on their tax bill. But because they had not made the right decisions in years prior about which tax code would be best for their situation, they were limited on how much they could save. The truth is that many decisions business owners need to make flow OUT OF the decision about which tax code to choose instead of the other way around. In the case of Sam and Teresa because they didn't choose the right tax code, they didn't have the right business entity design, didn't make the right decisions about how to run their payroll and didn't consider the right kind of qualified retirement plan to offer. They didn't understand how to make quarterly estimated tax payments or predict ahead of time what the result of their actions might be. And all of this went without notice until the big impact would come in 2025, when the business would grow to a new record and the pain became obvious and unbearable.

Where Entrepreneurial Fantasy Meets Reality—and How to Have Both

Many small business owners, if not most, become jaded on their journey. The pros of ownership and self-employment are far outweighed by the cons. Fantasizing and daydreaming about getting away, selling this thing, living the Tim Ferriss four-hour workweek. *Just get away . . .* Must be nice. But out of reach for most. Still, a brief mental vacation does a body good, and a brain.

But why do most business owners long for a break from their own business? And how can they finally get one without pressing *pause* on the entire thing? Both important questions—but these are symptoms, not root causes. This chapter is not about freedom from business obligations or building the right scale into your operations, but *why* there are such things desired. Usually, it's because the *pros* of entrepreneurship give way to the *cons* when the annual tax bill comes, those estimated quarterly payments are due, or penalties hit throughout the year without warning. And that's when all you want to do is "check out." The tax bill is *pain.* Uncertainty. Dread. I've not yet met a small business owner who didn't have a pit in their stomach when waiting for a draft return from their accountant. Enough years of this and it can feel easier to want to get away from the whole thing. But wouldn't it be better to just solve the root cause of the negative feelings? What if you didn't feel like your tax bill was a surprise? No more pit-of-stomach fear of the tax return? And what if you knew you were paying your fair share of taxes and not a penny more? What if you understood and selected the tax code that you wanted to use and you knew it was the best one for your family? Wouldn't that feeling of control and understanding provide unshakable confidence?

This is why I lead with the tax topic in this book—and for our private clients at Firmstride. I say, *zoom out* beyond just taxes. Yes, admittedly, the biggest bang for your buck from a book is to learn how to legally save money on taxes if at all possible and as often as possible so you needn't feel the daily need to just get a break from this thing you call your business.

But! Understanding taxes is *also* about a broader comprehension of how to retain more of your wealth . . . because taxes are likely your largest expense. So think of this as both a short-term and long-term impact on your ability to generate income, retain wealth, and outrun inflation as fast as possible.

So to reiterate: Saving money on taxes is all but a guaranteed return on investment of time, attention, and effort to learn how taxes *actually* work. But having a basic understanding of taxes *also* gives you a perspective on important business decisions because you learn how to optimize the entire system of your business. Now, we're not talking about making you as knowledgeable as a CPA; you need just enough knowledge to select which tax code is best for you and how to execute and optimize that decision.

Let the lessons begin.

It's Not All about Taxes; It's So Much More

To *mitigate* your taxes, you must first *manage* your taxes. Management covers understanding, planning, and yes, mitigating taxes. And management of taxes is a brother to *passive income* creation, which are together both empowered by *cash flow*. We want everything in this business set up in an organized fashion so taxes (and buying passive income) are rinse and repeat. So it goes like this, coming to understand your business so you "get it" when it comes to *everything else* that matters:

Manage taxes.

Mitigate taxes. Channel passive income.

Control your cash.

See? Zoom out.

Another benefit to this exercise—of reframing "lower tax bill" to "understand all the numbers in my business and how to adjust them"—is the greatest mind-shift of all, which is philanthropy. *Oh my God . . . I'm wealthy now!* This is where you will be and how you will live, live like you never thought possible; I'll help to bring you there. **So while tax mitigation is high-priority, it's actually the result of other activities and thus is not the most important discipline. Tax mitigation requires other foundations to be in place, such as cash control, proper entity structure, and a competent accountant.** Eventually in this book, we'll cover them all.

Now, coming back from *there* to *here*, the opening subject of taxes. To mitigate taxes you first have to understand how a business is taxed, which is not a one-tax-fits-all-sizes situation! So in the next chapter, we will talk about how businesses are taxed differently, why, and where your business fits into the picture.

A System for Everything

Back to Sam and Teresa. Working with their coach, the couple had a clear plan to get back on track with their business and their family finances overall. They completed the design of their business entity structure, finding a better model that not only fit their current needs but also allows for scaling as their business grows. They formed additional business entities and developed a plan to acquire real estate and lease it back to their operating business entities, all while protecting each entity from legal liabilities with separate control that all came back to the couple.

Sam and Teresa also organized their bank accounts and addressed concerns about cash held by the business. And of course, they also came to "grok" taxes, including how to calculate and make estimated tax payments even when their tax preparer wasn't accounting for the growth of their business. They also learned how to read both their business and personal tax returns, which led to (legally) reducing their taxes owed by $58,000 in 2024, with future savings coming year after year into the future. They will feel a larger impact in 2025 when their tax rate should drop from around 26 percent to approximately 20 percent, resulting in hundreds of thousands of dollars in tax savings in the years ahead. Of course, they are also able to well-predict their April true-up, make estimated tax payments (lower than had been previously), and take advantage of bonus and Section 179 depreciation (which you will soon learn all about) to bring overall taxes paid each year down even lower. All of this was done within a system they built to run their business and manage their family finances, a system that is repeatable and ensures everything works together smoothly. No more surprises.

In the midst of all this business education, Sam and Teresa also discovered how to collaborate more effectively as a married couple, managing the family's cash without feeling like they were cutting corners. This newfound teamwork empowered them to plan for upcoming cash needs with confidence—something Teresa particularly appreciated, knowing that Sam had everything under control and was providing for her.

Their lives changed forever. They're living the dream. All because they zoomed out from taxes. Firmstride was their trainer, coach, and sherpa.

CHAPTER 3

IF IT AIN'T BROKE, FIX IT ANYWAY (BECAUSE IT PROBABLY IS)

Matt grew up in northern California. In the 1960s, Matt's dad returned from military service, married Matt's mom, and started a soon-successful metal workshop to build industrial valves and custom pipe fittings. Within a few years, the company had twenty-five employees at the bench while Dad ran operations day-to-day. Meanwhile, Mom handled all financial matters and was *de facto* human resources director. In high school, Matt joined the company, cleaning and repairing the machines.

Having grown up in this gray collar family business, Matt decided to study mechanical engineering and would graduate college with a bachelor's degree. Instead of staying home, Matt entered employment at a publicly traded Fortune 500 company as an engineer. He got married, had kids, and earned promotions all the way up to mid-level marketing and sales manager for one of the company's most important product lines. But soon after Matt's fortieth birthday, his dad was diagnosed with a terminal illness. Matt and his wife knew one thing—Matt would have to take over the family business if it was to survive. So Matt left his corporate job to do just that.

Fortunately, Matt's father lived for another year. And during that precious time, he taught Matt everything he knew. Dad was a hands-on leader and found the perfect place for Matt's natural sales and operations talent. Matt quickly picked up on—and improved—how the company onboarded and delivered projects, thanks to his experience at the large corporation. When the time with his dad finally came to an end, Matt felt he could handle the business and hoped to even grow it beyond what his dad had been able to achieve.

Matt was now in charge as owner and CEO. His mom continued on in the business as the bookkeeper and HR manager; Matt took over everything else. The business continued at a steady pace because Matt was able to bring in new business and the team continued to execute well.

When Matt worked in corporate America as a mid-level manager, he earned around $225,000 a year with his salary and yearly bonus. But when Matt took over as family business CEO, he paid himself the same wage his dad had—$150,000 a year—and took the same monthly transfer out of the business account to his family account that his dad had been doing for years: $7,000 per month. This was about the same as Matt's old salary, adding up wages and the monthly transfers.

Everything went great the first year—until Matt got his tax return. That's when he finally saw the year's bill: almost $300,000. That was more than he had paid himself! The family tax preparer also notified Matt of enormous penalties he was liable for, which angered him. Why didn't anyone tell him? How could he have missed them? Something, clearly, was wrong.

Matt was desperate to get that federal tax bill lower the next year. Matt had previously thought that entering the family business would bring him the tax benefit of business ownership. But where was this benefit? And how could it be possible that he owed as much in taxes as he had earned?

Matt asked the family accountant what went wrong. But the accountant didn't think anything was wrong—which was even more alarming. Matt knew something was off, and he was desperate to find out what went wrong and how to solve it.

Matt had recently been introduced to a group of local business owners from his church that got together regularly for mutual support and skills training. In that group, Matt met someone whom he thought might be able to help. Over their first breakfast meeting together, Matt and this new mentor talked about what their businesses did, how they got into them, and how they were doing now. Matt's mentor asked Matt, "What type of entity is your business?" Matt was embarrassed to admit he didn't know. Within a few minutes, Matt went from feeling very proud of the family business to being uncertain he knew what he was doing at all. Dad had never talked about any of this; that year of focused training before his dad had passed was about how to work *in* the business, not *on* the business, to paraphrase the famous saying.

Matt's mom who did the books didn't know the answers either. She had always relied on the family accountant and attorney to handle those sorts of things. After all, they had been with the family since the 1960s when they had started out. She was just in charge of bookkeeping, running payroll, and taking care of personnel needs as they arose.

Matt next met with the family accountant, who explained that the business was set up to be taxed as a C-corporation. This was a decision Matt's dad had made in the 1960s when he started the business because he wanted to open a bank account. Matt figured out quickly that this was likely the biggest driver of his high tax bill. It turned out Matt didn't understand that he needed to make quarterly estimated tax payments for the business and for his family. While he was at corporate, he had withheld all his taxes from his paycheck. No one had ever explained to him how it worked for a business where he was the owner.

Matt also did not understand that the business needed to pay its own taxes. His dad had always told Matt's mom to make the estimated payments. She executed the payment and did not understand what they were or how they were calculated. So when Matt's dad was gone, she had not made any estimated tax payments for nearly a full year. Matt's dad never taught him about taxes or how they worked so it took a year for them to figure out that they were not taking the necessary steps.

Once they figured out what caused the problem, they were able to get on track. But what about the huge tax rate? Between the business and the family, they were paying nearly 35 percent in federal income taxes. They also owed more taxes for Federal Insurance Contributions Act (FICA), state, and property.

Matt learned that one of the drivers of their higher tax bill was indeed their C-corporation tax designation. Being a C-corporation was possibly the only option back when his dad started the business and no one ever re-evaluated the decision. Maybe it was time. It was possible to change from a C-corporation to something else. This was a complicated project because it would impact his taxes, his personal benefits, company inventory management, and Matt's tax filing schedule. It would also impact areas down the road and how he thought about the profits earned by the business. Every change would be significant.

After consulting with the family accountant, their business attorney, and Matt's mentor, Matt weighed the factors and decided it would be better in the long run to convert the family business from being taxed as a C-corporation to an S-corporation. It would in fact have been better had they converted before they bought their warehouse, but no one thought about it until now. That's just how these things usually go, but it doesn't need to be that way.

And that's what I told Matt.

A Mistake Nobody Knows Was Made

Before we proceed, I should tell you this:

For the sake of understanding and flow, from this point onwards, we are going to simplify—without compromising—the integrity of the concepts related to business entities. I didn't write this chapter for *your* specific business and family situation, so make sure you talk with someone who knows and understands your situation and goals—your accountant and attorney—*before* you make any decisions.

Now that the disclaimer is out of the way, I'm going to state the obvious: different businesses do business differently; the way your business is set up may or may not be ideal for what you're trying to accomplish. In fact, like Matt, you, too, may have a non-ideal business entity. What do we mean by "non-ideal"? You see, there are different tax rules for different entities. The wealthy understand how to choose which tax rules they want to play by to maximize their benefit. Your choice of which tax rules you are going to use to your full advantage is initially determined by your selection of your business entity. Even if you *did* nail your business entity from a tax perspective, you are still likely not operating the company according to maximum benefit legally and financially and legally (notice the repetition for emphasis).

Usually, a business entity setup issue is not noticed for years, decades even, as was the case with Matt's family business. The best way to mitigate a non-ideal business entity is to make a different choice from the start; the second-best way is to correct it immediately. And so if there *are* any parts of your entity structure that you want to improve, either a mistake that's costing you a lot of money *or* a mistake that opens you to uncomfortable legal liability, we're going to begin the journey of correcting them now. And to do that, we're going to give you a masterclass on business entities. This will be worth it.

(Let me give you a quick author's note for context: The tricky part about this is that a business entity that was ideal at one point in time can be non-ideal for another point in time or evolution of your business. Changing business entities too often is not recommended because it's expensive and can trigger taxes, so choosing what you'll stick with for a while takes some thought. We're about to give it some.)

Business Entities: A Useful Masterclass to Save You Time and Money

From my perspective, a proper business entity design is the foundation for minimizing your taxes and managing risk for your business activities. So, how do they work?

Well, I'm not going to teach you how to create new business entities because you shouldn't be doing that. You should be hiring an *attorney* to do that. And also I'm not going to teach you *all* the tax details top to bottom. But I will give you enough to be dangerous—including information about the tax burden you may be legally obligated to pay after setting or resetting your business entity.

Speaking of entity, the United States has established **three categories of subjects** that have rights, can own property, can enter into contracts, must file a tax return, can be sued, and are tracked with unique identifying numbers.

The **first** kind of subject is a *person*, and their rights are defined in the Bill of Rights within the United States Constitution. All people have the right to due process of law, freedom of speech, freedom from search and seizure, and so forth. People in the United States can own property, sign a contract, and be sued. People file a tax return, and people are given a tracking number—typically a Social Security number—that is associated with the Social Security welfare system for senior citizens, which the vast majority of employed individuals in the US will have paid into during their working years.

The **second** kind of subject the American system recognizes is a *company*. Companies don't have a Bill of Rights, nor are they defined in the US Constitution—in fact, they're not even mentioned. The rights and privileges of companies are established through case law. This means you can't look up the laws about companies—you have to study the history of lawsuits to see what precedents have been set by judges ruling one way or another and therefore interpreting (really, deciding) what the law is one way or another.

The **third** kind of subject is a *trust*. Trusts are different—they are written about in state law, which means they're well-defined and states have the ability to write the laws about trusts for what they think is best for their people. If you form a trust in the state of Delaware, the laws that govern that trust are going to be different than a trust in Wyoming or California.

Like people, companies and trusts must follow the tax code and file a tax return or report on the owner's tax return as a pass-through. Each company or trust is assigned a unique tracking number called an EIN. Companies and trusts also can own property, be bound by legal contracts, and can be sued.

Maybe this gives you an idea of why the business entity topic is so complex. Nevertheless, we will persist. As the legal rights of people are out of the scope of this book for obvious reasons, we will narrow our focus to companies (and trusts, as a matter of fact).

When you're forming a new company, there are generally **four** things you have to think about that fall into either **legal or tax attributes**, which can be combined in many ways so that we get to form the company the way we want for our greatest advantage, now and in the future.

The Four Attributes of a Business Entity

First is **legal protection**. Legal protection is all about what happens if the business gets sued and loses. Who's liable? Who has to pay out? Here in the United States, we can separate business assets from our personal assets so that we don't lose our personal assets—like our home—if the business gets sued and loses the lawsuit.

The opportunity to separate business and personal assets from a legal liability standpoint is actually essential to our economy if you think about it. By protecting our personal assets, we are free to take risks with the business property. This is not the case for all types of business entities in the US and is an important factor when considering what kind of business you want to form.

The **second** legal attribute is **ownership**. Who gets the profits of the company? The company itself? The owners? And how do the owners split up the profit? Let's say two friends and I start a lemonade stand, and we decide to split the profits evenly. That's a simple arrangement.

But maybe we decide we're not going to split the profit evenly; it's fairer to split up the profit based on how much time we each spend sitting out in the hot sun working the stand. If one of us decides to work the stand for 50 percent of the time it's open, we might want to pay that person 50 percent of the profits. Or maybe we prefer to split the profits based on how much we each spend to help set up the business. There really are endless approaches for how to split company profits, and the legal designation of the company matters for what options are available.

The **third** legal attribute is **control**. Who can write contracts and commit the company to debt? We need to be clear about who has that authority. The selection of the legal personality of the entity controls who has those powers.

Lastly, the **fourth** attribute is the **tax setup**. Who's going to pay the tax on the profits of our lemonade stand and what tax code are we choosing to follow? Are we also going to split that up, or do we want some other arrangement to take care of the tax bill?

These legal and tax factors lead us to select the right business entity for our needs. The most common options include **corporations, partnerships and limited liability companies**. As an aside, the legal designation of the company is handled through the state where it is formed. You don't have to form a company in the state where you are actually located; you can shop around and use the state that has the best laws to meet your needs and form the entity through that state's Secretary of State. Since states get to decide for themselves what is required to form the company, the process for setting up the legal personality of your business entity may vary from state to state. The **Beneficial Ownership Information Act** (a law passed to fight money laundering and terrorism) requires you to register with **FinCEN**, regardless of your state of business establishment.

Taxation setup is done at the federal level, rather than state, and is mostly independent from the legal decision for the company. This is where you first get to choose which tax code you want to follow. The most common tax code options are **Subchapter C** (which we simplify by saying "C-corp"), **Subchapter S** (which we call "S-Corp"), **Subchapter K** (which selects the partnership tax personality) and Subchapter F (for nonprofits). There is a default tax code for each legal entity choice and some combinations of legal and tax code choices are not allowed. Beyond that, you can generally combine legal and tax code choices in a way that maximizes the benefit for your situation. I'll get more into each combination shortly.

For now, know that your attorney and accountant are there to help you select what kind of legal personality and tax code is best for your business and family situation. They can either individually help you choose the best combination of legal personality and tax code based on what you want and what will lead to the best outcomes or sometimes one of those advisors understands enough to feel comfortable advising you. It's generally best to get both the legal and tax perspectives (from your attorney and accountant) before making the final decision about which combination is going to work best for your specific situation. You could, in theory and in practice, do it all yourself. But should you? Not if you want to maximize profit and minimize tax.

Legal and Tax Entity Combinations

Let's now walk through the different combinations of legal and tax personalities that can be combined when you form a company.

		Tax election Registered with the federal government				
		No tax election	Subchapter C (C-corp)	Subchapter K (Partnership)	Subchapter S (S-corp)	Subchapter F (501)
Legal designation Registered with the state	No legal protection	"Sole proprietor"				
	Corporation ("Inc")		Default "C corp"		Optional	Optional "Non-profit"
	Partnership		Optional	Default		Optional "Non-profit"
	Limited Liability Company ("LLC")	Default if 1 owner "disregarded"	Optional	Default if multiple owners	Optional "S corp"	Optional "Non-profit"

Table 1 - Combinations of legal and tax personalities and default business entity types.

If you don't form a legal entity for your company and you don't make a tax election, you are a **sole proprietorship**. This is common among people who want to run a small business and don't mind mixing their business and personal money. In a sole proprietorship, the owner is *personally liable* for any legal issues arising, and they pay taxes on all profits. The owner of the business must report their sales, expenses, and profits on Schedule C of their personal tax return. They don't get to take advantage of the tax rules and business deductions that help small businesses because they just aren't big enough yet. Think of a lawn care guy that runs around with a lawnmower in their truck; that's probably a sole proprietorship. One downside of a sole proprietorship business is that you have to pay self-employment taxes (Social Security plus Medicare) on the full amount you get from the profits. The current rate for that tax as of this writing is 15.3 percent.

Once you decide to form a company (and leave the sole proprietor world behind), you open the possibility of selecting which tax code you want for the business. Selecting the tax code you want is done by electing the tax personality of the business entity.

If you decide forming a **corporation** is what you need from a legal perspective, then the default tax code paired with that entity is **Subchapter C**. We don't typically say it like that—we just say "**C-corp**." Of course corporations do have other options for tax status. Perhaps the owner of that business decides they would prefer to use the tax code defined in Section 1 **Subchapter S**, so they elect "**S-corp**" tax status for the corporation instead.

A **partnership** is another legal designation for a company. A partnership can choose to be taxed under the partnership tax code (Subchapter K) and a partnership can also be taxed under Subchapter C instead—or as a non-profit (Subchapter F). But they aren't allowed to be taxed under Subchapter S. If the partnership is a General Partnership, the business legal liability also passes straight through to the partners. Other types of partnerships are available to control the legal risk flow-through.

In the standard partnership tax arrangement, the tax bill is usually split up among the owners based on how much each owns, the same approach to taxes as an LLC, which stands for "limited liability company" (more on these shortly). Partnerships are unique, though, because under a partnership, the profits don't have to be distributed to the owners according to what percentage of the partnership each owns. This makes a partnership the ideal option for companies where the owners and profit payouts differ by some attribute—perhaps how long the owners are willing to stand in the hot sun.

Since the mid-1990's, LLCs have been—and still continue to be—the most popular business entity for small businesses. If an LLC has just one owner, it has no tax status and is said to be "disregarded" because the entity is ignored for tax purposes. That means the tax bill just flows through to the one owner. If the LLC has more than one owner, by default it is taxed like a partnership in that the tax bill goes to each owner based on what ownership percentage that person has. If the LLC is a partnership the owners pay self-employment taxes (Social Security plus Medicare) on the full profits in addition to the individual federal income tax (based on tax tables).

Subchapter S changes that. If you choose to have your LLC taxed under Subchapter S, you must run payroll, which includes the self-employment tax, but the rest of the profit is only subject to ordinary income tax (the tax tables for each of the owner households). This means that the profits after payroll are taxed *less*. There are additional tax deductions under this tax code which makes it popular for small businesses because it tends to leave more cash in the pockets of the owners at the end of the tax year.

You could become an expert on all these tax rules—there are over 4 million words in the US tax code to keep you busy. Or you could just ask your accountant. If you don't have an accountant yet or you don't feel comfortable running this past them, that's OK; Firmstride is here for you.

And finally, if the goal of the corporation is to be a charity, either religious or secular, they would instead apply for non profit tax status under Subchapter M section 501. The company's legal entity applies for nonprofit tax status with the IRS by filing the appropriate form. Unlike the other tax elections, a business has to apply to be tax-exempt and they must justify the reasons they think they are eligible. This is why forming a charity requires specialized attorney work.

Proper Terminology

Now that we've looked at how legal and tax personalities of companies can be combined, let's look at the proper way to describe the kind of business you have so there's no confusion when you talk to legal or tax professionals.

If you just say you have an **LLC**, that doesn't say how it is taxed. "A single-member LLC" is closer to a complete picture. But saying you have a "disregarded LLC" is the most accurate. And if you say you are an "S-corp," does that mean your legal entity is a corporation, a partnership, or an LLC? "LLC taxed as an S-corp" would be clearer. If you wanted to sound like a lawyer, you could even say you're an "LLC that has elected to be taxed under Subchapter S."

The people who own an LLC are called **members**. An easy way to remember this is to think of it like an investment club. You could be a member of the club if you had enough money.

Members of LLCs don't have shares (more on those in a moment). They track their ownership through **membership units**. Many LLCs are small businesses and many times the members are active in day-to-day operations. Sometimes they delegate the day-to-day to managers who act on their behalf. If you combine both methods you get an owner that is active day-to-day alongside managers, with the owner being called a **managing member**. If the LLC is big enough, there might be a whole hierarchy of people, then the highest leader is called the **managing director**.

The distributed profits from an LLC are called **draws**.

I know this might be the first time you're seeing all these words on one page, and it might seem like a lot. You've probably heard all these terms before and may have tried to use them. Many people use these terms interchangeably, not realizing they can be useful for precise communication for legal and tax ideas. This can be dangerous. Let's say you work with a vendor who sells you paint you use on your product.

Are they your "partner?" That's sloppy, if you are trying to communicate that they sell you something you need. Partners own part of the company and are entitled to profits. Is that what you mean to say? Or are they a "vendor?" We've got to get the language right. In business, math matters. So do words and for the same reason—a shared reality. No shared reality, no adherence to legal or tax requirements.

To further clear the muddy waters, let's talk about the corporate-LLC overlap before we get to partnerships. Because corporations with C tax status are so common, most people just say they have a C-corp, which as you know is short for "corporation taxed under Subchapter C." But now you also know you could have a partnership or an LLC taxed under Subchapter C tax status. A legit way to say that might be, "I have a partnership taxed as a C-corp."

Partnerships are weird to describe for reasons you're about to read. You'd never hear someone say, "I have a partnership taxed like a partnership," though technically that would be correct. People just say "I have a partnership." But then if they have a partnership taxed some other way, like the last C-corp example, they'd just call that out.

If the company is a legal entity called a partnership, ownership is not tracked through stock, but through **partnership interests**, and owners are called (duh) **partners**. People who can sign contracts in a partnership are either called **partners** or **agents**.

If the partnership is big enough, there may be a hierarchy of decision-making, and the top people are called **managing partners**. Often, there is more than one, and they oversee their own departments of the company. When you hear someone tell you that they "made partner" in a firm, what they are saying is they have proven their talents and loyalty enough that they got invited to buy partnership interests from the other partners. They typically have to buy the partnership interests; these are unlikely to be given for free. Then they'll get part of the profit of the business in addition to their wages. Those profit payments are either called **guaranteed payments** if they are regular and, well, guaranteed, or just **draws** if they are irregular and based on how well the company performs.

Now, if we're working with a **corporation** entity, the owners of the corporation are called **shareholders**. They track their ownership percentage through **shares**. You can become an owner in some of the bigger corporations by purchasing shares, commonly called **stock**.

If you buy stock, you own part of the company—so as an owner you'll be asked to vote on important decisions or let the **Board of Directors** vote on your behalf. The Board of Directors is required to exist in corporations as they represent the shareholders in the day-to-day decisions. Most corporations don't let all employees sign contracts that commit the company. Only assigned **directors** can do that.

The top boss of a corporation is called the **Chief Executive Officer**. Technically, only corporations have CEOs, but we like that term so we often apply it to other legal entities, especially to LLCs. Profits from a corporation are called **dividends**, and they may be given to shareholders or retained by the corporation for ongoing business investment.

When you express your business entity and its attributes fully and accurately, your advisors will notice. The words you use indicate you know what you're talking about—and have the potential to be one of their best clients (meaning superior service for you!). But if you're sloppy with your words, then your advisors may assume you don't know as much as you actually do. It goes beyond properly labeling your business. So does managing the business itself. Is your entity the best one right now for you to achieve the outcomes you care about? Have you stepped back and evaluated? These are the questions. Let us find the answers.

Selecting the Right Legal Designation (For You)

The answers to four questions help us decide which legal entity best fits our current needs.

1. *Who owns it?* Corporations, partnerships, and LLCs can be owned by people, other companies, and nonprofits, either domestic or foreign. The exception is S-corps. Only US citizens and certain trusts can own an S-corp.

2. *How many owners?* A notable difference between LLCs and corporations (or partnerships) is the number of allowed owners. Historic lawsuits have set the precedent that LLCs cannot have more than 100 owners. If you intend to have more than 100 shareholders (i.e. you want to go public), you will likely want more than 100 shareholders and thus would be a corporation or a partnership.

3. *Are there share classes?* Share classes are how companies designate certain shareholders to have different rights within the company. Perhaps the better shares entitle the holder to get paid the profits first or have better pricing on shares. Only corporations can have formal share classes. Partnerships follow the tax code that allows them to pay out the profits differently than ownership percentages. The code that applies to

LLCs is simpler and can only pay profits based on ownership percentages.

4. *How complex is the company?* Corporations are the most complex legal entity. They must create and maintain documentation, hold regular meetings, and make formal notifications. Partnerships, on the other hand, are the most simple administratively. They only need a partnership agreement that describes how they'll share profits. LLCs are a bit more complex but still relatively simple. That little bit of complexity comes because many LLCs select to be taxed under Subchapter S—which requires them to run payroll. Do you want that complexity? Does it serve your goals?

Compliance

Those four questions and the subsequent answers that came to you as you read have probably already collectively brought you the answer—which entity your business should be. Perhaps we've confirmed your situation is what's currently best for you, or there's work to do to change things. Either way, we haven't covered areas of business entities that will otherwise put the fear of God into you. These include **compliance, legal liability**, and **taxation**.

First (next), we'll touch on company compliance which is all the documentation and procedures you need for staying compliant with the typical state and federal laws.

LLCs

LLCs require a certificate of formation, like a partnership will, as well as a document that describes the business operations called the operating agreement.

Because many LLCs are S-corps, they will need to run payroll, which brings additional work. It's not a big deal with a good payroll service. LLCs may need to file taxes if they have more than one member, or make a tax election. Disregarded LLCs don't need to file a tax return because the tax liability is reported on the owner's tax return (even when that owner is a parent business).

Partnerships

Partnerships are the easiest from a compliance perspective. A certificate of formation and a partner agreement are signed at creation, then the only ongoing paperwork is tax filing.

Like corporations, the form to file depends on the tax election. The partnership may also need to submit payroll paperwork if it chooses to run payroll, which is optional for a partnership.

Corporations

Corporations have the most compliance work to do because they need corporate bylaws and meeting notes from the annual shareholder meeting and a regular board of directors meeting. If your corporation is closely held, meaning you own it only within the family, then holding the annual shareholder meeting and the board of directors meeting can be a great excuse for a party. Just make sure you take official meeting minutes and save them. Operating corporations also need to file taxes—the tax document to file depends on what tax election the shareholders made.

If your company is a publicly-traded corporation, you will need to file other Securities and Exchange Commission (SEC) reports such as a 10-Q, which reports quarterly earnings. Dividends are reported on Form 1099-DIV, which needs to be filed each year with the IRS.

Company Legal Liability

Unless you've been through a lawsuit with your business, you may not have looked carefully at how business legal liability works. Let's look at an example to illustrate how your entity structure impacts your legal risks.

Imagine you own a popular and successful coffee shop in town, Coffee Shop, LLC. Your coffee shop has a bank account with $100,000 in it. You own some equipment, employee uniforms, and furniture. However, the biggest asset you have is the cash in the bank, and you keep it there for payroll and for buying materials to operate—like coffee beans and cups. You also keep a little of the cash as a reserve to cover payroll because some weeks can be slow based on local weather.

But here's how a legal challenge can change everything.

Scenario 1: External Legal Risk

Figure 1 - scenario 1 business entity

A customer comes in and gets coffee. They sit down at one of your fancy tables, and one of the chair legs snaps and the customer falls onto the floor. Of course you feel terrible, and you give them a month of free coffee. But they are pretty upset, and they make a big fuss on social media about the situation.

Then two weeks later, an official-looking man comes into the shop asking to see the owner, you. He introduces himself and hands you an official-looking document. It's a complaint from the customer that got hurt and a notice for you to appear in small claims court. You hire an attorney to help you, and when the day of the court case comes up, you get dressed up in your best suit and go to the courthouse. Your attorney does all the talking, but the judge awards the injured customer $20,000.

You lost.

Does your customer get $20,000? Who pays that?

Well, your business pays the full $20,000 amount out of your operating account. You are not personally liable and the payment comes from the cash held by the business. Ouch.

Scenario 2: Internal Legal Risk

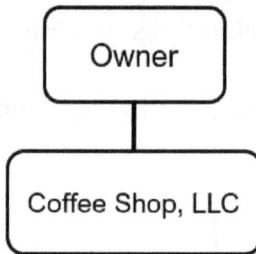

Figure 2 - scenario 2 business entity

Now let's change the scenario a little. Suppose it wasn't a customer that got hurt, but one of your employees. You feel terrible about this because this employee is someone you know personally. They still sue the business, and they still win. You owe $50,000. Who pays?

The business pays the employee $50,000. The employee never comes back to work; after getting the money, they quit. Ouch. Ouch.

Scenario 3: External Legal Risk, Revisited

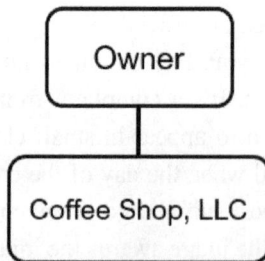

Figure 3 - scenario 3 business entity

Let's change the scenario to make it more interesting. Suppose we're back with $100,000 in the business account and the customer gets hurt very seriously—and this time, they were permanently disabled from the injury. They sue your business for $500,000 and win. How much does the customer get?

The business has to pay the $500,000 out of its assets. What assets does the business have? Well, it has $100,000 in cash plus a few thousand dollars in equipment, uniforms, and furniture, plus coffee beans and cups. The court could force you to liquidate the assets of the business to pay the disabled customer. They wouldn't get the full $500,000 because the business doesn't have that much in assets.

This would bankrupt your little coffee shop—bringing all accounts and all assets to zero—and you would be forced to close.

As bad as closing your coffee shop sounds, at least the liability of the business *didn't flow to you personally.* You still have your personal assets like your home and checking account. If this business were a sole proprietorship, there would be no legal business entity to shield you, and the court would likely order you to liquidate your personal checking account and sell your home—if that's what it took—to pay the disabled customer.

We're oversimplifying this scenario to illustrate how business legal liability works. If this situation were real, you would likely be settling with the injured customer outside of court and using insurance. But if you don't have insurance or you don't hire an attorney to help you settle, you might find yourself needing to close up the business.

Scenario 4: External Legal Risk, Building Ownership

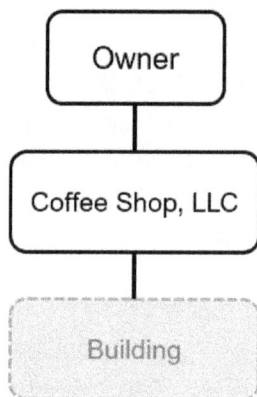

Figure 4 - scenario 4 business entity

Now suppose that Coffee Shop LLC owns the building; it's not rented. What happens if damages are awarded to the customer for $500,000? Does the customer get the $500,000 if all the cash in the coffee shop bank account is $100,000?

It turns out that the court can pull from *all* the business assets to pay the legal liability owed to the disabled customer . . . including the building. So in this case, the customer would get the $100,000 cash held by the coffee shop and the courts could order you to sell the building to cover the rest of the $500,000.

What makes this scenario even more painful is that when you liquidate the building to pay the legal bill, you'll have to pay taxes on the profit from the sale. Ouch. Ouch. Ouch.

Scenario 5: External Legal Risk, Building Self-Rental

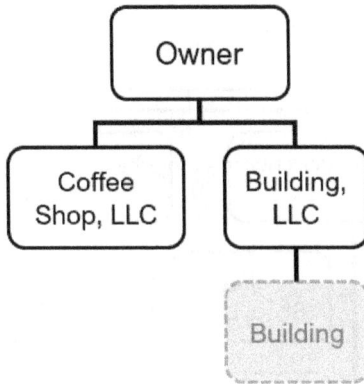

Figure 5 - scenario 5 business entities

Here's the same situation as Scenario 4, but now we've got the building in one legal entity called Building, LLC (which you own), and the operations of the coffee shop are in Coffee Shop, LLC.

When the customer sues Coffee Shop, LLC, they can get access to the assets of Coffee Shop, LLC—which is only the cash in the bank account. The assets of Building, LLC are *not* liable in the judgment against Coffee Shop, LLC, so the building isn't up for grabs. *Phew!*

By putting the building into a separate business entity, it is separate from the assets of Coffee Shop, LLC. Thus the customer gets all the cash in Coffee Shop, LLC's bank account, but the building itself is safe. Maybe you want to open a new coffee shop, Coffee Shop II, LLC? Just buy better furniture next time!

Scenario 6: External Legal Risk, Holding Company

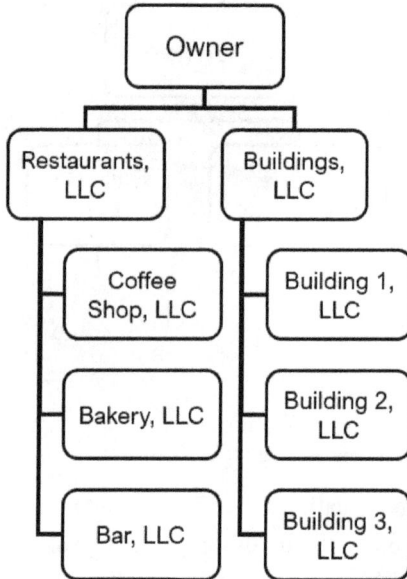

```
                    ┌──────────────┐
                    │    Owner     │
                    └──────┬───────┘
             ┌─────────────┴─────────────┐
      ┌──────────────┐            ┌──────────────┐
      │ Restaurants, │            │  Buildings,  │
      │     LLC      │            │     LLC      │
      └──────┬───────┘            └──────┬───────┘
             │  ┌──────────────┐         │  ┌──────────────┐
             ├──│   Coffee     │         ├──│  Building 1, │
             │  │  Shop, LLC   │         │  │     LLC      │
             │  └──────────────┘         │  └──────────────┘
             │  ┌──────────────┐         │  ┌──────────────┐
             ├──│ Bakery, LLC  │         ├──│ Building 2,  │
             │  │              │         │  │     LLC      │
             │  └──────────────┘         │  └──────────────┘
             │  ┌──────────────┐         │  ┌──────────────┐
             └──│  Bar, LLC    │         └──│ Building 3,  │
                │              │            │     LLC      │
                └──────────────┘            └──────────────┘
```

Figure 6 - scenario 6 business entities

Let's consider a more complex enterprise. Say you own three popular restaurants in a holding company called Restaurants, LLC—and Coffee Shop, LLC is just one of those. You also own three buildings under Buildings, LLC. Coffee Shop, LLC still only has $100,000 in the bank's checking account.

If the customer wins a $500,000 judgment against Coffee Shop, LLC, they can't get assets from any other of the businesses. You've isolated the risk to each respective restaurant by putting each into a separate entity. Smart.

Scenario 7: Internal, Holding Company

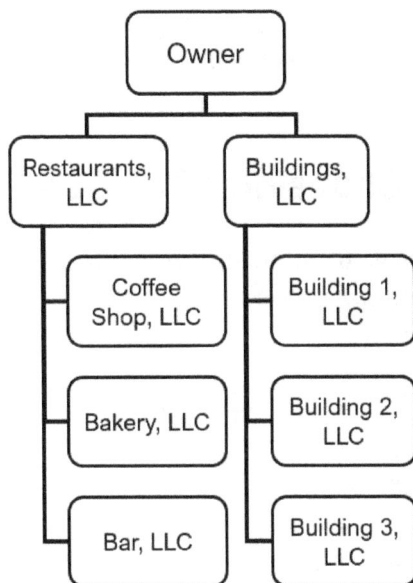

Figure 7 - scenario 7 business entities

Now let's look at what happens when the scenario changes and the liability flows into other business entities.

Suppose we now have a holding company called Restaurants, LLC. That entity owns Coffee Shop, LLC, Bakery, LLC, and Bar, LLC. Each business is isolated from a legal perspective, except for one thing: You have an employee of Restaurants, LLC, the holding company. Let's say they are your bookkeeper for all your businesses. For whatever reason, they sue and win a judgment against you for $500,000. Because they're an employee of your holding company, they now have a legal right to $500,000 worth of assets owned by Restaurants, LLC, which includes the assets of Coffee Shop, LLC, Bakery, LLC, and Bar, LLC. If you don't have enough assets in Restaurants, LLC's bank account, the court will force you to take assets from other businesses held by that main parent company. And if you don't have enough, you'll have to liquidate whatever is needed from Coffee Shop, LLC, Bakery, LLC, and Bar, LLC to pay the employee $500,000.

At least you set up a separate holding company, Buildings, LLC, for the *buildings* you own that are legally separate entities from Restaurants, LLC and the three entities it owns.

Choosing a Tax Code

With the scarier topic out of the way, let's now visit the most important decision that business owners get to make—which tax code they want to use.

Subchapter A

First let's get something important out of the way. You pay personal taxes under a certain tax code called Subchapter A. This section of the tax code defines who must file, rules for withholding from your W-2 wages, when taxes are due, what is counted as income, what personal tax deductions are allowed and what tax credits are allowed (e.g. Child Tax Credit). This tax code uses a progressive tax scale and the US Treasury publishes the tax brackets (which they adjust every year). Subchapter A provides the foundational structure for determining how households and individuals calculate their taxable income, apply deductions and credits, and ultimately determine their tax liability. The IRS provides Form 1040 for calculating and reporting your taxes according to Subchapter A.

Did you know you can choose to have your business also taxed under Subchapter A? This is called a *sole proprietorship*.

Sole Proprietorships

Sole proprietorships are extremely effective when you're getting started with a new business, especially because many businesses start off operating at a taxable loss. Sole proprietorships are easy and low cost to operate. A sole proprietorship is the only kind of business that allows you to take your full business loss and directly offset other income you have in your family.

For example, suppose you want to start a business that makes candy using your grandmother's recipes. You need to buy $10,000 in equipment, pay someone to make you a logo and a website and you just aren't sure if everyone will love your grandmother's caramels as much as you. You start as a sole proprietorship, buy everything you need, and in the first year—because you are learning to make industrial-scale candy and you don't yet have a distribution channel to sell it—you end up with a business loss of $40,000. Luckily your wife's job at a local technology company provides enough income for ends to meet while you get everything dialed in. At tax time because your business was a sole proprietorship, you can take that $40,000 loss directly against your wife's $200,000 salary for a total household taxable income of $160,000. If you had formed any other kind of company the losses from your business may have been limited.

But there's a catch (and isn't there always a catch?). A sole proprietorship is not a legal business entity—it's actually the absence of a legal business entity. If you got sued in your new candy business, you would be personally liable. And if you go out and buy a bunch of equipment, you are signing up to be personally liable for the debt. When you buy equipment you cannot depreciate it (more on that later). Only you can decide if those risks and foregone benefits are worth the tax savings.

It may be a good approach for your business to start as a sole proprietorship—which means you are choosing to tax the business under Subchapter A (the personal tax code). As the business grows you'll find yourself wanting the legal and financial shield you get from forming a proper business entity. We use the rest of this chapter to look at the additional tax code options that are only possible when you form a legal business entity.

Choosing the right tax structure depends on what you're trying to accomplish with your business. Here are a couple of short-hand tips. You can also contact your attorney to discuss these options and your situation in more personal details.

- **Subchapter S** is designed for a family-run lifestyle business. This just means that the goal of the company is to provide income for a family (or a few families) to live while minimizing taxes. This is the most common tax selection for small businesses.
- **Subchapter C** is ideal for large or fast-growing businesses needing unlimited shareholders and multiple stock classes (typically a requirement if you are seeking venture funding), but it faces double taxation on corporate profits and dividends. This double-taxation sounds bad on the surface, it sometimes turns out to be less taxes than Subchapter S—so don't judge this book by its cover.
- **Subchapter K** provides unmatched flexibility in allocating income, losses, and deductions among owners, with no restrictions on ownership types, but it comes with potential self-employment tax on earnings.
- **Subchapter F** of the Internal Revenue Code governs the taxation of exempt organizations such as charities, nonprofits, and certain other tax-exempt entities. These organizations are typically exempt from federal income tax under IRC Section 501.

Let's dive deeper into each tax code choice so you can make the choice that's best for your situation.

Subchapter C

You can elect this tax status for LLCs, partnerships, and corporations. A corporation is the most common choice of legal entity when an owner wants to be taxed under Subchapter C. Subchapter C is a flat tax—which means you can calculate your taxes simply by taking your taxable income times the rate. As of this writing, profits are taxed at a flat 21 percent (In the 1960s, the US Treasury had it as high as 52 percent). Many US states impose their own corporate tax on top of the federal corporate tax, and those states tend to use a flat tax approach also.

Companies pay their own corporate taxes, not the owners, and they file tax Form 1120. The profits of the company post-tax when given to the shareholders are called *dividends*. Dividends are paid to the shareholders based on the number of shares they hold and are taxed under Subchapter A as either long-term capital gains or short-term capital gains based on how long the shares were held. Short term gains are taxed as ordinary income which means you get to use the tax brackets (if non-qualified). Dividends are also subject to an additional 3.8 percent **Net Investment Income Tax** (NIIT) depending on how much your household earns that year. We typically say that C-corp profits are double taxed but are actually taxed three times if you count NIIT.

1. Once under Subchapter C (the profits of the company)
2. Once under Subchapter A (dividend)
3. Once under NIIT (capital gains)

Selecting to be taxed under Subchapter C is likely to be the best choice when you want to start a business, and reinvest the profits back into research and development. Product-based companies often start off using Subchapter C because they only pay a flat 21 percent on taxes. It doesn't pass through to the owners, and the company doesn't have to distribute the profits to the shareholders. That means they can keep the profit in the business and reinvest back in for product development.

Subchapter C also allows some amazing tax opportunities when selling, and many people who start a company with the sole intention of selling it will select Subchapter C.

Running a company under Subchapter C can also be better for very large amounts of income. While companies under Subchapter C experience double taxation, where the first level is 21 percent and the second level is either at the ordinary income of the owner or at the capital gains rate, sometimes this is actually less in total taxes than other options. If you're earning many tens of millions of dollars a year and you have selected Subchapter S or K for your taxes, most of that profit will be taxed in the highest bracket (37 percent). Suddenly a 21 percent tax rate with a ten or twenty percent capital gain starts to look like a better deal.

Subchapter C also allows different tax deductions. One of the most popular is personal benefits. Some of these benefits can be important to the family or executives and these perks are not tax deductible under other tax codes. Subchapter C allows the company to buy and take a tax deduction on certain life insurance policies, for example.

Subchapter K (Partnerships)

Subchapter K (and Subchapter S) create a company that is called a **"pass-through entity"** because the tax code for each passes the tax liability on the profits directly through to the owners instead of the tax being paid by the company. Tax code Subchapter K can be selected for LLCs and partnerships—the most common is the partnership legal entity. Subchapter K allows owners to allocate profits, losses and deductions in a way that does not strictly match ownership percentages. This is useful for companies where contributions (e.g., capital, labor, expertise) vary and partners agree on how to share the business results—including the tax liabilities. Profit distributions under a partnership are simply called **distributions**. If the distribution is regular and guaranteed like a salary, then it is known as a guaranteed payment.

Subchapter S

Subchapter S is good for what we call *lifestyle businesses*. You may have heard the term lifestyle business before and may even have a bad impression of it. The term just means that the business exists so that the family can earn income and profits to live their lifestyle. That is what describes most successful businesses in the United States.

Subchapter S also has excellent business deductions available. These deductions are simple and generally allow business-owning families to keep more of the money that they've earned than if they chose to be taxed under a different tax code. While the family making tens of millions of dollars who are living well below their means might be looking at Subchapter C, most families will probably choose Subchapter S for their business.

If the business is taxed under Subchapter S, then the distribution is called a **draw**.

Subchapter F (Non-Profit)

Subchapter F tax code governs the taxation of exempt organizations, such as charities, nonprofits, and other entities that qualify for tax-exempt status under Section 501. These organizations are typically exempt from federal income tax because they operate for purposes such as charity, religion, education, science, or public safety. Subchapter F outlines the requirements for obtaining and maintaining tax-exempt status, including limitations on political activity, restrictions on lobbying, and the need for operations to primarily serve public interests rather than private gains. While exempt from income taxes, these organizations may still be subject to tax on income unrelated to their exempt purpose through the Unrelated Business Income Tax (UBIT). Subchapter F also establishes reporting requirements, such as filing annual Form 990 to ensure transparency in finances and operations. Compliance with Subchapter F provisions is critical for organizations to retain their exempt status and continue benefiting from the tax advantages it provides.

Qualified Business Income (QBI) Deduction

The QBI deduction, introduced as part of the Tax Cuts and Jobs Act (TCJA) of 2017, represents one of the most significant changes to small business taxation in decades. Signed into law by President Donald Trump in December 2017, the TCJA aimed to stimulate economic growth by reducing taxes for businesses and individuals. There were a few key features of this law. One was the reduction of the flat tax rate under Subchapter C from 35 percent to 21 percent, benefiting large corporations. The second was the introduction of the QBI deduction to extend tax benefits to businesses that had selected to be taxed under Subchapter A (sole proprietorships), Subchapter S and Subchapter K. The QBI deduction allows you to take a deduction on your personal taxes of up to 20 percent of your taxable business profits. This deduction can be limited a couple of ways, the most common reason being your total household income and the type of business that the owner operates. If the business revolves around the talents of one individual such as a surgeon, lawyer, entertainer, or professional athlete, they are known as a **Specified Service Trade or Business**, or SSTB. If your business is an SSTB then the amount you can take as a QBI deduction will be limited based on your total household income (if over $483,900). The QBI deduction can also be limited if your business has crazy-high margins or you own a lot of valuable real estate. There is a whole tax form (Form 8995) to figure out if your QBI deduction is limited by those factors. You'll likely see this form in your personal tax return if you need to do the calculation for limitations.

This deduction was intended to level the playing field between corporations and small businesses while fostering job creation and investment in the U.S. economy. However, the QBI deduction is temporary and will expire in 2025 unless extended by Congress. As of the authoring of this book this tax deduction has not been extended.

Taxes on Company Profits

Now let's take a look at the tax differences and similarities based on how we select tax codes to minimize our taxes. Let's repurpose our earlier coffee shop example to do so. This will be enlightening.

Scenario 1: Business taxed under Subchapter C

In this first example, let's say Coffee Shop, Inc. is a corporation and it has selected Subchapter C tax status. The business had sales of $5 million and earned $1 million in profits last year. Who owes the taxes for those profits? How are those taxes calculated?

Well, multiple people owe taxes. First, the company owes 21 percent of a million dollars. After those taxes are paid, there's a remainder of $790,000 in profit in the business.

Let's say, for the sake of this example, the owner takes the full $790,000 out as a dividend. So now the owner of the coffee shop owes capital gains tax on $790,000, which is $158,000 (assuming owner has held the stock long enough to qualify for long-term capital gains), which is 20 percent.

So if you take the 21 percent flat tax and you add it to capital gains tax, the total tax burden is 37 percent. The profits on the coffee shop were taxed *twice*—first at the company level and again at the owner's capital gains level. In addition, the owner is going to owe 3.8 percent NIIT as well (another $38,000), bringing the total federal tax burden to $406,000—or 41 percent. We did not calculate any state or FICA taxes on their W-2 wage in this calculation to keep it simple.

Scenario 2: Subchapter S

Let's look at an example where the coffee shop selected to be a corporation for its legal designation and chose to be taxed under Subchapter S. There's still $1 million in profits for the year. Who owes taxes, and how are they calculated?

In this case, the tax liability flows through to the owner. The coffee shop does not pay taxes on its own, so the owner gets to bear the full brunt of all the taxes. But the owner gets to enjoy that QBI deduction of 20 percent. So 20 percent of $1 million is $200,000, which means that the remaining amount to be taxed is $800,000.

If we run that through the tax tables for someone with no other income, then the owner would owe $222,126, or about 28 percent. In the previous example under Subchapter C, the owner owed 41 percent. So it's substantially more tax-efficient for the owner to choose to be taxed under Subchapter S (an S-corp) rather than choosing to be taxed under Subchapter C (a C-corp) for this particular business.

Scenario 3: Corporation taxed under Subchapter S with Disregarded LLC

Now let's change things a little bit. Imagine Coffee Shop, Inc, is a corporation that has selected Subchapter S (we will now just call this an "S corp"). And the owner owns the building, held by Building, LLC, that is disregarded from a tax perspective. Initially, we'll ignore building depreciation.

Coffee Shop, Inc. had the same operations and paid Building, LLC $50,000 in rent. So the profit of the coffee shop is $950,000 and for the sake of simplicity let's assume the profit of Building, LLC was the entire $50,000. The total profits on the enterprise are the same $1 million as the prior example. And just like the last example, the owner still gets the full 20 percent QBI deduction on *both* the profits of the coffee shop *and* the profits of the rental building. The total profit is the same so he'll get the same QBI deduction and the same tax bill. Just because the owner pays himself rent doesn't make a net change from a tax perspective.

But it does make a huge difference from a legal perspective. Remember that prior example of the legal liability flowing between the owner's coffee shop and his building? It is for this reason that business owners typically separate operating business entities from asset-owning entities. It's not to save on taxes but to create a shield between assets so they are all protected from each other.

For real estate—especially buildings—things get even sweeter when the owner brings depreciation into the picture. Depreciation is treated like an expense from a tax perspective and doesn't have any impact on the business cash. If the owner makes less taxable profit, they owe less in taxes.

Scenario 4: Multiple Business Entities

Let's make things a little more complex. Say our hypothetical business owner has three popular restaurants and no buildings. Coffee Shop, Inc. is a C-corp; the Bakery, LLP (limited liability partnership) is taxed under Subchapter K (as a partnership) that he started with his best friend next door who's a fabulous baker; and then he has Bar, LLC where he selected Subchapter S for taxes.

Now how are taxes calculated? Who pays them?

Let's use a table to simplify the complexity.

	Tax Choice	Tax Liability	Tax Calculation
Coffee Shop, Inc.	Subchapter C	Company	21 percent flat rate
Bakery, LLP	Subchapter K	Partners	Partner's income
Bar, LLC	Subchapter S	Owner	Owner's Income

Table 2 - how this complex enterprise will be taxed

Coffee Shop, Inc. is a C-corp. It's going to pay the twenty one percent flat tax. And then the profits that remain in Coffee Shop, Inc are going to be taken out as a dividend and that will be taxed at the owner's personal capital gains rate.

Bakery is a partnership with the neighbor, taxed under Subchapter K (a partnership). So in that particular case, each partner is going to pay the tax liability for the percentage of the partnership that they own. If they split the partnership profits and taxes fifty fifty, then half of the tax liability will flow through to the owner while the other half flows through to his neighbor.

And then of course there's the Bar, LLC. Who pays the taxes on the bar? In this particular case, it's under Subchapter S, so the tax liability is going to flow through to the owner of the bar. It'll be taxed as ordinary income, meaning the tax liability will be calculated from the tax tables.

Common Approaches

Not all business owners want to grow their business to be large, so oftentimes they'll stop at various points in their business's evolution. When you think about business entities, instead of trying to pick the right entity for you forever, try to think of what is the right business entity for the *phase* you're in right now and for the foreseeable future based on what you know.

That said, changing business entities is not a cheap endeavor. Oftentimes you have to engage the services of an attorney and an accountant. Furthermore, converting between tax codes may be a taxable event. And some conversions are not allowed. So you don't want to just change business entities willy-nilly.

However, it is reasonable every two to three years to reevaluate your business entities to see if you need to change something in the structure. And don't forget that tax codes are just laws passed by Congress—they can change as the political winds shift.

A tax entity that makes perfect sense right now for you may not make sense in your future.

So let's look at what is the most common generic pattern that a business might evolve through.

It starts off with the owner that has a Big Idea. Oftentimes the owner starts off with big hopes but no certainty about how big that Big Idea really is. But the owner with the Big Idea wants to find out so they set up a business. In this case, it often benefits to be a *sole proprietorship.* A sole proprietorship is great for getting started because if the business has a loss, then the owner can take the loss against their other income. Generally speaking, sole proprietorships will be under $100,000 of profit. But for this choice to make sense, the owner has to be willing to shoulder the legal burden of the company because sole proprietorships provide no legal shield for the owner's personal assets because they are not technically business entities.

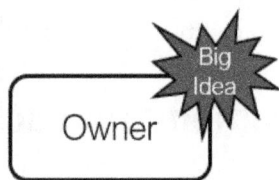

Figure 8 - a future business owner gets a big idea

Once the business is earning about $100,000 a year, it frequently makes sense for the owner to form an LLC or a corporation. Most small family businesses will be LLCs, and they'll choose to be taxed under Subchapter S (an S-corp). It doesn't always make sense to be a formal business entity until the business is making approximately $100,000 to $150,000, since the additional expenses to run an S-corp (i.e. payroll and filing another tax return) doesn't exceed the potential tax savings (more on that later). The LLC taxed as an S-corp is the usual next stop for most businesses until they reach about a million dollars in an annual profit. This would look like Figure 9.

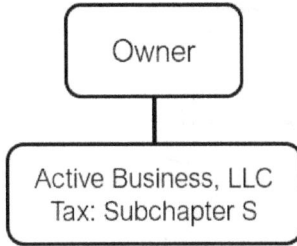

Figure 9 - next stop for a growing business is to form an LLC taxed as an S-corp

When a business gets larger than $1 million dollars in annual profit, oftentimes they're going to look at buying the building where they're operating or they're going to start to invest in real estate that is either in the family or supports the business operations. At that level of income families recognize that they have different income-producing assets with different risk profiles and they start to worry about how to use appropriate business entity structures as a way to shield those income-producing-risk-generating assets from one another. At that point the family will typically put the real estate into its own disregarded LLC and they'll separate those LLCs from their active business entities.

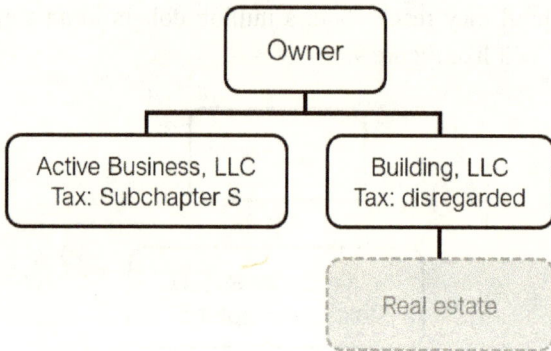

```
          ┌─────────────────┐
          │      Owner      │
          └─────────────────┘
         ┌──────────┴──────────┐
┌──────────────────┐  ┌──────────────────┐
│ Active Business, LLC│ │  Building, LLC   │
│ Tax: Subchapter S  │ │ Tax: disregarded │
└──────────────────┘  └──────────────────┘
                              ┌──────────────┐
                              │  Real estate │
                              └──────────────┘
```

Figure 10 - separate real estate from active business entities to isolate risks

This isolates risks so that the family doesn't have a legal liability in one business that causes them to lose assets in another. There's no magic income level where this is a requirement—it just tends to become a concern for families as they cross the $1 million per year threshold. Some families may hit the point of concern earlier; some later.

Owning the building where you operate your business can also be efficient for taxes and is known as a Self-Rental structure. A Self-Rental opens the door for additional tax strategies and even bigger tax savings.

Many families will continue to add businesses as they grow their business assets, often adding additional operating businesses and real estate assets as opportunities arise. As the family adds these, typically they'll be kept on a flat level like the Self-Rental until they get about three entities.

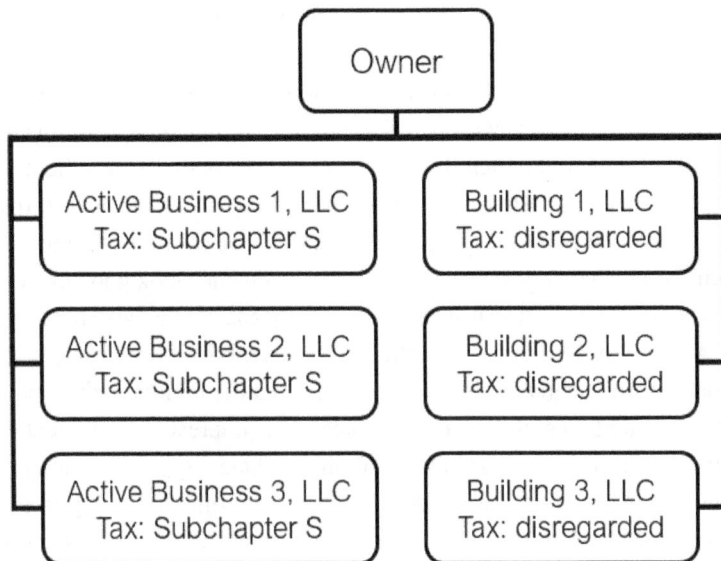

Figure 11 - a growing family enterprise will tend to stay flat until around the forth operating business is added

When a family has more than three operating businesses and each one is its own separate business entity, the family may form a holding company over those entities to improve the pricing on their employee health insurance. In recent years many healthcare companies don't require that kind of consolidation to give better pricing. You're not required to form a holding company for legal or tax reasons once the family has more than three operating businesses - it's just the way it tends to work out.

Now keep in mind that a company that has chosen Subchapter S for taxes must be owned by individuals that are US Citizens or resident aliens or certain types of trusts. Typically these companies will essentially surrender their Subchapter S tax choice, and they'll move under a holding company by converting to a **Qualified Subsidiary** (to convert from Subchapter S to a disregarded tax status, business owners typically do what's called an F-reorganization, called "F" due to one of the subsections of the tax code where that kind of change is defined). That holding company typically elects to be taxed under Subchapter S, and it's from there that either payroll is run, though it could be run at the individual business level depending on how the owners want to segregate and report on the profit and loss of each entity. Many families don't need the structure because they only have one or two operating entities, and three is not a magical number other than it generally saves the family money to consolidate the tax returns into a holding LLC, rather than filing individual tax returns.

Unfortunately, holding LLCs do create a lot of bookkeeping complexities and challenges. So while holding companies look good on paper, often the implementation just adds complexity and headache to the family.

As families build more wealth and accrue more business assets, they become more sensitive to the information about the family that's in public records. Oftentimes, they want to protect their interests in the event of a death of one of the spouses by bypassing probate - typically a long and expensive legal process at an inconvenient time. Imagine trying to operate a business when the bank account is frozen due to the death of the owner, for potentially months on end.

Many families do not wish to have the value or the knowledge of their assets recorded in any public fashion, so they'll form a trust. Not only does a trust shelter the family's name from public record by bypassing probate, but also it creates a faster way to pass assets to heirs. Trusts execute the transition of assets owned by the trust much faster, which means no frozen bank accounts and business as usual. This only works if the trust is set up correctly and it owns the assets of concern. And because the trust owns the assets, the individual owner's names are kept out of public records.

Case Studies

To help reinforce the business entity legal and tax code selection concepts, let's look at a couple of case studies.

Case Study 1: Car Body Shop

This is a lifestyle business owned by a husband and wife that produces $400,000 per year in taxable profit. Now it's a car body shop, which means that there's a lot of cutters, grinders, welding equipment, and other specialized equipment. They've also got about twenty-five employees.

The husband and wife wish to isolate their business assets from their personal assets to protect themselves from the legal liabilities resulting from the dangerous work that their business does. Someday they hope to sell the business and it's unlikely that they're going to sell anytime soon. The husband and wife currently rent the building where the body shop operates and recently the landlord contacted them and asked if they wanted to buy the building because he wants to retire. The goal of the husband and wife is to buy the building and keep as much of the wealth as possible as they go through the rest of their working life, which means minimizing taxes.

What does the ideal business entity structure look like for this family?

The family needs to achieve strong legal protection from legal liabilities balanced with saving on taxes. We're looking for an approach that accomplishes both.

The best tax code to select for running a lifestyle business like this is Subchapter S or Subchapter K (partnership). This allows the best tax benefits and will support the business goals—family lifestyle. Because there are no other partners that need to be included, Subchapter S will work fine and isn't as complicated as Subchapter K. So whatever legal designation should allow the family to select Subchapter S for the business. Let's look at the other factors to decide which legal entity choice would be best.

Only the following types of legal entities can choose to be taxed under Subchapter S—

- Limited Liability Company (LLC)
- Corporation

A corporation can have more than 100 shareholders and they have more formality as a result - like a board of directors and annual meetings.

That is not only unnecessary for this family—it is unwelcome. The LLC choice for the legal personality of the business makes the most sense in this situation.

The husband and wife team may want to buy the building to secure that asset for the family and the continuity of the business. This means becoming their own landlord. Assuming the family wants to do that they would segregate the building off into its own entity in order to separate legal liability of the building from the operating business. And then they're going to lease the building back to the business at market rate. The most common approach to the entity for a Self-Rental situation is a disregarded LLC owned by the family (not the body shop).

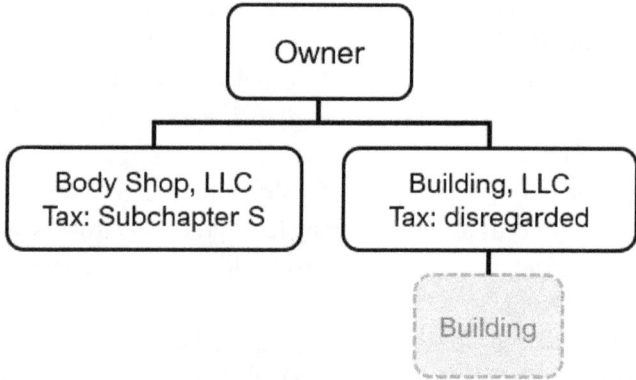

Figure 12 - business entity structure for a body shop that owns the building where it operates

The family would set up a will or trust to secure the business in the event of the death of the owner for the other spouse.

Case Study 2: Software Startup

This one is a bit more complicated. Suppose there are three friends that come together that decide to start up a software company. They're going to build a software solution that is software as a service or SaaS, and they plan to not only run a website and smartphone app offering the service, but also sell the software to other companies as well so that they can deliver their own white-labeled version of the service. So they have two objectives. They'll set up two separate entities. But first, they have to form a partnership.

They'll form a holding company structured as a partnership, and they're going to assign ownership rights based upon how much each of the friends puts into the business to get it started. They don't have to be the same since they're a partnership, so each of the friends is free to put in as much money as they choose. The amount they put in will determine how much they own.

The holding company partnership then owns a disregarded business that operates the website and the smartphone app services. The holding company also owns a company which owns the software intellectual property, which would be best under Subchapter C—structured that way because the friends hope to sell that software IP one day. And if they're able to sell the software after holding the company for five years, they hope to qualify for the Qualified Small Business Stock tax deduction, meaning that if they're able to sell the business, they might be able to take the profits of the sale tax free.

And that can be very attractive if they can sell the business for $10, $20, or $30 million. But if they sell the software, they will want to continue to operate the website and smartphone app that runs off the software, by separating the website and smartphone app business entity from the software-owning entity, they are now free to sell off the software intellectual property asset while retaining the service website and smartphone app business. This will give them flexibility and options in the future.

Now that the friends have identified their goals, selected the tax codes best for those goals and which tax personality to get for each entity, the friends now need to select the legal personality of each business entity.

A well-organized, well-documented business is easier to sell so they'll select a corporation for the IP-holding company and then follow the corporate requirements and formality that type requires. For the website and smartphone app, a disregarded entity would be ideal because then the partnership can file the website/smartphone operating company under its tax return and not require additional fees paid to the accountant. If the website/smartphone company was going to have employees of its own, it would need to choose some other tax code (likely Subchapter S). Here is the completed entity design for their situation.

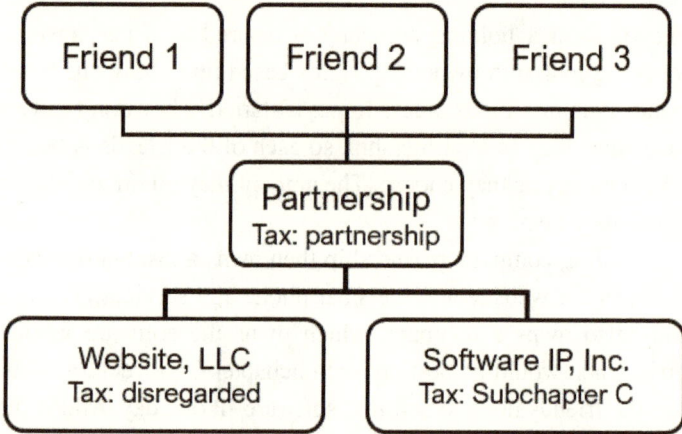

Figure 13 - business entity structure for a software startup example

Special States

States have the authority to form the legal side of a business entity. Some of these states are special and have different rules. Let's highlight a few of those differences now so if you have one of these special circumstances, you can consider one of these states to form (or reform) your business entity.

Delaware

Delaware does not have a state level corporate tax, nor does it levy any kind of franchise tax at the state level on corporate profits for LLCs or pass through entities.

It also offers charge order protection, which means that in the event that you are sued and you lose, the assets of the business are not given directly to the plaintiff. Instead the assets must first be removed by you from the business before they become the property of the plaintiff. The advantage of this is that if you have cash sitting in your business, you can threaten to leave it sitting there in perpetuity. Now you have a new negotiation lever with the plaintiff to whom you owe a lot of money.

Delaware is good on privacy, but the challenge with using Delaware is that the corporate law is governed by the Chancery Court, where they hear business cases related to corporations and such. At the time of the writing of this book, they've been setting very dangerous precedents as that court is very woke. More and more large corporations that used to be domiciled in Delaware are now moving out of the state and reforming in other states like Indiana, Florida or Texas.

Wyoming

While it doesn't have any state level corporate or or pass through entity state-level taxes, Wyoming has more case law around charge order protection, which means that it is the state of choice for forming trusts. Wyoming is also known for the best privacy laws in all the states of the union. You can even form an Anonymous LLC—meaning there is no personal information in the public records. This fact plus the strong case law makes it a desirable state for trusts that can pass behind the probate lines privately so that the public cannot find out who the owners of the businesses are. If you want to form a trust, Wyoming is likely your best bet. Wyoming requires a local registering agent (a company that acts as the point of contact for the business) so that will cost a little more.

Nevada

Nevada has no state-level corporate tax or pass through tax. It offers charge order protection for companies, and it has decent privacy, but what makes it popular is that it does not have state tax on vehicles and that it has excellent land protection provisions inside entities. Nevada's one of the few states besides Texas that recognizes land trusts, including land trusts for businesses and for primary residents.

Texas

Texas has no state-level corporate tax, but it does have a pass through entity tax that is known as a franchise tax, though that's a relatively small amount. Texas offers charge order protection, but it does not have any special privacy laws.

The nice thing about Texas is that they provide excellent tax breaks to large companies. Oftentimes, those tax breaks aren't seen at the federal level but they are provided locally for city and local taxes. This is why companies like IBM, Google, Intel, and Tesla choose to domicile in Texas.

South Dakota

South Dakota is known as *the* low-cost state. There are no state-level corporate taxes or pass through entity taxes, though the state does not offer charge order protection. South Dakota is not only inexpensive but is also excellent for laws around trusts, specifically land trusts.

Florida

Florida is also a well known and popular state for businesses. They're very friendly to large corporations, much like Texas and some other states are. They do have a state level corporate tax and a state level pass through entity tax, and they do not have charge order protection.

But they are most known for the protection of homesteads and retirement funds. If you think about the people that tend to live in Florida (i.e. retirees), that makes a lot of sense.

Converting

Changing your business from one tax code to another is a big decision. This requires careful handling by an experienced professional. The formal change is actually quite easy - the hard part is understanding how to manage all the repercussions. To change tax codes for your business your books have to be absolutely up-to-date and reconciled with high confidence. You can make a conversion for either the current year or, if you're still around the time before the year ends, you may be able to make a conversion for the prior tax year as well. Changing tax codes for your business can trigger one time tax bills and have significant tax consequences down the road.

So you don't want to do a conversion like this without understanding and researching the full tax impact from a professional that's done it before. However, though these kinds of conversions can be a one time taxable event, oftentimes there's going to be ongoing tax savings in the future that can support your lifestyle and offset that one-time conversion expense. So you have to weigh the short term and the long term tax impact carefully.

Having walked business owners through this transition, I can warn you that you will likely underestimate the impact of a tax code conversion in a few ways. You will probably underestimate how complicated the decision is. You will probably also be surprised by how easy it is, yes, *easy*, to implement the decision once you've made it. Converting from a business taxed under Subchapter C to a business taxed under Subchapter S is almost *too* easy.

It can also be freeing. People generally don't anticipate the feelings they find they have about their business after they complete a conversion to a more favorable tax code for their situation. I've found that families can feel trapped by Subchapter C. And that's because they're afraid of double taxation. They know if they take money out, it's going to be a taxable event. They also feel trapped by the formality that they need to maintain in order to keep the business healthy. If you convert to Subchapter S, and oftentimes if you even convert to a different type of legal entity, you no longer have the burdens of those administrative things and fear of loss. In addition, you can start to think about the business money as being your own personal money that you can take out or leave in, at will. Oftentimes, converting from Subchapter C to Subchapter S helps you to see the bigger picture of the wealth of the family. These kinds of conversions force you to rewire the way you think about your wealth. And if you rewire your brain to think differently about money and your business, this is often a path to more wealth.

$100,000 Savings in Year One

So how did things turn out for Matt? Well, the following year after the big change the business had solid performance. The conversion from Subchapter C to Subchapter S went smoothly under the guidance of an experienced accountant and attorney. Matt was able to continue his $150,000 per year salary and take the same monthly draws. So while the conversion was a change in how they operated the business, the family finances didn't see much of a change at first.

Until they got their family tax return. The tax return for the family business—now taxed under Subchapter S—was reported on their personal return. Their total average tax rate had dropped from 35 percent to 22 percent. That savings accounted for nearly $100,000 of savings in the first year. The single largest impact on their tax bill was their selection of which tax code they were going to use—a decision that had been made nearly sixty years ago and had not been revisited since.

This is why the wealthy pay attention to which tax code they want to use—it usually makes a huge difference.

There was one additional consequence for keeping the Subchapter C status until now—but it wasn't directly tax-related. The family now needs to hold the business and the building for five years before selling. This is fine for the family because they currently want to keep the business in the family as long as possible. Matt's experienced advisors helped him understand that important rule about the conversion.

Matt wished he would have known about this years earlier so that his mom and dad could have kept more of their income. Matt also wished that he had learned earlier how to correctly read the three critical financial statements because that would go on to change how much Matt would pay himself.

Maybe you would say the same.

CHAPTER 4

THE THREE MOST IMPORTANT FINANCIAL REPORTS AND HOW TO READ THEM

Matt's story continues.

Recall how Matt took over the family business when his father became ill and then passed away about a year later. During those final months together, Matt learned everything about the business operations, clients, projects, and the day-to-day that he could. Matt's dad had delegated the finances to Matt's mom and their accountant long ago, so Matt felt comfortable skipping those lessons because they were being handled and he had limited time.

Matt's college degree and corporate product management experience would serve him well. He'd developed basic management skills in corporate and knew how to run a business given a budget. Small business was similar and different from his prior experience and he was confident he could learn from his dad with the time he had remaining.

Matt first learned how to use a profit and loss report to develop a feel for how things were going in the business. Every few days, he looked at the profit and loss statement to see how things were going. Every morning he logged into the bank accounts and checked the balances. Many times, he'd check the bank balance again at night before heading home just to see what had happened throughout the day. He was a good business operator and had his finger on the pulse of operations just like his dad had been showing him.

Here comes the "but."

But there was always something nagging at Matt when payroll came. It was odd that the profit and loss report usually showed it was going to be tight. This just didn't line up with what he was seeing in the daily glances at the bank balances. It bothered Matt that his profit and loss report was so far off and he could not explain it. The business' operating checking account was always so flush with cash so Matt didn't worry about it much with everything else going on. It was just one of those constant annoyances Matt didn't have time or energy to chase down. It turns out the difference between his P&L and bank balances was not an indication of a problem—but of Matt's lack of knowledge.

At some point Matt finally got fed up with the contradictory realities and the issue of not lining up made his list of cares. So he brought it up with his mentor to see what he would say. His mentor told Matt that all business owners go through this anxiety until they learn to look at and understand their **balance sheet** and **cash flow statement**—those other two key financial reports. Matt had seen these reports in the bookkeeping software but didn't really know what they were for. His dad or mom hadn't spent time explaining them either, so he just assumed they were optional nice-to-know reports. That was about to change because as a small business owner, Matt now needed the full picture to make better decisions.

Matt learned about the business balance sheet and the cash flow statement. These reports provided the understanding Matt needed to know why things always looked tight on the P&L around payroll time and why the profit and loss statement was so far off the bank account—and how he could change that, for the better, forever. What surprised Matt was how his new understanding opened a bunch of new doors he didn't see before.

Almost an MBA

This will sound harsh. I kind of mean it to.

In my experience, many business owners don't make good financial decisions because they don't fully understand the three foundational financial reports of every business: profit and loss statement (which we will now call the "P&L"), balance sheet, and the cash flow statement. Business school graduates study these like lost ancient literature and can read them forwards, backwards, in invisible ink, and in seven languages (well, maybe not seven). But most small business owners don't have an MBA. That's OK (for you, reading this) because this chapter is going to give you the next best thing—the only-what-you-need-to-know-to-be-successful "scoop" on these three critical documents. Read yours and prosper!

But first, let me teach you how I'll be teaching them to you.

Financial Statements Are Your Car's Dashboard

Understanding your financial statements is like using the dashboard of a car. Each instrument provides a specific type of information, and together, they help you navigate and manage your journey effectively. Just as focusing on one gauge in a car could lead to trouble, relying on a single financial statement can create blind spots in managing your business. By using all three reports— P&L, balance sheet, and cash flow statement— you gain a comprehensive view of your business's performance, much like monitoring your car's dashboard while driving.

Profit and Loss: The Rearview Mirror

The P&L (sometimes also called "income statement," "earnings statement," "statement of operations," or "statement of financial performance") is like your rearview mirror—it shows you where you've been.

This financial report tracks your business's performance over a specific period, highlighting revenue, expenses, and profit. It provides insights into the efficiency of your operations and helps identify trends.

- **Why it's like the rearview mirror:** Just as the rearview mirror shows what's behind you, the P&L reflects past business activity. It doesn't predict what lies ahead but helps you understand historical performance, such as whether last month's sales met expectations or if recent cost-cutting measures improved profitability.
- **Pitfall of over-reliance:** Driving while looking only in the rearview mirror is dangerous. Similarly, relying solely on the P&L can leave you unaware of your business's financial health or challenges coming up around the corner.

Balance Sheet: The Gauges

The balance sheet is like the dashboard gauges of your car, showing your speed, RPMs, and engine temperature. It provides a snapshot of your business's current financial position by summarizing assets (what you own), liabilities (what you owe), and equity (what belongs to you as the owner).

- **Why it's like dashboard gauges:** Just as your car's gauges show real-time data—how fast you're going, how hard the engine is working, or whether the car is overheating—the balance sheet reflects your current business financial health. It shows whether you're solvent, whether you have enough assets to cover liabilities, and how much equity you've created.
- **Pitfall of over-reliance:** Monitoring only your speedometer or engine temperature while driving might cause you to miss obstacles ahead. Likewise, focusing solely on the balance sheet can make you overlook operational inefficiencies or liquidity issues revealed by the other reports.

The balance sheet is so important that there is an equivalent for your family finances. This is called a *Personal Financial Statement* or *Net*

Worth Report. If you have an investment manager they probably provide you with that on some regular basis.

Cash Flow Statement: Fuel Gauge

The cash flow statement is like the gas gauge in your car, showing how much fuel you have. This report tracks the movement of cash in and out of your business, divided into operating, investing, and financing activities.

- **Why it's like the fuel gauge:** Your car won't run without fuel, and your business won't operate without cash. The cash flow statement helps you see where your cash is going in your business. You can use this to reveal whether you're adding cash or burning through reserves. This can help prevent surprises like running out of money to pay bills. This report shows you how the cash balance in your bank account maps to your P&L.
- **Pitfall of over-reliance:** Watching the gas gauge exclusively while driving your car won't tell you how fast you're driving, how your engine is performing, or what's behind you. Similarly, focusing only on the cash flow statement can mask deeper operational issues and overall financial health of the business. This would basically be like looking at the cash balance in your bank account each day and thinking everything is hunky dory in your business.

Alright, now let's "back up the car" so we can get ready for our trip. Where are we going? To state the obvious (which is worth starting anyway), let's put it this way:

The goal of all companies we are discussing is to generate profit by taking care of customers in some way that they value and will pay for. There are many ways to do that, either through products or services. Different types of companies have different profit margins and goals, and different industries have varying expectations of how much profit a company should produce. However, let's agree for now (until the non-profit chapter) that the goal of every company is to produce profit by taking care of customers.

We're going to look at an example of a fictitious business - and the financials of it - to illustrate how financial statements can give you different perspectives on what's happening within a business.

The company we'll be using is made up. It's called My Furniture LLC. This is an example of a business that resembles many others we work with here at Firmstride. This business makes and sells customizable high quality hand-made furniture for homes. The business has a strong online brand, takes all orders online and builds the furniture from high quality raw materials. We have been profitable for three years and cash flow positive (which means we collect enough cash each month to pay for all our operations). The goal of my business is to provide income for my lifestyle and family.

In this example, the company is large enough to have a team of employees. As the owner, I've decided I want My Furniture LLC to be a stable employer. So we not hire and lay off employees as orders ebb and flow month-to-month.

For this example, let's say my business generates $1.2 million in sales per year. We'll get into more details about what that looks like in terms of profit. The point is I have a reasonably good company that's been around for several years, with a loyal customer base and a fairly stable, growing market of customers. There are certainly months with more sales than others; for the most part each month is profitable - it just depends on how much.

Now, I mentioned that we take orders online from customers and ship them beautiful furniture. But what happens inside the company is much more complex than that. When we receive an order, we collect all the money up front. Then once we get paid, we make the customized the design for the customer's selections and then cut, assemble, and build the furniture. We use high quality materials such as solid wood, brass fasteners and pulls, and the highest quality varnishes. In addition to those expenses that depend on the number of orders we get, we have other expenses that are fixed and shared among all orders—like our saws, clamps, and workbenches. We don't need to buy more of those right now to take on our growing demand for orders.

Of course, we have people that work at My Furniture LLC. They build each customer's furniture with love using our tools and the raw materials we buy from our suppliers.

Let's suppose I've been running this company for a few years and the business is stable. But I still don't have peace of mind because there are three questions that consistently plague me as the owner. I'd like to get my hands around all three of these questions—not just once, but on an ongoing basis and any time that I want.

1. The first question I really care about is **how profitable my operations are**. Are orders up last week? How much profit did we earn from that recent batch of orders from that marketing campaign we tried? I'm always trying to improve our production operations—completing orders faster, reducing expenses without compromising our product quality. I want to know if the changes I like to measure whether the changes I make in the operations are beneficial or not. I'm also always trying to get better deals from my suppliers—maybe by buying in bulk or taking advantage of bargains I find on raw materials.

2. I constantly worry about **whether or not the business has enough cash to operate**. I like to run a pretty lean shop, and I prefer to take the pay and profits from the business out to my personal account so I can take care of my family's needs. But I don't like running things so tight that I have to worry about missing payments to vendors or not being able to make payroll. I like enough buffer so that I don't have to worry. So how do I manage the amount of cash my business needs to avoid creating undue stress for myself?

3. I want to know how well the business is doing and how much I get to pay myself as the owner. In short—is this worth it? Is all my work paying off?

Fortunately, the first question about operations is answered by the **P&L**. This report gives us a perspective on how efficiently my operations run in my company. I can see the impact of my ideas as I try them.

Another way to put it is: How efficiently can I take a dollar earned from a customer and turn it into profit?

If I earn a dollar from a customer and deliver the furniture to them, do I earn five cents of profit? Twenty cents? Fifty cents? And as I want to change and grow my company, how does that affect the amount of money I earn as my income increases along with my sales? If I double my sales do I also double my profit?

The second nagging question is answered by the **statement of cash flows**. This report gives me a perspective on how well I'm managing the cash in the business bank account—the economic lifeblood of my business.

The last nagging question is how well my business is doing overall. While I feel it's doing well, I'd like to quantify that. Can I get some numbers to back that up? That's where the balance sheet comes in. The **balance sheet** tells me how the business is performing at a specific point in time. It also tells me how much I can take home for my pay as the owner of the business.

Now let's revisit each topic for a small business owner's deep-dive; here's what you should know that you know some of, but probably not all. By filling in the knowledge gaps, we will change everything for you. This will be worth your time.

The P&L, Revisited

The P&L provides a clear picture of your business's profitability over a specific period of time. It's the go-to report for understanding how efficiently your business turns $1 dollar of sales into profit. Think of it as a snapshot of the financial efficiency of your operations. When you compare different windows of time on your P&L you can get some idea about what benefit (or injury) you had from changes you made or were forced upon your operations.

At its core, the P&L follows a simple formula:

Revenue - Expenses = Profit

Let's break down the main components using our furniture company example.

Revenue ("Income" or "sales")

The top line of the P&L is your total revenue—essentially, all the money your business earned from sales during the reporting period. For example, if My Furniture LLC took $100,000 worth of orders last July, that amount represents the business revenue for the month and will be at the top of my P&L when run for that month.

Cost of Goods Sold

Next on the P&L comes expenses. Those are divided into Cost of Goods Sold (COGS), which represents the direct expenses required to produce the products or services that were sold, and then fixed expenses. COGS fluctuate based on sales volume. Examples in my custom furniture business of COGS include the wood, screws, brass fittings, labor directly tied to order fulfillment, and shipping costs. In our example, if My Furniture LLC spent $28,000 on materials and direct labor to fulfill the $100,000 in orders in July, $28,000 is the COGS for the month.

Gross Profit

Gross Profit is the term for what you earn when you take Revenue minus COGS. That's how much money is left to cover other expenses - the expenses that are fixed - after the direct costs of production are accounted for. In our example, with $100,000 in revenue and $28,000 in COGS, the gross profit is $72,000. Gross profit is a key indicator of operational efficiency of my business, showing how effectively I'm managing the costs directly tied to producing the furniture.

Fixed Expenses (Overhead)

Fixed expenses, also called overhead, are the costs of running your business that don't vary with production levels. These include rent, utilities, salaries for administrative staff, insurance, and marketing. For My Furniture LLC, let's assume fixed expenses amount to $47,000 during July. These costs remain relatively stable, even if sales fluctuate. I'm not allowed to skip paying rent on the building if orders drop by 20%. I also don't have to pay more during the end-of-year rush when orders are generally up.

Operating Profit

Subtracting fixed expenses from gross profit gives you operating profit, also known as operating income. This figure reflects the profitability of my core furniture business. For My Furniture LLC, the operating profit for July is $72,000 gross profit minus $47,000 fixed expenses, or $25,000. In summary, I collected $100,000 in sales and with the COGS and operations expenses subtracted out, I'm left with $25,000 in profit from the core business.

Other Income and Expenses

Other income and expenses are financial activities unrelated to your core operations that can generate income or add expenses but these are not directly related to your core business. In this example, My Furniture LLC earned $4,000 in interest from the bank account in July. This $4,000 is income for the business and therefore it is included on the P&L for the month. It is categorized as "other income" because it's not directly tied to the business's main activity—producing and selling furniture.

Net Profit

Finally, we arrive at net profit, also known as net income or the "bottom line." This is what's left after all expenses, including COGS, fixed expenses, and any other income or expenses, are accounted for. For My Furniture LLC in July, the net profit is $25,000 operating profit plus $4,000 other income, or $29,000.

So we sold $100,000 in sales in July and the business earned a profit - before taxes - of $29,000.

Why the P&L Counts

The P&L provides critical insights into your business's operational efficiency and profitability. By analyzing it regularly, you can identify trends, pinpoint inefficiencies, and make data-driven decisions to improve performance. For example, if COGS increases unexpectedly, you might investigate supplier costs, production efficiency, or product mix. Similarly, if fixed expenses rise, you can review overhead spending for potential savings.

P&L Pitfalls (and How to Avoid Them)

While the P&L is a powerful tool, it's essential to use it correctly. Here are some tips:

1. **Avoid Over-Reliance:** The P&L reflects profitability but doesn't show cash flow or long-term financial health. Pair it with the balance sheet and cash flow statement for a complete picture.
2. **Understand Timing Differences:** The P&L doesn't indicate - or align with - your cash balance in the business bank account. For example, if you purchase inventory on credit, the expense may appear on the P&L even though cash hasn't left your account yet.

3. **Focus on Trends:** Reviewing the P&L monthly or quarterly helps identify patterns and evaluate the impact of changes because the ups and downs from the weekly numbers gets smoothed out with averaging.

But *why* are these tips helpful? That may seem obvious to the point of trite, so let me explain it—because many small business owners completely miss it.

While it's good to look at absolute dollars to know how much we earned, many owners prefer to look at percentages instead. Percentages are useful because when you're comparing month-to-month or year-over-year performance, it's often easier to interpret and compare percentages than raw numbers. Of course, we don't get paid in percentages—we get paid in absolute dollars—so we need to pay attention to both.

Percentages are expressed as *margins*. Gross margin, operating margin, and net margin express profitability as a percentage of revenue, allowing you to compare performance over time or against industry benchmarks. For example, let's look at COGS to see how the margin is helpful. If I spent $28,000 building furniture in July and took orders for $100,000, my cost of goods sold is 28 percent of sales. So my gross margin would be 100 percent sales minus 28 percent COGS, or 72 percent. My fixed expenses were $47,000 for the month or 47 percent of sales. My operating margin is $25,000 which could be stated as 25 percent operating margin. I had $4,000 in other income so my net profit is $29,000 or 29 percent net margin.

Margin makes it easy to express the performance of a business. I can say: "My gross margin is 72 percent, my operating margin is 25 percent, and my net income margin is 29 percent." This is an effective way to describe how the business is performing.

If you like seeing both the absolute numbers and the percentages side by side, that's a standard report in QuickBooks called "Profit and Loss as a Percentage of Income." You can run it for any time period you want and see exactly this type of information.

Now that we understand how to calculate margin and dollars, the goal over time is to see the business perform in a consistent and predictable way. This helps us compare changes, evaluate whether they're good or bad, and estimate what the future might look like. This is called a company model or business model. Business owners often use this term to describe the percentages they aim to achieve every month. Having a business model is essential for two reasons:

1. If your results don't align with your model, you want to understand why. Did you do something that was more successful, or did you try something that hurt your business performance?
2. Having a model helps you plan.

Let's look at an example. Suppose my business operating model is as follows:

- Sales: 100 percent
- Gross margin: 75 percent
- Operating margin: 30 percent
- Net income margin: 30 percent

Now let's see what happened in our July month example. My sales were $100,000, but COGS were $28,000, or a 28 percent margin. According to my model, I expect my COGS to be 25 percent. In July, I saw a performance of 28 percent. What happened? I overspent.

I'd like to figure out why. Perhaps the mix of orders changed, and I sold a higher percentage of low-margin products. Maybe I hired a new employee who isn't skilled with the tools yet, resulting in more mistakes and thus more waste. Maybe the price of lumber went up. Or perhaps I bought something this month that I don't buy every month—like a year's supply of varnish. I need to ask: What changed? What caused this? Do I need to adjust something?

If my COGS went up in July, my gross profit goes down—it's just math. I was off by three points. When we say we're "off by three points," it means my gross margin was 72 percent when I wanted 75 percent (75—72 = 3). Saying "three points" avoids confusion, as saying "three percent" could mean something different.

Now let's look at fixed expenses. In July, my model predicted fixed expenses to be 45 percent of sales, but they ended up being 47 percent of sales. That's another two points off. When I look at my operating margin, I achieved 25 percent, but my model is 30 percent. How did this happen? I gave up three points in COGS and two points in fixed expenses—three plus two equals five. I gave up five points on my operating margin.

Thankfully, I got lucky—my bank paid the business $4,000 in interest, which is four points of sales. So instead of losing five points, I only lost one. My net profit margin ended up being 29 percent instead of the expected 30 percent. What really saved me wasn't my operations but the unexpected interest payment from the bank. I'd want to investigate why my business was off by five points and ensure I correct it for next month instead of just being happy that I earned $4,000 in interest.

For example, if I find that the higher COGS in July was due to buying a year's supply of varnish, I'd expect my COGS to be slightly lower next month when I don't need to buy varnish. If August is not better, I'd dig deeper to understand why—perhaps I overspent on wood. By tracking these trends, I can make informed decisions about my operations so that I continuously improve.

The same applies to fixed expenses. For instance, if July was a particularly hot month, my air conditioning costs may have been higher. Or maybe there was more overtime because of a record month for orders. In that case, overtime for the team assembly the furniture would make sense. If I notice I'm paying over time regularly, perhaps I should hire more staff for the growth in sales.

Your P&L is where you dig into these numbers. In most bookkeeping software, like QuickBooks or Freshbooks, you can click on numbers for a detailed breakdown. If you can't explain why numbers are off your model, it means either your model is wrong or you don't have a good enough handle on your business operations and you might want to get more involved.

Many business owners start their understanding of financial reports with the P&L because it reflects the day-to-day operations—which are familiar to them. When businesses are just starting, they may not be profitable. The goal is to become—and stay—profitable, so the P&L becomes the primary tool for tracking progress early on.

However, many business owners fail to move beyond the P&L to look at other financial reports, which are equally—if not more—important. The P&L is a standard financial report so all bookkeeping packages will have a similar version of it. While the format may vary slightly, the structure remains consistent. Remember, the P&L is retrospective—it shows past performance for a specific period, such as last week, last month, last quarter, or last year.

Keep in mind that not all transactions are recorded immediately in the P&L. There's often a delay, so you need to understand when your reports are accurate. Most businesses aim to have all transactions processed and reconciled with bank statements by the 11th or 15th of the month. That way, reports run after that date are known to contain all the transactions (they may still not be categorized correctly—that's a different problem). Ensure your bookkeeper meets these deadlines so you're not working with erroneous or incomplete data when making a decision about your operations.

One key aspect of the P&L is its ability to compare actual performance against your model. Continuous improvement is crucial. If you don't have an operating model, you can start by averaging the last six months of data and using that as your baseline, refining it over time as you gain more experience with your particular business.

Finally, keep in mind that the P&L doesn't exactly reflect what happened or what's going to happen in the business bank account. For example, if I used in-store credit at the lumber yard to buy wood and the store issues the invoice on the 15th, running my P&L on the 1st won't show those expenses yet. This is why the P&L cannot be used on its own—it tells you about operations, not cash flow.

That said, the P&L is a useful tool for estimating taxes. While it won't give you exact tax figures, it's a good proxy. Your business tax return will look quite similar to your profit and loss statement, so you can use it as a guide to estimate tax obligations. Keep in mind that not everything shown on your P&L can be included as a tax deduction on your business tax return and not everything on your business tax return may appear on your P&L. Depreciation is one common item that can have a big impact on taxes and does not typically appear on a P&L (unless you decide to add it for your business).

The Balance Sheet, Revisited

Next up, the balance sheet.

The balance sheet is a financial snapshot of your business at a specific moment in time, showing what your business owns (called "assets"), what it owes other people ("liabilities"), and what remains for you, the owner after the business pays everyone it owes ("equity"). Unlike the P&L, which tracks operational performance over a period, the balance sheet provides a freeze frame of your financial position. Its primary purpose is to answer a fundamental question: *How financially healthy is my business at a specific moment in time?*

At its core, the balance sheet follows a simple equation:

$$\textbf{Assets = Liabilities + Equity}$$

This equation ensures that everything your business owns is accounted for, whether it's funded by debt (liabilities) or by your ownership stake (equity).

Ultimately, any given business will boil down to what the company has and what it owes to other people. In a perfect world, the company has more than it owes. When the opposite happens—when the company owes more than it has—it becomes insolvent, which can lead to bankruptcy. To avoid this, we need to make thoughtful decisions and maintain a balance between what the business has and what it owes. I'm not saying that debt is bad. In fact, debt is often a valuable tool for helping businesses grow. However, it's important to manage debt wisely so the company doesn't become unbalanced.

The balance sheet helps us quantify and measure this balance. Let's explore the balance sheet in detail.

Assets: What Your Business (Actually) Owns

The first thing we want to know is what the company has. What are some of the things the company owns?

Well, at my hypothetical furniture company, I have tools. I also have a building, though there's still a mortgage on it. I have wood, materials, finishes, and everything else in inventory for building products. I have a bunch of orders in my queue that are already paid for, and I also have a bank account with cash in it. These are all things My Furniture LLC owns.

These are called *assets*. The assets I just described generally fall into two categories. The way we categorize and organize a company's assets on the balance sheet is based on how easily they can be converted to cash. That's because, at the end of the day, the business runs on cash. If I run out of cash, I'll need to convert some of my assets into cash to keep the business running.

And so all assets are categorized into two groups:

1. **Current Assets:** These are assets that can be easily converted to cash within a year. Examples include:
2. Cash in your operating account.
   - Accounts receivable (money owed to the business by customers that have placed orders).
   - Inventory (materials, finished products not yet shipped, etc.).

Current assets are your most *liquid* resources, meaning they're the easiest to convert to cash to be used to cover short-term obligations.

3. **Fixed Assets:** These are long-term investments that help your business operate but aren't easily converted to cash—or if you had to convert to cash quickly it would likely be painful. Examples include:
4. Buildings, machinery, and vehicles.
   - Furniture and equipment.
   - Land and property.

Fixed assets are crucial for long-term growth and productivity but require careful management as they are less liquid. These assets also often depreciate over time.

For example, if My Furniture LLC has $185,000 in current assets (cash and receivables) and $556,000 in fixed assets (building, tools, and equipment), its total assets are $741,000.

Liabilities: What Your Business (Definitely) Owes

My furniture business, like all businesses, runs because I owe other people money. I don't operate debt-free. When I owe money to others, those obligations are called *liabilities*. There are many ways to organize liabilities, but we're going to organize them based on how quickly I intend to pay people back.

1. **Current Liabilities:** These are obligations you plan to settle within the next 12 months. Examples include:
2. Credit card balances.
    o   Accounts payable (money you owe suppliers).
    o   Short-term loans or lines of credit.
3. **Long-Term Liabilities:** These are debts that will take longer than a year to repay fully. Examples include:
    o   Mortgages on buildings.
    o   Equipment loans.
    o   Long-term lines of credit.

In our example, My Furniture LLC might have $299,000 in current liabilities (credit card bills and supplier payments) and $115,000 in long-term liabilities (mortgage and equipment loans), resulting in total liabilities of $414,000.

Equity: What (Really) Belongs to You

Equity represents the portion of the business that belongs to the owner after liabilities are subtracted from assets. It's essentially your stake in the business, including any profits retained in the company and the initial capital you invested. Equity typically includes:

1. **Owner's Equity:** The starting balance of funds you've invested in the business.
2. **Retained Earnings:** Profits reinvested or kept in the business over time.
3. **Distributions or Draws:** The money you've taken out for personal use, reducing the overall equity (hence why this is typically a negative number).

Let's look at what the balance sheet would show. If My Furniture LLC has $741,000 in assets and $414,000 in liabilities, the equity is what is left when you subtract the two amounts, or $327,000. This is the value that remains after all debts are settled, and it belongs to me, the owner.

How a Balance Sheet Works

The balance sheet balances because of its structure: Total assets must equal the sum of total liabilities and equity. If they don't, there's an error somewhere.

For example, if My Furniture LLC has total assets of $741,000, liabilities of $414,000, and equity of $327,000, the balance sheet is in harmony:

Assets ($741,000) = Liabilities ($414,000) + Equity ($327,000)

#BSM: Balance Sheets Matter!

The balance sheet provides a comprehensive view of your business's financial health and stability. It helps answer critical questions, such as:

1. **Am I solvent?**
   A business is solvent when its assets exceed its liabilities, ensuring it can meet obligations without financial strain.
2. **How much equity do I have? (i.e How much does my business owe me?)**

Equity growth over time indicates that your business is building value and wealth for you.

3. **What's my liquidity?**
   Current assets compared to current liabilities show your ability to cover short-term obligations—a critical measure of financial stability.

How to Use a Balance Sheet to Make Business Decisions

The balance sheet is invaluable for making informed business decisions, including:

- **Assessing Risk:** If liabilities grow faster than assets, it's a red flag that you may be over-leveraged and can't withstand a surprise downturn.
- **Securing Financing:** Lenders often review your balance sheet to determine your creditworthiness.
- **Strategic Planning:** Knowing your equity and liquidity allows you to reinvest profits or take distributions confidently.

For example, if My Furniture LLC's equity grows steadily each year, it may signal that the business is on a strong financial trajectory, allowing me, the owner, to reinvest in new equipment or take a larger draw.

Now, let's look at another example of how a balance sheet rolls over values each year.

Let's say that as of January 1, my retained earnings is $250,000. That year My Furniture, LLC earns net income of $290,000. I've taken a shareholder distribution of $140,000 because that's how much I withdrew from my equity in addition to my wages. If I add up all these numbers, I get $400,000 as my total equity as of December 31.

Now, it's January 1—one day later. What's changed? Not much—but a few things have rolled over and reset on my balance sheet. The net income of $290,000 the business earned in net income from the previous year has been reset to zero, my distribution for the year has been reset to zero (I haven't taken anything out yet) and the difference between what the business earned last year ($290,000) and what I took as a draw last year ($140,000) has been "retained" or kept in the business and thus was added to retained earnings. My total equity on January 1 has not changed.

	As of January 1	As of December 31	As of January 1
Retained Earnings	$250,000	$250,000	$400,000
Net Income	$0	$290,000	$0
Distribution Taken	$0	$(140,000)	$0
Total Equity	$250,000	$400,000	$400,000

Table 3 - total equity

We can use the balance sheet numbers to understand how the business is performing (net income) year-to-date, how much we've taken out year-to-date (distributions) and how much more might be available to take as a distribution. And just as a reminder: Who does that $400,000 of equity belong to? It belongs to me, the owner. This is why it is so great to see total equity increase consistently over time.

The Balance Sheet in Action

Moving on to a different example, the same hypothetical company, let's imagine it's May 31st, and I've closed the month for My Furniture LLC. The balance sheet shows:

- **Assets:**
- Current Assets: $185,000 (cash, receivables, inventory).
    - o Fixed Assets: $556,000 (building, tools, equipment).
    - o Total Assets: $741,000.
- **Liabilities:**
- Current Liabilities: $299,000 (credit cards, supplier payments).
    - o Long-Term Liabilities: $115,000 (mortgages, equipment loans).
    - o Total Liabilities: $414,000.

- **Equity:**
- Owner's Equity: $256,000 (starting balance on January 1).
  - ○ Retained Earnings: $71,000 (current year net profit).
  - ○ Total Equity: $327,000.

With these figures, you can assess that the business is financially healthy, has more assets than liabilities, and provides a solid equity base for me, the owner. My equity has increased since January 1.

Special Topic: Depreciation

You've probably heard the term "depreciation" before, and it's actually a surprisingly complex topic. There's an entire section of the tax code written about it. Depreciation is a way for businesses to recognize that equipment wears out, becomes obsolete, and is used over long periods of time to deliver goods or services.

Depreciation is the cost of an asset spread over time, based on how it tends to wear out or lose value. If you don't depreciate something, it's like having to pay for it all upfront, like cash. The challenge with that is it doesn't reflect the reality of how you use the asset or how it wears out. There are different perspectives on depreciation, and it's important to keep all of them in mind to understand how it affects your business.

Perspectives on Depreciation

1. **Cash Perspective**: From a cash perspective, depreciation doesn't exist. Nobody writes you a check for depreciation, and you don't have to pay anyone for it.
2. **Tax Perspective**: Depreciation is very important for taxes. It's a tax deduction against taxable business income (meaning that it's treated like an expense). As your equipment wears out, depreciation allows you to reduce the taxable profits of your business, recognizing that your assets are wearing out—even though the cash portion may have been already paid in full. Depreciation only applies to business assets; personal property cannot be depreciated.

Why Depreciation Matters

Depreciation is common in business because companies need equipment to deliver goods and services to customers and equipment wears out over time. Politicians often use depreciation as a tool to stimulate the economy. During economic downturns, the government may offer special depreciation bonuses to businesses. These depreciation bonuses lower the taxable profit from your business and thus lower your tax bill because you only pay taxes on profit. The beauty of depreciation is that it lowers your taxes without requiring any cash to leave your bank account. Lower taxes means more cash in your pocket which can make investment in your business easier.

Depreciation Methods and Schedules

Depreciation is based on an assets useful life. For example:

- **Cars** typically depreciate over five years.
- **Buildings** depreciate over 27.5 or 35 years, depending on their use.

Even within a given time frame, there are different methods to calculate depreciation:

- Some assets, like vehicles, wear out faster, so you might use accelerated depreciation to deduct more in the first year.
- Others depreciate evenly over time, so you'd use a straight-line depreciation schedule.

The most common depreciation schedule used by businesses is **MACRS** (Modified Accelerated Cost Recovery System). It provides schedules for everything from laptops to buildings. There are other methods and you get to choose which one fits your situation best. Once you choose a method you have to stick with it until the asset is fully depreciated (meaning it is all used up).

Capital Assets vs. Non-Capital Assets

Not everything can be depreciated. For example, pens are not capital assets because they don't significantly add value to the business or become less useful over time. In contrast, buildings and machinery are considered capital assets, which are typically depreciated.

Where Depreciation Is Reported

Depreciation schedules are usually tracked in your accountant's software. While some accountants provide detailed schedules as part of your tax package each year, it's not common. Depreciation is reported on your tax return (Form 4797, attached to your 1040). However, this form doesn't break down assets line by line; it aggregates them. If you have many depreciable assets, it's a good idea to get a detailed report from your accountant each year to understand the schedules of each asset. Each asset owned by your business is tracked separately and has its own depreciation schedule. This information is helpful for estimating current or future depreciation, which in turn aids in tax planning.

Profit and Loss vs. Balance Sheet

Most businesses report depreciation on their balance sheet because it acknowledges that assets lose value over time. On the balance sheet, depreciation is typically listed below the asset section, often labeled "zDepreciation" to ensure it appears at the bottom (balance sheets are often sorted alphabetically).

However, some businesses—especially those in construction, metalworking, or manufacturing—prefer to report depreciation on their profit and loss (P&L) statement. This is because it reflects the real cash spent on maintaining equipment. For example, in my furniture company, where I spend heavily on keeping equipment in working condition, listing depreciation on the P&L makes the most sense for the way I like to plan.

Whether to report depreciation on the P&L or balance sheet depends on how you want to view your business operations. If you report it on the P&L, it's typically listed under fixed expenses, but you might consider moving it "below the line" (after operating profit). This is because potential buyers of your business are often more interested in **EBITDA** (Earnings Before Interest, Taxes, Depreciation, and Amortization) than depreciation itself. Most businesses put depreciation on their balance sheet (the way to say this is "Depreciation is a balance sheet item.")

Depreciation's Impact on P&L and Taxes

If you put depreciation on your P&L, it makes the statement less reflective of your bank account or business operations since depreciation isn't a cash expense. However, it can make the P&L more reflective of how you need to spend money to keep equipment working or make your P&L more tax-focused because depreciation is tax-deductible. Whether it's on the P&L or the balance sheet, your CPA will report depreciation on your tax return, so you'll still benefit from the deduction. You can decide for yourself what you want to see on your P&L so that you make the best decisions possible for your business.

Depreciation Recapture

When you sell an asset that has been depreciated, you must account for **depreciation recapture.** Essentially, you add back the amount of depreciation claimed over the asset's life to calculate the profit on the sale of the asset. This ensures you don't get a double tax benefit.

There's no "free lunch" with taxes—you'll either pay taxes now or pay them later. You get the depreciation deduction while owning the asset, but you must reconcile that when you sell. You'll only get one deduction, along the way or at the end when you sell the asset, not both.

Statement of Cash Flows, Revisited

The cash flow statement is your business's financial "honesty report," showing how cash moves in and out of your business over a specific period. While the P&L focuses on operational efficiency and the balance sheet highlights financial stability, the cash flow statement answers one critical question: *Do I have enough cash to keep my business running?*

Even a profitable business can fail without sufficient cash to meet its obligations. That's why this report is essential—it bridges the gap between profitability and liquidity.

The Three Sections of the Statement of Cash Flows

The cash flow statement breaks down cash activity into three distinct categories:

1. **Operating Activities:**
   This section covers cash generated or spent during normal business operations. It includes:
   - Cash received from customers (income on the P&L or accounts receivable on the balance sheet).
   - Cash paid for operating expenses like payroll, rent, and materials. This includes items on your P&L and items still sitting on your balance sheet (e.g. cash still sitting in your payroll account because payroll hasn't fully run yet).

For example, My Furniture LLC might collect $100,000 in customer payments while spending $28,000 on raw materials and $47,000 on fixed expenses, resulting in a net positive cash flow from operations.

2. **Investing Activities:**
   This section reflects cash used for or generated by investments in the business, such as:
3. Purchasing or selling equipment.
   - Buying or selling property or long-term assets.

If My Furniture LLC buys a $6,500 piece of machinery, that amount appears as a cash outflow under investing activities.

4. **Financing Activities:**
   This section tracks cash flow from borrowing or repaying debt
   and from owner distributions (you can think of equity like a
   loan from the owner), including:
   - ○ Taking out or paying down loans.
   - ○ Paying yourself (distributions or draws).

If My Furniture LLC pays $1,000 toward an equipment loan or if I as the
owner take an $11,000 draw, these amounts appear as financing activities.

How the Cash Flow Statement Works

The report begins with the cash balance at the start of the period, adds
or subtracts changes from the three categories (operating, investing, and
financing activities), and ends with the cash balance at the end of the
period. This simple structure provides a clear picture of how cash is flowing through your business.

For example, imagine My Furniture LLC starts the month with
$130,000 in cash. During the month:

- Operating activities generate $17,000 in net positive cash flow.
- Investing activities result in a $6,500 cash outflow for new
  equipment purchased.
- Financing activities result in a $11,000 cash outflow, reducing
  cash by that amount.

After accounting for these changes, the ending cash balance is
$129,500. This report explains exactly where the cash went, providing
transparency into the business's liquidity.

Crucial Cash Flows

The cash flow statement is crucial because it reveals whether your business has the liquidity to cover expenses, invest in growth, and handle
unexpected challenges. Even if your P&L shows a profit, you could still

run out of cash if revenue is delayed, expenses spike, or investments are poorly timed.

For example, My Furniture LLC might show $29,000 in net profit on the P&L for the month, but if the business spends $28,000 on materials and $11,000 on draws, the cash flow could turn negative. This discrepancy underscores why the P&L and cash flow statement must be used together.

Let's revisit My Furniture LLC's financials for June. The company's cash flow report looks like this:

- **Starting Cash Balance:** $130,000
- **Operating Activities:** +$17,000
  - Customer payments: +$83,000
  - Payments for materials, wages, and expenses: $(66,000)
- **Investing Activities:** $(6,500)
  - Equipment purchase: $(6,500)
- **Financing Activities:** $(11,000)
  - Loan repayment: $(1,000)
  - Owner draw: $(10,000)

If you add all these items up, the net change in cash for the month is $(500). The ending cash balance in my business bank account is $129,500, reflecting a slight decrease due to investments and draws.

Common Cash Flow Challenges

Cash flow problems are one of the most common reasons businesses struggle, even when profitable. Here are a few common scenarios and how the cash flow statement helps:

1. **Revenue Timing Issues:**
   If customers delay payments, cash flow can dry up even if the P&L looks strong. Reviewing the operating activities section highlights whether receivables are being converted into cash quickly enough.

2. **Overinvestment:**
   Purchasing equipment or inventory without sufficient cash reserves can strain liquidity. The investing activities section tracks these expenditures, helping you avoid overextending. Businesses often use a line of credit to help address this challenge.
3. **Debt Burden:**
   Excessive loan payments can deplete cash reserves. The financing activities section reveals whether debt is consuming too much of your cash flow.

Planning for Cash

The cash flow statement is a powerful tool for planning and decision-making. It helps you:

- **Manage Liquidity:** Ensure you have enough cash to cover payroll, rent, and other obligations.
- **Plan Investments:** Decide when to purchase equipment or expand operations based on available cash.
- **Control Distributions:** Balance personal draws with the business's cash needs.

Here's an example. If My Furniture LLC sees that cash flow from operations is consistently positive, I would feel confident reinvesting in the business or increasing my draw. Conversely, if cash flow is tight or negative, I may delay investments or reduce my distributions to maintain a healthy cash buffer in the bank account.

The Bigger Picture: The Role of Cash Flow in Business Success

The cash flow statement ties together insights from the P&L and balance sheet, providing a complete view of your business's financial health. It ensures that profitability translates into liquidity and helps you avoid running out of cash.

By regularly reviewing this report, you can proactively address cash flow issues, make informed decisions, and keep your business on a stable path to growth. Combined with the P&L and balance sheet, the cash flow statement forms the foundation for sound financial management. This is continuous improvement, and this is what separates "meh" business success from greatness. You know better, so you do better. But first, you must be willing to *know better*.

Three Financial Statements, One Big Picture

The three primary financial statements—P&L, balance sheet, and cash flow statement—are interconnected tools that together provide a complete picture of your business's financial health. Individually, each statement answers specific questions. The P&L shows how profitable your operations are, the balance sheet reflects overall financial stability, and the cash flow statement reveals liquidity. However, relying on just one report can lead to blind spots. When analyzed together, these reports highlight patterns, reveal inconsistencies, and offer actionable insights.

Back in the early days before we had fancy accounting or bookkeeping software, accounting was done by the cash register. It was super simple because you would collect cash from customers and pay suppliers out of the same cash register. If the cash in the register when it was time for the store to close each day went up a little bit —and you don't take any out to slip in your pocket, just leave it all in there—you would know you're profitable. That's the "poor man's P&L" because it is so simple and effective.

The cash flow statement hails from that legacy. It's the way to know you're on track because the P&L doesn't tell you the full truth. I already mentioned that the P&L doesn't exactly reflect what's going on in your bank account. You could have a great-looking P&L with all positive, beautiful numbers—and still face big problems because the business is running out of cash.

The same goes for the balance sheet. It doesn't show how well you're operating your company. You could actually be running your company into the ground and still have good numbers on the balance sheet.

But you will never have good numbers on the P&L, good numbers on the balance sheet, and good numbers on the cash flow statement if your business isn't doing well. These three reports together form a triad to confirm that your business is healthy. That's why you must run all three. Because:

- If your P&L shows a positive net income (meaning you're earning profit),
- If your balance sheet shows increasing equity and more assets than liabilities,
- And if your cash flow statement shows a positive cash delta (meaning your cash is increasing every month),

. . . then you know you're good. And you know that you know.

But it gets interesting when one of the reports shows good news, and another shows bad news. Those situations are relatively easy to chase down—you can drill into the numbers, figure out what's going on, and correct it. The most challenging scenario, however, is when you get mixed news across all three reports.

Now, let's explore how these statements work in harmony, using examples to illustrate when they may present conflicting signals.

Example 1: A Profitable Business That's Running Out of Cash

Imagine that My Furniture LLC's P&L shows strong profitability for the month. The company generated $100,000 in revenue, with $72,000 in gross profit and $25,000 in operating profit. At first glance, everything looks great—revenue is healthy, and operations are efficient.

However, the cash flow statement tells a different story. Despite the $25,000 operating profit, the business's cash position decreased by $10,000.

- **Investing Activities:** The company purchased $15,000 worth of equipment.
- **Financing Activities:** The owner took a $20,000 distribution, further depleting cash reserves.

The balance sheet confirms the situation. While total assets increased (reflecting the new equipment), current assets—especially cash—declined. The liabilities section also reveals that credit card debt increased, likely because cash was too tight to cover certain expenses.

Insight: This is a classic case of a business appearing profitable but running into liquidity problems. Without sufficient cash to meet obligations, the company could struggle to pay suppliers or make payroll, even though the P&L looked strong.

Action Plan: The owner should:

1. Reevaluate the timing of equipment purchases to align with cash availability.
2. Reduce distributions to preserve cash.
3. Consider financing equipment purchases rather than paying cash upfront.

Example 2: Strong Cash Flow But Poor Profitability

Now imagine another scenario where My Furniture LLC has a net positive cash flow of $10,000 for the month. The cash flow statement shows that operating activities generated $5,000, while financing activities (such as a loan) added another $15,000. At first glance, this might seem like a healthy situation—cash is increasing.

However, the P&L reveals a problem: The business operated at a loss of $10,000 for the month. The cost of goods sold and fixed expenses exceeded revenue, eating into profitability. The balance sheet reflects this as well, showing a decrease in retained earnings, indicating that the business is depleting its equity to cover losses. This means that me as the owner is financing that shortfall out of what belongs to me.

Insight: While the cash flow looks strong, the business is borrowing money from third parties and me, the owner, to stay afloat. This is not sustainable in the long term, as the growing debt will eventually outpace the company's ability to repay.

Action Plan: The owner should:

1. Analyze the P&L to identify operational inefficiencies, such as high COGS or bloated overhead expenses.
2. Focus on increasing revenue or cutting costs to restore profitability.
3. Use the balance sheet to monitor debt levels and avoid overleveraging.

Example 3: A Stable Balance Sheet But Inconsistent Operations

In this example, the balance sheet shows that the business is in good shape. Total assets of $750,000 exceed liabilities of $400,000, leaving $350,000 in equity. The company is solvent, with sufficient assets to cover debts.

However, the P&L tells a more volatile story. Revenue has been inconsistent over the past three months, fluctuating significantly from $100,000 in one month to $60,000 in another. This inconsistency affects operating profit, which swings between positive and negative values. The cash flow statement confirms the issue, with cash reserves shrinking during low-revenue months.

Insight: While the balance sheet reflects stability, the business is struggling with operational consistency, which could eventually impact financial health. If low-revenue months persist, cash reserves and equity could be depleted, jeopardizing the business.

Action Plan: The owner should:

1. Analyze sales trends to identify seasonal fluctuations or customer retention issues.
2. Improve cash flow management by setting aside reserves during high-revenue months.
3. Focus on marketing and customer acquisition to stabilize revenue.
4. Consider moving to a different accounting method (move from cash to accrual[2])

I think we've made our point. These examples highlight the importance of viewing all three statements separately yes but also and especially together.

Driving Your Business with Confidence

Let's return to our favorite car metaphor. We now think of these reports as the dashboard of your business. The P&L is your rearview mirror, showing where you've been. The balance sheet is your speedometer and gauges, reflecting your current state. The cash flow statement is your fuel gauge, showing how far you can go. By glancing at all three, you can drive your business with confidence, making informed decisions that balance profitability, stability, and liquidity.

Now, imagine driving while only focusing on one part of your dashboard—whether it's the rearview mirror, the speedometer, or the fuel gauge. You'd miss crucial information and increase the risk of going off the road. Managing your business is no different. You need to glance at all three financial statements regularly to maintain balance and ensure smooth operation.

Quick examples to drive this home:

---

2 - There are different accounting methods that can help you create reports that more accurately reflect your business operations so that you can make better decisions. Accrual accounting method is especially helpful when you have highly volatile sales and it takes a long time to complete an order or finish delivering a service. With Accrual accounting you don't count the sales as revenue until you ship the product or complete the service. Talk with your accountant to discuss if a method of accounting other than cash would help you better manage your business.

- If your **P&L** shows strong profits but your **cash flow statement** reveals declining cash reserves, you may be overspending on investments or distributions.
- If your **balance sheet** shows stable equity but your **P&L** reflects operational losses, you may need to address inefficiencies before they erode long-term stability.
- If your **cash flow statements** show positive cash flow but your **balance sheet** indicates growing liabilities, you may be relying too heavily on debt to maintain liquidity.

Remember, we said "regularly." Glance *regularly*. What does that mean? Here's what it means.

How Often to Review Financial Statements

Just like you glance at different instruments on and in your car at varying intervals, you should review the P&L, balance sheet, and cash flow statement at different frequencies based on the type of information each provides. Regular reviews—both individually and collectively—help you maintain a clear picture of your business's health, spot trends, and address potential issues before they become serious problems.

Here's a recommended schedule.

Daily: Keep an Eye on Cash Flow

- **What to Review:** Focus on cash balances from your bank account and, optionally, a summary of inflows and outflows.
- **Purpose:** Liquidity is the lifeblood of your business. A quick daily check of your bank account balances ensures you have enough cash to cover immediate obligations, like payroll or supplier payments.
- **Tools:** Most bookkeeping software, like QuickBooks and Freshbooks, syncs with your bank and credit card accounts to

give you real-time cash balances. This is also quick and easy to do with your bank's website or their smartphone app.

Example: Imagine logging into your bank account to see $50,000 available for operations. You know your weekly payroll is $25,000, so you're reassured that you can cover it without issue. If the balance were lower, you might decide to hold off on a discretionary expense.

Weekly: Review Key Metrics

- **What to Review:**
  - P&L summary for revenue and expenses.
  - Cash flow statement to check net cash changes.
- **Purpose:** Weekly reviews help you monitor short-term trends and ensure operations are on track. They're especially useful for spotting anomalies in sales, unexpected expenses, or cash flow issues that might need immediate attention.
- **Focus Areas:** Look at top-line revenue, gross profit, and net cash changes.

Example: If sales dropped this week compared to last, you might investigate whether a marketing campaign underperformed or if there were delivery delays. Alternatively, if cash flow is negative, you could adjust the timing of payments or collections.

Monthly: Conduct a Detailed Review

- **What to Review:**
  - Full P&L to evaluate profitability and margins.
  - Cash flow statement to analyze liquidity changes.
  - Balance sheet to assess financial position.
- **Purpose:** Monthly reviews give you a broader view of your business's performance. By comparing actual results to your operating model, you can identify what's working, what's not, and what needs to change.

- **Key Questions:**
  - Is the business profitable?
  - Is cash flow positive?
  - Are assets growing faster than liabilities?

Example: If the P&L shows an unexpected drop in operating profit when compared with your ideal business model, you can drill into variable and fixed expenses to pinpoint the issue. If the balance sheet shows a rise in accounts payable, you might review payment terms with suppliers to avoid overdue penalties. If you see a big number in accounts receivable you could look into which customers are not paying on time and give them a call.

Quarterly: Strategic Evaluation

- **What to Review:**
  - Balance sheet to identify long-term trends in assets, liabilities, and equity.
  - P&L and cash flow statement for the quarter as a whole.
- **Purpose:** Quarterly reviews are ideal for spotting patterns and evaluating the effectiveness of strategic initiatives. These reviews also align with tax and compliance cycles, making them a good time to prepare for quarterly tax payments.
- **Focus Areas:** Compare actual performance to goals and projections, and use insights to adjust your strategy for the next quarter.

Example: If quarterly results show consistent revenue growth but declining net profit, it may be time to renegotiate supplier contracts or cut overhead expenses. Or perhaps you hired ahead of when staff was actually needed. Alternatively, strong equity growth might indicate an opportunity to reinvest in expansion.

Annually: Big-Picture Assessment

- **What to Review:**
    - Balance sheet to understand year-over-year changes in financial position.
    - Annual P&L to assess overall profitability and business operating model.
    - Cash flow statement to evaluate long-term liquidity trends.
- **Purpose:** Annual reviews are ideal for big-picture planning, setting new goals, and preparing for tax filings. They're also a time to reflect on the business's progress and make adjustments for the coming year.
- **Key Questions:**
    - Did the business grow as expected?
    - Is the company positioned for future growth?
    - What changes are needed to improve next year's performance?

Example: If annual reviews reveal that your gross margin has consistently declined, you may consider raising prices, renegotiating costs, or discontinuing low-margin products.

When to Review All Three Together

While each report has its own review cadence, it's essential to evaluate them together periodically to ensure a cohesive understanding of your business. Here's how to align their reviews:

- **Weekly or Monthly for Small Businesses:** Review all three reports together if your business has fast-moving finances, such as daily sales or fluctuating cash flow.
- **Quarterly for Established Businesses:** Mature businesses with steady operations may only need a comprehensive review of all three statements quarterly.

- **Before Major Decisions:** Always review all three reports when making significant decisions, such as expanding operations, securing financing, or adjusting your pricing strategy.

Benefits of Regular Reviews

1. **Stay Proactive:** Regular reviews help you spot issues early, whether it's a cash shortage, declining profitability, or growing debt.
2. **Monitor Progress:** Consistently reviewing your reports allows you to track how well you're meeting goals and staying aligned with your operating model.
3. **Make Data-Driven Decisions:** A clear understanding of your finances ensures that every decision—whether it's hiring new staff, purchasing equipment, or scaling operations—is backed by reliable data.
4. **Tax Preparation:** Frequent reviews keep your books in order, reducing stress during tax season and ensuring compliance.

The Bottom Line

Just as you wouldn't drive a car without glancing at your dashboard, you shouldn't run a business without regularly reviewing your financial statements. By adopting a routine for examining the P&L, balance sheet, and cash flow statement—both individually and collectively—you can navigate your business with confidence and control, staying on the path to long-term success.

Oh—and remember Matt? Well, here's what he learned from his three most important financial reports.

Tight at Payroll

Back when the business was getting started, Matt's dad, together with the family accountant, had decided to include depreciation on the P&L. This is a non-cash item that reflects the tax nature of depreciation and the reality of how the business equipment would wear out over time. Equipment depreciation had been a big deal to the business, being a pipe fitting and valve manufacturer with equipment that naturally wore out and, well, depreciated over time. By including depreciation on the P&L, Matt's dad had intended to intuitively plan and set aside cash for equipment wear and tear. Matt had been using the P&L for something entirely different—he was using it to get a cash perspective around the time of payroll. Once he understood what the P&L was showing him, everything made sense.

Once Matt learned how to correctly read the P&L generated by his bookkeeping software—and learned to read the business balance sheet—he looked for a way to better understand the cash changes in his business operating account. The answer led him to the cash flow statement. This report explained item-by-item what had happened in his bank account and how those transactions were reported on the P&L and the balance sheet. Understanding each transaction in the business bank account gave him much needed confidence that the business was healthy overall.

The collective result of Matt's business finance education was this: He realized that his equity in the business was about $1 million! That meant he could increase his monthly dividend—an emotional break-through, to say the least—as compensation for the difficult work he was doing as the business owner. It had actually been there all along—he just hadn't known it. If only he'd learned to read that balance sheet months ago! There was also sadness from the lost opportunity for his dad.

But—sometimes in business there is another "but"—Matt's business was still a C-corp. His accountant told him that withdrawing that nearly-million bucks would be a taxable event. Fortunately, Matt's mentor explained a way to soften that blow. And that was the next lesson, which you, too, will learn—how to manage your cash flow.

CHAPTER 5

CASH FLOW CONTROL
FOR FUN AND PROFIT

Brad and his wife Jenny operate a successful business in the American midwest. Their story picks up at the empty-nester stage of life; the kids are already out of the house, and the couple is financially stable. Yet they, as most couples looking toward their golden years do, worry about their finances. The ups and downs of even a good business are felt in daily life at home. But especially in April every year, on tax day. That's when the surprise tax bill hit. And they've been getting bigger and bigger each year. The shock's grown as well. Brad and Jenny have had to cash out investments early or steal from their savings nest-egg in order to pay the tax bill. Meanwhile, their business has remained successful. Something's not right here.

Brad and Jenny had tried for years to manage their cash situation to keep the ups higher and lows lower. Perhaps unexpected tax payments were just the natural consequence of owning a business. Perhaps. Or perhaps not.

To manage cash flow early in their marriage and long before the kids were grown (or born), they'd used the envelope method. As we've read previously, this works—for a while. But it doesn't work if you don't do it and at some point it will break down as you earn more money. As you'd expected, yes, Brad and Jenny drifted; they no longer use envelopes.

They, too, ended up with multiple bank accounts—five, to be exact. Each checking account held money for one of their expense "categories." One was for food, one was for the loans against the mortgage on the home, another for the lake house mortgage, one for the car, one for entertainment, one for household expenses, and one for saving. Wait—that's seven bank accounts. Maybe they had seven. Shoot . . . yeah. They had seven. They didn't even know how many bank accounts they had!

So as you can imagine, it took a *lot* to stay on top of all the balances. They frequently had to transfer money between and among multiple accounts multiple times a week to keep any number from going negative. I remind you once again—their business was *successful*.

Brad and Jenny also gave generously to their church. They'd typically donate a monthly amount based on how much they thought they had left over at month's end. Sometimes this felt like a lot; other times, the balance was negative until Jenny made a rush transfer out of another account before close of business that day. As devout believers, the couple felt this approach to cash management didn't let them give the amount or in the way they believed they were called to. It felt terrible overall, even aside from charitable contribution inconsistency. Not only was there a lot of time wasted maintaining balances, there was constant fear of running out of money. This took a toll, particularly on Jenny. She constantly worried about the balances in the accounts because these were *her* responsibility. She wanted to do a good job and be a good steward of the money Brad had worked so hard to earn. She often felt like they needed to cut back and spend less. This changed how she felt when they would go out to eat or go on a vacation. Brad didn't like that Jenny felt insecure; he wanted her to know that he was providing for everything they needed. But she didn't feel that way. Because, frankly, he wasn't.

But that was about to change.

Other Strategies for Handling Cash

Managing cash sounds so simple, right? It's just cash, just a checking account. It's not so easy for business owners, for a couple reasons. If you are challenged or frustrated managing personal family money, it's not because you're not capable of doing it but because you probably have different needs and face unique challenges as a business owner.

You have a unique risk profile since your business is both your largest source of income *and* your largest source of risk, and the income your family earns from the business likely has variability. Sometimes it's a feast, other times, a famine. And because you own your own business, you have more options than a standard W-2 employee for what to do with your personal cash. You get to choose between, "Do I invest in my family's future?" and "Do I invest in my business' future?" You're probably always thinking about your business; you may spend certain hours in the office, but it's always on your mind. So now, the choice between a new investment in the business for future profit or a nice vacation with the family is not so easy. It can weigh on you emotionally.

And if it weighs on you, it probably weighs on your spouse.

As a business owner, you also have a unique experience with taxes. In addition to withholding taxes through your paycheck like everyone else, you get to make quarterly estimated tax payments. Let's not even get started on the stress that can come from the April tax bill true-up. All of this creates unique challenges.

All these competing priorities and challenges create a need for awareness how to control cash that other people frankly don't need. How you handle cash is going to be the foundation of the skyscraper of your family finances.

But before I show you the **Cash Consolidation Process**, let's talk about how you probably handle cash right now—the way most business owners do. And there are a few different methods.

How Most Small Business Owners Manage Their Money

Approach	How It Works	Pros	Cons
Envelope method popularized by Dave Ramsey's Financial Peace University	Envelope for each spending category Put cash in at start of month When envelope is empty, stop spending	Helps couples eliminate bad debt when resources are scarce Helps couples work together Simple and low cost to implement	Does not scale with income One spouse often feels guilt (especially the one that is taking care of the household) Promotes mentality that there isn't enough to go around
Debt snowball— strategy for paying off debt that focuses on eliminating the smallest balances first, while making minimum payments on larger debts	List debts, make minimum payments on all Make extra payments on smallest debt Once small debt is paid off, move to next largest one Repeat until all debts are paid	Systematic Brings couples together as a team Effective at eliminating debt, especially high interest bad debt	Not a cash-management system Doesn't prioritize based on cost to the family (small debts may not be the most expensive)
Debt avalanche—	Like debt snowball but start with biggest debts first	Same as debt snowball	Same as debt snowball
Pay-Yourself-First— parallels the approach outlined in the book "Profit First" by Mike Michalowicz	The basic idea of the book is that the first and highest priority of sales is to pay the profit to the owner. While this might be a good mentality for viewing your business as a cash engine, it doesn't work well as the business grows and scales. It fundamentally ignores a scalable business model and creates the illusion of profit when the business might not be ready to provide that level of profit to the owner. The parallel with the family is based on income. It prioritizes saving within the family.	Feels good	While saving is generally important and this is a good way to learn that discipline, this method completely ignores the ebbs and flows of living expenses that most business-owning families experience. It also does not provide guidelines and boundaries for long-term financial planning and leads to a scarcity mentality where excess in one area is needed to make up for the deficit in another.

Approach	How It Works	Pros	Cons
Budget	Money is planned for the categories the family needs and then spending is tracked against those planned expenses.	Parallels business budgeting and therefore feels familiar to business owners Provides way to hold emergency funds Easy to understand	Only works in hindsight Doesn't account for the large cash needs that can surprise a family Can cause unspoken stress between spouses—what happens when the grocery category is over budget and the hobby budget is under?
Living Expense Account	Paychecks and draws are deposited into a single account that feeds all other expenses (credit card payoff, subscriptions, auto-debits, etc). Expenses are often put onto "autopay" either through credit card monthly payoff or auto-debit.	Works Is the most common method among families with sufficient income to cover all typical monthly debts Tends to create harmony among couples with relatively stable expenses as they don't have to worry about spending Cash is very liquid (means it can be easily and quickly transferred to other accounts)	Tends to stockpile money (not put excess to work for the family) Money in checking accounts doesn't earn respectable interest Doesn't plan ahead for big cash needs that business-owning families tend to face or want to do (like a big well-deserved vacation with the kids) Doesn't explicitly create an emergency reserve (and often does this by accident by stockpiling) Doesn't provide a process that moves money to an intentional purpose. Doesn't promote the ideal giving mentality. Tends to promote laziness in families as they don't need to check account balances or discuss spending on the regular.

Table 4 - many ways to manage money

However, the number-one most common method most business owners use to manage cash is none at all! Usually, this is because they started with some method, and as the business grew in complexity, and their income grew along with it, the system they were using either no longer worked or it was too difficult to sustain. There's not really any good side to this, and the bad side is obvious; there's no system. You can't teach it to somebody, and you're spending time thinking about it. There's just a lot of bank accounts and money transfers flying around.

The second most common method I see, and one I see often since I work with a lot of faith-based business owners, is the *envelope system*. Popularized in America by Dave Ramsey and his Financial Peace University, most people I've seen who use this are aware of Ramsey from their church. It's very good, actually, when you're starting out or want to focus on reducing debt. The way it works is that you have multiple envelopes (you start with physical envelopes), one for each category of personal spending. At the beginning of each month, you put money in, and then spend out of that envelope. Once the money is out, you stop.

But it's not designed for people who make a lot of money and have moved beyond eliminating bad debt. You get tired of handling cash, so you start creating accounts for each of your expenses to maintain some semblance of the method. Or you've got a monster spreadsheet to track them all. It's still the envelope system. Even if you're doing it electronically, it's the same system, and it doesn't scale up to the level of income you're at.

The next system I've seen is the *budget system*. If you're reading this book, then you've had a successful business, and to have a successful business, you've had to have learned how to budget on some level and manage your expenses. A lot of people take that system, which works for the business, and mistakenly try to apply it to their family. *How much do I spend on clothing? How much do I spend on food? How much is entertainment? Can't spend more than that! Get that number lower!* This creates a scarcity mindset. It's designed for running a profit-maximizing business. Running a family is different. It's emotional. The goal isn't maximizing profit, but living abundantly.

Another one I've started seeing —and it's a little concerning to me— is this method called "Pay Yourself First," based on a very popular book called *Profit First*. The basic idea is that, when you earn income, the first thing you do is pay yourself. Then, with whatever is left over, you deal with the other responsibilities you have. It works when you have a lot of money but not when you have to make hard decisions. And I absolutely do **not** recommend it.

I've had to correct more businesses that had gone off the rails because they followed that book and implemented the "Profit First" mentality than I have had to correct for people who had no direction and didn't know what to do. In fact, I had to coach a business owner using this method. He was paying himself an incredible couple hundred thousand dollars a year for his salary, but couldn't understand why his bank account kept going down. He had bankrupted his business with this method. He couldn't produce a balance sheet or a P&L or any standard financial business report.

The Cash Consolidation Process

So what method do I recommend? I call it the **Cash Consolidation Process**, and there's a reason I chose this name.

First, it's about *cash*. Not debt, not credit, nothing but cash. Second, it's about *consolidation*. Rather than dividing and subdividing, we're combining and putting things together to manage efficiently. And lastly, it's a *process*. It's a machine, and if you follow the rules, it will produce consistent, repeatable, and delightful results.

I didn't invent it; my financial advisor taught it to me nineteen years ago, and have been using it since. And since my wife and I have been using this, I've measured how long this process takes to operate each month by the number of cups of coffee I can drink while the coffee's still hot. This is a one coffee cup job, once a month.

There are five main goals—the amazing outcomes you get to experience—by implementing this system.

First, every dollar that your family earns is assigned a purpose. There's no money sitting around getting moldy, as I like to call it. No stockpiling.

Second, you eliminate surprises, especially the uncomfortable ones. As a business owner, there's all sorts of surprises around every corner, and every three months you get to make a quarterly estimated tax payment.

Then you get the April true-up surprise plus your property taxes. All these surprises will go away and will be replaced with the confidence that comes from having a plan.

Third, you get clear visibility in how much you spend each month in living expenses *without* slipping into a budget mentality. I want you to live abundantly, blessed with a business you're stewarding.

Fourth, you need to generate passive income and build for the future. You can't just earn money today, because eventually, you won't want to be responsible for your business anymore. And when that happens, you need a plan, and that plan needs to be roughly in place years ahead of time because it will need time to grow large enough.

And **fifth** and finally, you want it to be easy to give. This creates happiness. And to do that, you need a support system.

How does it work?

First, the family generates income from a number of sources. Right now, we'll focus on three: paychecks, distributions (when the owner takes a portion of the profit due to them from the business), and rental profits. These sources of income are then consolidated and allocated towards three specific purposes: giving, living expenses, and investing.

Giving is the money you choose to give to other people, whether that's through charity organizations or specific things. Right now, we'll focus just on giving cash, not property, stock or anything else.

Living expenses include the cost of all things you need in order to live your lifestyle today. This is your home mortgage (if you have one), car payments (if you have any), bills, credit cards, entertainment, groceries, etc. Your living expenses are the things that you need every month in order to live the life you want to live.

Investing, in this case, is code for *passive income*. Consider it to be an investment now for your future income.

Your income is consolidated into a bank account called the Cash Consolidation Account. Not only does this hold the money that will be distributed towards those three purposes, it will also hold your Big Cash Needs, what I call "lumpy expenses." These are the expenses that you need to plan for, greater than $5,000, and due within the next six months. Quarterly tax payments, for example, or vacations, or an emergency fund.

The money from the Cash Consolidation Account is then allocated into accounts for those three purposes.

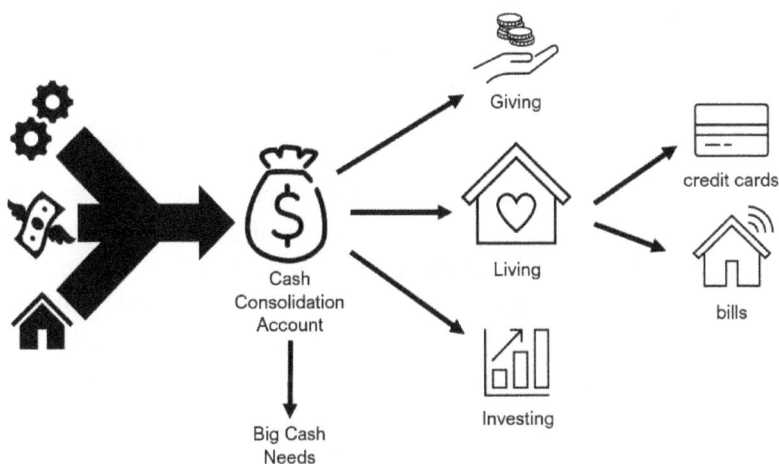

Figure 14 - overall view of the Cash Consolidation Process of cash

Let's break them down, and for the sake of this image, let's pretend all the income comes in before the first of the month. It'll never happen that way, but for the sake of this discussion, let's say it does.

First thing you do is transfer over the money required to live your lifestyle for a month into the account that pays your living expenses (your Living Expense Account). This account will have at least one month of living expenses in it already as a buffer. At its lowest, it should have one month's worth of average living expenses left in it, and usually that is by the end of the month, when you're about to replenish it. Once replenished (each month) it will have two months of average living expenses as the starting balance.

The next step is to identify the upcoming six months of Big Cash Needs (expenses that are above $5,000). Perhaps that might include your next quarterly estimated tax payment. Or maybe a big family vacation. At minimum, it includes your emergency reserves. This amount of money is how much you will leave in the Cash Consolidation Account once you have assigned and transferred money for giving, living and investing. For the rest of the explanation of the steps let's assume there is more in the

Cash Consolidation Account than you need for your next six months of Big Cash Needs.

Next you transfer money from your Cash Consolidation Account into the giving account (if you choose to have a dedicated account for giving) or transfer directly to the charity or organization that you support. Then with the excess left over in the Cash Consolidation Account, you move into your investing account.

These accounts—the Cash Consolidation Account, the Living Expense Account—are just checking accounts; if you went to your bank and asked to open a Cash Consolidation Account, they'd look at you like you were crazy. Investing accounts may be different, and this will vary according to your needs; this could be a 401(k) or an IRA or a brokerage account, but for the sake of this chapter, we'll treat this like another bank account. Same with your Giving Account; we'll assume this is cash, given to either a church or other organization.

Let's look at an example: Say we have a hypothetical family. In their Cash Consolidation Account, they have $100,000, and have a Living Expenses Account with $20,000 in it. Their living expenses average $20,000 per month. Let's say they run a successful business, and this month, earned $30,000 total from their W-2 paycheck and profit draw.

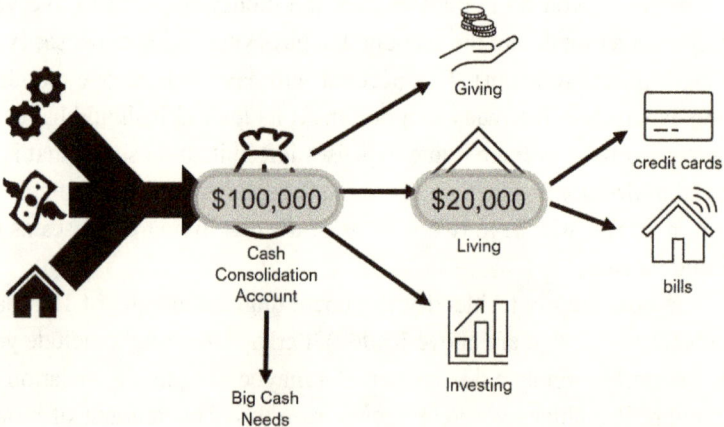

Figure 15 - starting balance of Cash Consolidation Account and Living Expense Account

The $30,000 from their paycheck and their draw is first deposited into the Cash Consolidation Account, raising the balance from $100,000 to $130,000.

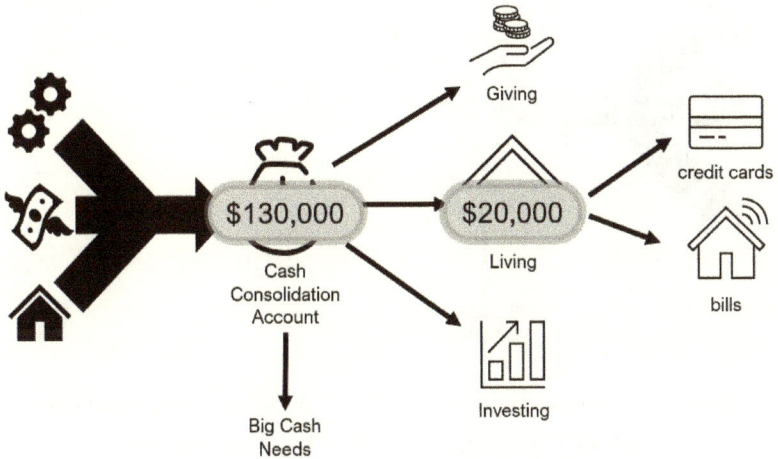

Figure 16 - balance in accounts after paycheck and draw from business that totalled $30,000

Now, the first thing they do is transfer $20,000 out of the Cash Consolidation Account into their Living Expense Account to take care of their upcoming month of living expenses. Now, the Cash Consolidation Account is down to $110,000, and the living expenses account is up to $40,000.

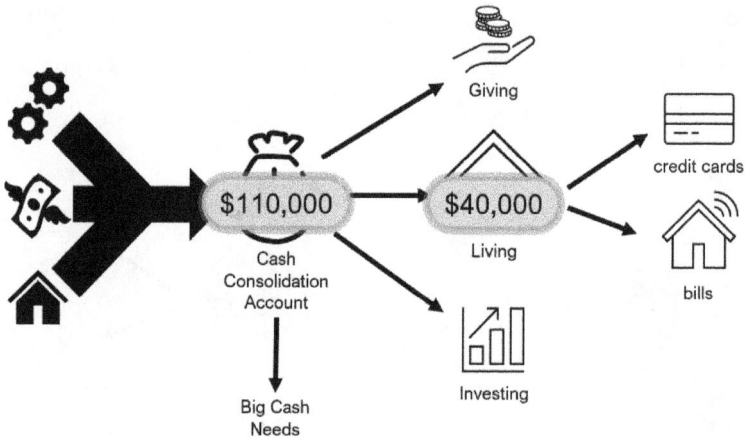

Figure 17 - balances after transfer of $20,000 out of Cash Consolidation Account to cover upcoming monthly living expenses

They also choose to give $3,000 as the next step, so the Cash Consolidation Account goes down to $107,000 and the Giving Account goes up by $3,000. The new totals are shown in Figure 5.

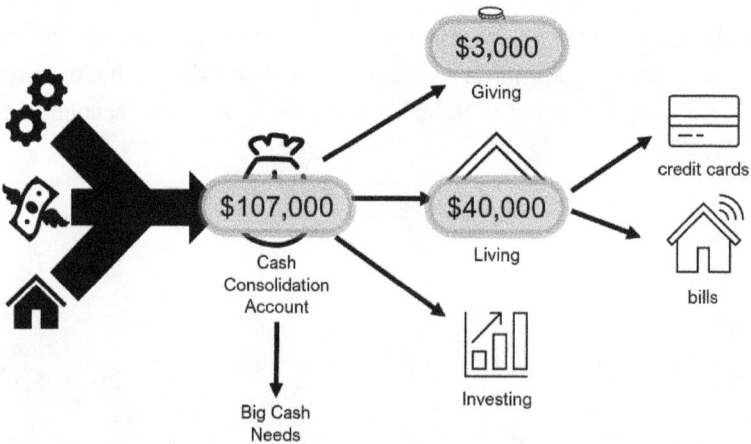

Figure 18 - balances after family gives $3,000 (which they chose to do before looking at Big Cash Needs)

This month, the family plans $100,000 to cover the next six months (which includes a quarterly estimated tax payment plus a family vacation plus their emergency reserves). So the $7,000 of excess in the Cash Consolidation Account goes into the Investing Account. The new balances are shown in Figure 19.

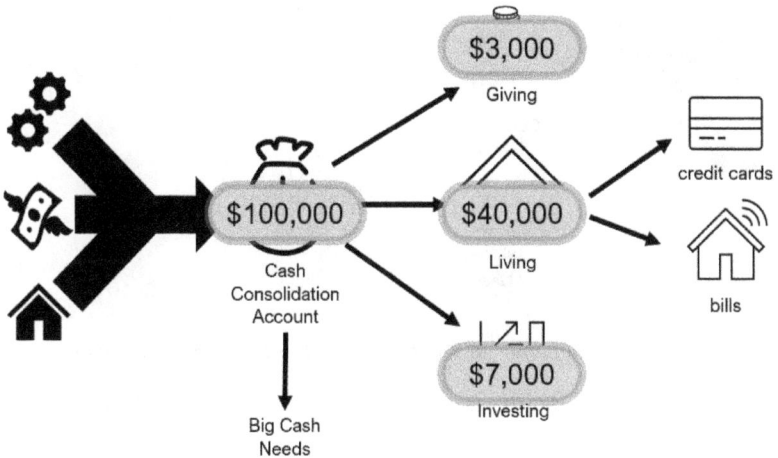

Figure 19 - balances after $7,000 of excess is transferred into investing account (note that family determined balance in Cash Consolidation Account for upcoming six months was $100,000)

Now the month proceeds as normal. The family pays their mortgage, their credit cards and all their bills. This is how the balances look at the end of the month.

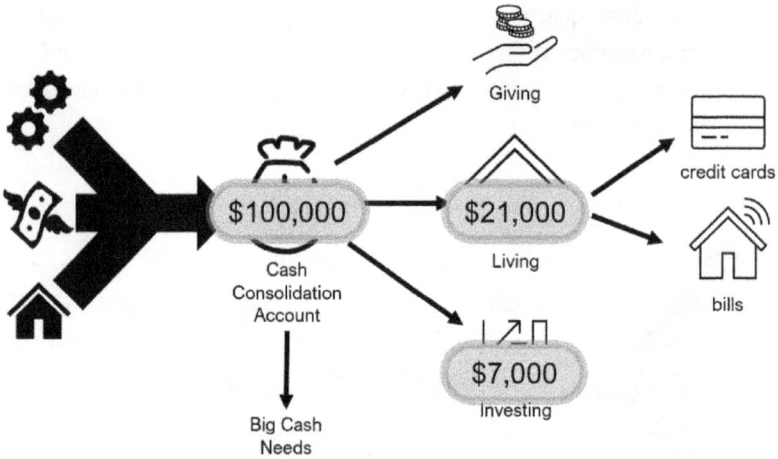

Figure 20 - balances at end of the month in all family accounts

Now that the family is at the end of the month, what can they conclude?

First, the Cash Consolidation Account hasn't changed, since no big cash payments were made out of that account. The Living Expense Account now has $21,000 in it, meaning that while they paid off credit cards, paid their mortgages, paid their bills, and lived off of the proceeds, they only spent $19,000 ($40,000—$21,000), while the average they usually spend is $20,000. They underspent by $1,000 during the month compared to average so the Living Expense Account contains that extra.

Now, the cycle starts all over again, and this time, they bring in $35,000 from the business in W-2 paycheck and profit draw. Let's pretend all that income arrives on the first day of the new month. The new balances look like Figure 21.

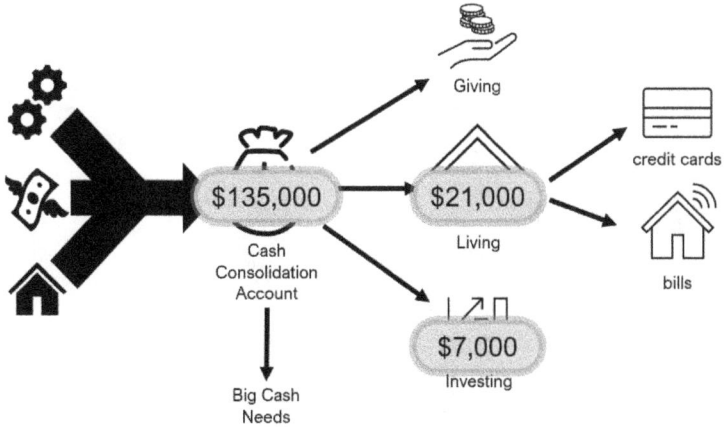

Figure 21 - balance on start of the new month after adding $35,000 from the business (paycheck and draw)

Despite having a $1,000 surplus in the Living Expenses Account from the last month, they still transfer $20,000—their average living expenses—from the Cash Consolidation Account into the Living Expenses Account. Balances are shown in Figure 22.

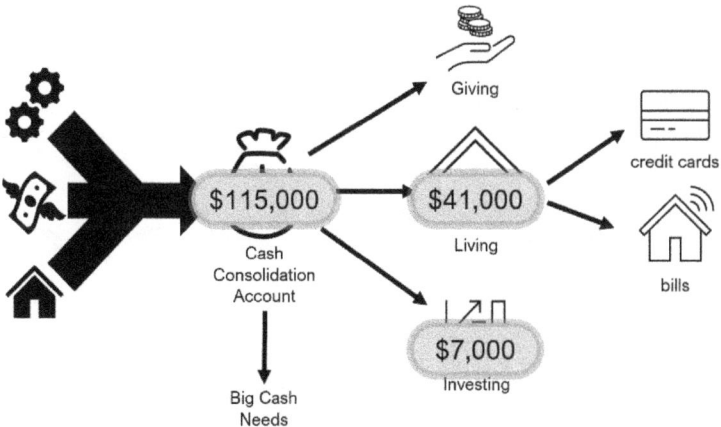

Figure 22 - balances after transfer of $20,000 to cover upcoming month living expenses.

They also give $3,000 to charity like the prior month.

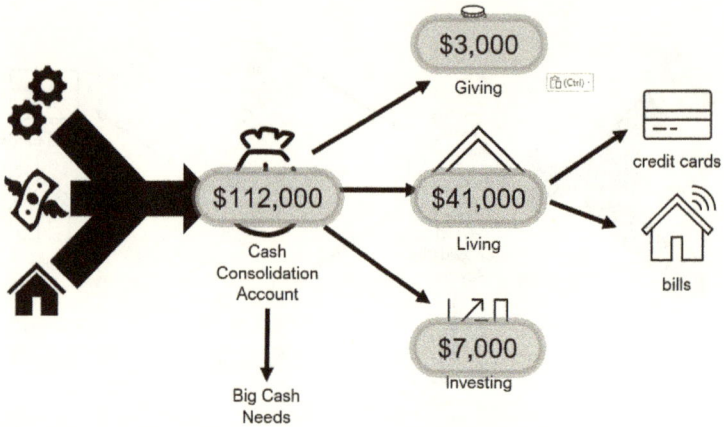

Figure 23 - balances after charity gift of $3,000

Suppose for the upcoming six months to cover the Big Cash Needs the family determines they need $100,000 again. This is the target balance in the Cash Consolidation Account. So there is an excess of $12,000 that is moved into the Investing Account. Everything is done and the balances for the start of the new month are shown in Figure 24.

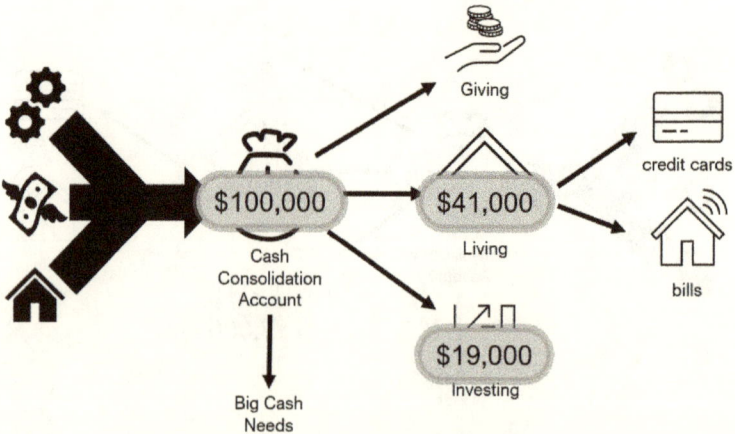

Figure 24 - starting balances in new month

In this second month the family pays $25,000 for a big vacation from the Cash Consolidation Account, which they have been saving for as part of the planned Big Cash Needs. Out of the Living Expense Account they also pay their mortgage, bills, and credit cards.

At the end of the month, the balances are shown in Figure 25.

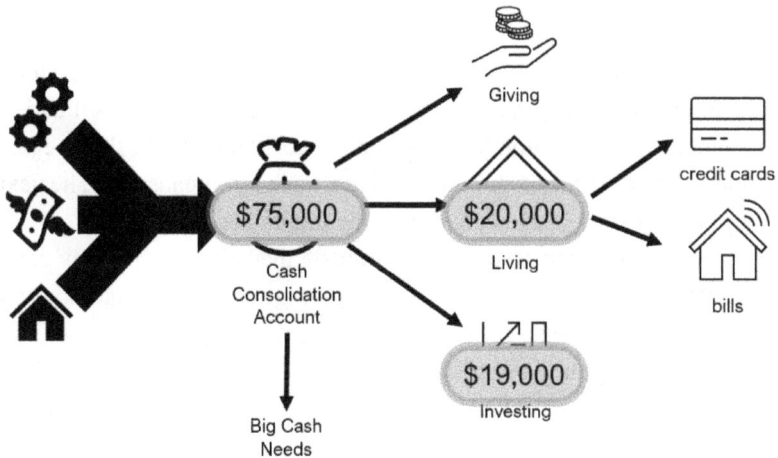

Figure 25 - balances at end of month after paying for $25,000 family vacation plus mortgage, all bills and credit cards

By the end of the month, their Living Expenses Account has dropped to $20,000, meaning they overspent on living expenses by $1,000, which was corrected for in the normal process.

Family Priorities and Adjustments

Did you notice the order the family allocated the transfers out of the Cash Consolidation Account? Why that order and not some other? Why immediately deposit for living expenses, then giving, then investment? It depends on your family priorities and where you want to put your monthly excess. Do you want it to go to investing or giving? My wife and I prioritize giving first, and then living expenses, and then big cash needs, and then investments. A family might prioritize debt reduction or giving, then focus on big cash needs, then investment. The system can handle any of your priorities and the beauty is that you have to decide.

Your priorities can change and the system continues to work. All you do is make a simple change to how you handle the excess. My advice, if you don't have a solid idea, is to prioritize either living or Big Cash Needs, and then put giving last. Some people aren't prepared for giving off the top, and they need time to work into that approach.

I set this up on the first Saturday of every month, and the first thing I do is check my Big Cash spendings out of the Cash Consolidation Account the previous month. Some I update to "Paid," others that are just coming up in the next six months I add to a tracking spreadsheet. The next thing I do is to review the balances of the family accounts.

I use a web-based service to consolidate the balances of all my bank accounts so I can see all investments, giving, cash consolidation, and living expense accounts in one place. I recommend you find a tool that will do that for you. I use a spreadsheet to keep track of my Big Cash Needs, and I use it to calculate how to balance the Cash Consolidation Account after all the transfers are done.

I will check the list with my wife of our upcoming Big Cash Needs, and we'll discuss the big payments we made the prior month. This keeps her involved in the big decisions. Sometimes, I can get some of these Big Cash expenses cheaper, like when I saved $2,000 on the purchase of a new car we were planning. Other times, I've not been comfortable with, say, how much a vacation costs, and those conversations help my wife and I reach a good compromise. Sometimes our monthly conversations just end up as, "Hey, can you please look over the list of what I think is coming in the next six months and make sure I didn't miss anything?" "Sure!"

Each month my wife and I could discuss what we want to do with the excess in the Cash Consolidation Account. We used to do that when we initially started. But after a while we just started doing the same thing (transferring our excess into the Investing Account) so now I simply can confirm "same old' same old?" after reviewing the list of upcoming Big Cash Needs.

Some of these monthly transfers you can eventually automate, like your Living Expense Account transfer, and you do not want to automate those from the beginning. Other things, like quarterly tax estimates, you can't easily automate.

One of the keys to this working is having an estimate for your average monthly living expenses. While this can change with major lifestyle shifts, generally, you want to see the month by month amount wiggle up and down a little rather than any upward or downward trend. How is your estimated monthly living expenses calculated? Well, there are three ways. A good way, a better way, and a best way.

The **first** method—the good approach— is to **guess**. Add up all your big known expenses, like your mortgage, your car payment, things like that, and add some buffer on top. How much is that buffer? What's the average? Nobody knows. It's a hard number to pin down, and it's very hard to get an accurate estimate for this, but it's still worth doing. It may get you about 40 percent to 50 percent near the real number.

The **second** method—the better approach—is to use a **living expense calculator**. These can be apps; some you take and enter your bank account information, make a few adjustments, and it does the math for you. It's reasonably accurate and will get you within about 20 percent of the true number.

The **third** approach is to use something like **Mint** or **Monarch Money**. You can run reports on these and they are likely the most accurate estimate of all approaches. I advise running multiple reports and then averaging, then sitting down with your spouse and discussing the estimates and what feels right. Selecting the amount to transfer from the Cash Consolidation Account to the Living Expense Account isn't a permanent number, and you'll likely readjust after a few months. Don't think of this as getting the right number, think of it as the number you're going to start with.

If a family is seeing their Living Expense Account balance increasing each month, that means that they're living below what they estimated for their living expense needs, and they either have to decrease the monthly amount they transfer a bit, or spend more on their lifestyle. If the account balance decreases regularly, then it means that the family is living beyond the estimated monthly living amount, and has to either spend less on expenses, or increase the average transfer from the Cash Consolidation Account.

This should also be a generalized number. Round up by five thousand or two thousand or a thousand dollars; trying to get within a thousand dollars is too tight. And every three months, re-evaluate. Make changes slowly. These are things that you want to discuss with your spouse if things change; if your kid moves out, or you get an increase in income. Don't just decide one month to change the amount you pull out, and don't jump drastically by $5,000 one month. Change it by $1,000 for three months, and then re-evaluate.

When Your Income Increases (or Decreases)

When I say income, I am not just talking about your paycheck. This includes your draw and other things that can go up when your business grows. Let's say it increases. That's what's supposed to happen, right? Your business is growing, you're making more money.

If you're following this method, the system will automatically handle the change in your income. You'll notice you have a lot more for investment or giving this month. What you want to do is do your best to keep your living expenses level. Don't go buy the new house. Don't go buy the new boat. Don't go buy the new RV. Take that money and stuff it in investments, and when you do decide to get that RV, treat it like a Big Cash expense, and discuss it with your spouse.

One of the benefits of this system is that it protects you from yourself.

What if the opposite happens? What if your income starts to go down and doesn't come back up in a reasonable timeframe? Maybe your business gets into a tough season. Or maybe you've acquired a new business and have a new note you have to pay down. Again, this is handled by the system. You'll start to notice you have less and less excess every month. What you need to do is take a break, take a breath, and take another look at your situation.

Go back to your Big Cash Needs and update the numbers. Each month, you should review them, but I've found a lot of people won't update those planned costs, especially the quarterly tax payments. If your business income is going down, then those taxes should be going down too. If you have a new business, you may not even need to make them, your expenses may be so great.

As a last resort, you can tighten your belt and decrease your living expenses.

What if you get what I call a **blue bird**? When you get a sudden large cash blessing? They're rare, but they happen. I had one when I made a stock investment that blew up. We made a hundred thousand dollars in a day, because we bought a share at four dollars and sold it at forty. Or maybe you sell your business. Or maybe it's inheritance. Or maybe a really big bonus. Or maybe you got a lot back from the IRS because your tax strategy worked better than you had planned.

Let's suppose you get a really, really big blue bird? I mean a really big one—like the kind that changes the game for your family permanently.

The **first** thing you do is **protect** it from you. With a number that big, you think to yourself, "Yes, I *could* buy a private jet." No. You get that cash out of sight. You put it somewhere. Now it's in the family's control, but not in the system, it's out of the equation for a short time. What I often recommend is to open up a brokerage account with your wealth manager, and park the money there for a short time to let yourself breathe and figure out what to do with it.

But then, after you've had some time to think about it, you're going to **allocate** that money for different purposes. Maybe you take care of some debt. Maybe you give some of it away, or maybe you invest it in passive income, or invest back into your business. Some things, like a Real Estate Investment Trust (REIT) or Qualified Opportunity Zone (QOZ), give you only 180 days, or six months, so you'll have to think relatively fast.

And you *will* need **professional help**, and I am not talking about just someone like me. Depending on how much money, you might need a psychologist or some other kind of mental counselor. Then you need the right kind of wealth advisor, and the right kind of CPA. But you do need some breathing space to get all these things lined up.

Transitioning from Active to Passive Income

Active income is what you earn by the sweat of your brow. You go into an office, you take responsibility. But at some point, you probably want to stop that and transition to living off your investments.

When the time comes, it's really simple. You move your investments over to become your source of income. You still operate the process, but now you can much more tightly control how much money comes out of your account. And now you can take out just enough to cover your living expenses, your big cash needs, and your giving.

This is a prime strategy for those over the age of fifty-nine and a half, as now you can draw from your retirement accounts without incurring any penalties.

Passive income is so meaningful to business owners that we're going to give the subjects its own chapter—the very next one!

The Emotional Blessings

I preach doing this whole Cash Consolidation Process once a month, because that is the right frequency to keep from driving yourself (and your spouse) crazy. If you're in the frying pan, then you might need to run this system every two weeks.

But if you review this too often, or try to get the numbers exactly right, you can slip back into the budget mentality and risk surrendering some of the emotional benefits of the Cash Consolidation Process.

You also want as few bank accounts as possible. More accounts tend to create waste and unnecessary complexity, which brings with it an emotional cost.

One of the other benefits of this method is that it opens communication with your significant other. I find that people tend to underestimate the emotional impact of money on their partner, and by including their spouse, this actually builds up the marriage. Imagine that, rather than finances stressing you and your spouse out, or even hurting your marriage, it's a place where you can come together and feel peace.

You will probably screw this up at first. But give yourself (or your partner) grace, and then you'll have this down in no time. There will be times of income excesses each month but also falling-short, if you are like most small business owners. Do. Not. Panic. That's what the "extra" months are for, enabling you to even things out. Good advice I've heard on the topic before is—don't let the *good* months go to your head, and don't let the *bad* months go to your heart, as in, cause an unwanted cardiovascular event! (Aren't they all though?) The point is that as you measure what you manage, the very fact that you're now measuring it via the Cash Consolidation Process means you will be a better manager of it all, meaning you will also see potential shortfalls incoming and be able to adjust marketing, sales, and business expenses as needed so that ultimately, impact of that otherwise cash crisis in your business will be none at all to your family. Bestselling author and entrepreneur Scott Adams refers to foreseen crises like these as "slow-moving disasters," which are able to be mitigated or prevented altogether with the right . . . system. This is yours for managing your family cash.

Where Are They Now?

How did things go with Brad and Jenny? Sure enough, they implemented the Cash Consolidation Process. They learned to predict their Big Cash Needs **six months** in advance and so became ever-prepared when expenses came due. They knew how much they needed each month and had unshakable confidence that they would have it—and they did. Jenny understood her family's real versus perceived needs and was able to see with absolute clarity that Brad was taking excellent care of her. The couple also got feedback each month about how much they were spending, which gave them just enough feedback to adjust with plenty of time to spare—no more balance-shifting to escape going negative in an account with only hours to spare. One particular day while shopping, Jenny realized she'd lost the feeling that they had to skimp. There were no more fears around money. She was free. What an amazing gift.

With fear gone, the realization they had all they needed and wanted entered. Brad and Jenny felt *wealthy*. They had gratitude—and a renewed desire to give to those around them.

Not only had the Cash Consolidation Process given them an easy way to identify how much they could give each month, it opened the possibility that there was a more meaningful way to give. Instead of giving from what was left over at the end of the money, they could start giving from what they received. This shift, though small, created even more gratitude for the blessings in their life. Giving had gone from a left-over activity to a primary source of joy.

CHAPTER 6

(ALMOST) EVERYTHING YOU NEED TO KNOW ABOUT PASSIVE INCOME

Austin is a fifteen-year restaurant industry veteran and operates two successful restaurants. His wife Liz, as most small business owner wives do, helps out. She manages the family finances and devotes as much time as she can to their children and grandchildren. A couple of years prior to the inciting incident that ultimately brought their story into this book, Austin and Liz decided to buy a lake house. They envisioned long, relaxing weekends with extended family and close friends. They deserved it. They'd "made it."

And yet—you probably know what's coming—something was "off." Austin and Liz felt like they were doing well in business. But they didn't *know*. They didn't have the data or numbers beyond the occasional glance at checking accounts. And this didn't feel good. Austin and Liz had a very low-resolution image of their cash flow. Restaurant revenue seemed steady, and they were able to give more than 10 percent of their income to their church. What was left over afterwards usually seemed to be enough for living expenses, plus occasionally more. And when that left-over would accumulate into several thousand dollars, they'd contact their financial advisor to invest it on their behalf. But that's when the visibility ended and the anxiety began. Austin and Liz didn't *know* what happened to that money afterwards. The money was growing . . . probably. But how much? Relative to what alternatives? Better than or worse than? How did that money, whatever it amounted to, fit into their lake house plan—and beyond, to an eventual retirement? Was there enough to cash out and buy rental properties and whole life insurance? Were those even a good idea? Again, compared to what?

You would think that getting this kind of information out of a financial advisor would be easy, but you'd be wrong. Austin and Liz felt like they knew they didn't know, and it always bothered them, even though life seemed to be going their way. But they didn't just sit there and worry; they got moving.

Surprise! Passive Income Is Useful

You own and operate a business for many reasons, and most likely, one of them is to generate wealth. We are fortunate to live in a country with an economy that provides multiple benefits to business owners that are not available to typical W-2 employees. But if you don't channel the cash you earn from your business into passive income you will be working in your business for the rest of your life.

That may sound like something you're willing to accept, but at some point, you may want to do something different with your energy. Getting passive income is about buying future income now so that it's there when you want or need it. If you can't control your cash, or you're one disaster away from losing it all, or you're losing everything in taxes, you can't build passive income as quickly.

Passive income is what you buy when you have excess leftovers from your Cash Consolidation Process each month.

The Basics of Passive Income

OK, let's start off with a basic idea of what passive income is. In short, **passive income is all money not earned through your own direct**

labor. If it's not a wage, a salary, a commission, a fee, or a tip, it's passive income. Any money earned through the sweat of your brow is *active* income—going to the office, working with employees or customers, growing your business, and all the other hard things of business and careers and jobs and work.

With passive income, you live off of the fruits of the upfront investment. You probably have some passive income right now, just from stashing cash in the bank and earning interest. While it's good that you're doing that, you can't live off of it. If you want to reach the point where you don't have to work by the sweat of your brow, you need a way to increase your passive income, and the good news is that you have options in that regard.

A solid passive income frees you up to do whatever you like—charity work, ministry, vacations, or anything else. But before we get there, we need to cover some basic concepts that undergird passive income.

Compounding

Let's start with the most straightforward of these: **compounding**. If you understand compounding, you understand why passive income takes time to build.

Let's say we start with $100,000 at the beginning of the year, and you get to earn 10 percent interest on that $100,000. How much more do you have at the end of that year? The answer would be $10,000, because that's 10 percent of $100,000. You'll still have the original amount you started with, so in total you now have $110,000. Let's say you decide to let this go again for another year.

At the end of the next year, suppose you got the same 10 percent interest again. This time, because you started with $110,000 and the interest compounded on that, the amount you earned in interest was $11,000. At the end of the second year your total is $121,000.

When you repeat this process again and again, the amount you get at year's end gets bigger and bigger. Growth accelerates because each year you are starting with a slightly larger number. Once you've done this for twenty years, you will have almost $700,000, and this came from a mere $100,000 that you started with and simply *left* there, doing nothing else.

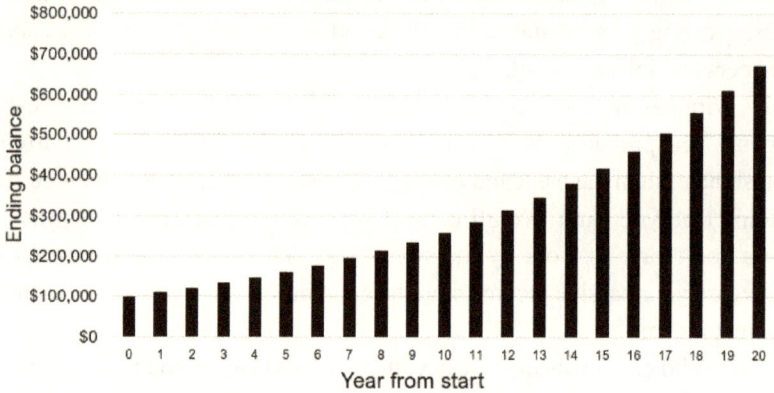

Figure 26 - compounding of $100,000 for 20 years at 10% annual interest

This is magic! It's the magic of compounding.

If I did the same thing as before—started with $100,000 with 10 percent interest paid to me at the end of the year—**but** then threw an extra $12,000 in as well plus the interest earned, I'll have ended up with $122,000. That figure comes from the initial $100,000, the $10,000 earned from interest, and the $12,000 extra. Next year, I earn 10 percent of $122,000, so $12,200, but I also toss in another $12,000, bringing the total to $146,000. If we keep doing this for twenty years, we get $1.36 million. In total, we put $240,000 in plus the starting $100,000, and the number got **so** much bigger.

But wait! There's more. It gets better—when you put the $12,000 in as $3,000 per *quarter* instead of a lump sum at the end of the year, the money grows even faster since the $12,000 becomes part of the compounding effect instead of just being tacked on. Doing it that way gets you $1.47 million in twenty years. An extra $106,000 was earned just because we increased the frequency of payment.

That's a *lot* of free money.

And this is what makes compounding so useful. Not only does it grow every year, but if you add money and add it frequently, the compounding effect gets stronger, giving you more money at the end.

Rule of 72: The Math of Compounding

We need a quick way to calculate these compounding effects so that we don't have to spend forever inputting a ton of formulas in a spreadsheet or hitting the times button on a calculator over and over.

The best way to estimate compounding is the "Rule of 72," in which you take the number 72, then divide it by the growth rate as a whole number to estimate how long it takes something to double. So if the growth rate is 10 percent, we take 72 divided by 10, meaning that it will take about 7.2 years for the investment to double.

Going back to our $100,000 at 10 percent interest example, you end up with $194,000 at the end of year seven, which is pretty close to the $200,000 estimate we get using the Rule of 72. While the Rule of 72 is not precise, it's quick and easy. And we're not trying to be precise for now because we're talking about the future and big numbers.

If I have a dollar today, and it earns 5 percent interest each year, I divide 72 by five to see how long it takes to double into two dollars. The answer is about fourteen years because 72 divided by five is about 14.

But it works in the opposite direction, too. If I promise you $4 in fifteen years at an interest rate of 10 percent, it will take about seven years for that $4 to lose half its value. Plus, because we're paying back over fifteen years, it will halve two times. So by the end of the period, the value of that $4 will be more like $1 today.

Now that we know how to calculate the value in the future and calculate today's value for something we expect in the future, we can make important decisions about our money.

Which would you rather have: $4 million in fifteen years or $1 million today? Think about this for a minute now: What would *you* personally want? At 10 percent interest, which is the average long term return in the stock market, these two options are mathematically the same.

Do they feel different to you? Would you take the $1 million today because you think you can get better than 10 percent return each year? Do you need the money now? Can you afford to wait fifteen years?

How much risk are you willing to take to get $4 million in fifteen years if all you have is $1 million today?

I agree that compounding is "the eighth wonder of the world," as others have said. Once you understand the basics of compounding it unlocks additional concepts and trade-offs that are important in finance.

But as we briefly touched on earlier, compounding has an evil twin—anti-compounding, or "drag."

The Dark Truth about Anti-Compounding

Anti-compounding will do everything possible to get in the way of your financial growth. You must always be wary of what will be taken from you without you even realizing what's going on.

The number one anti-compounding is **taxes**. When I work with my clients, I always look for ways to shave taxes down at least three points per year every year. While it may seem small, that's 3 percent every year for the rest of your life that doesn't get in the way of your 10 percent growth return.

That helps you outrun the next issue, which is inflation. It's hard to know the exact number, but the **Consumer Price Index** is the government's best guess at estimating inflation. But why is inflation so hard to estimate? Because it shows up in how much extra we pay for gas and groceries and things like car insurance. Inflation is not set by the government; it just happens. There are some times when negative inflation happens and prices drop. In general, inflation tends to be about 2.5 to 3 percent per year over the long-term, but there's no specific way to know.

Let's be conservative. If inflation is 4 percent and you are earning a 10 percent return in the market, you're only earning 6 percent net at the end of the day when the chickens come home to roost. To see how much you're losing to inflation, take your 10 percent minus inflation for what your money is actually worth.

The other major issue is the recurring fees that you pay investment professionals to invest your money for you. Those fees are usually 1 percent per year of the value of the assets, which doesn't sound like much, but it adds up.

Since you're losing your 10 percent gain to 4 percent inflation and 1 percent fees, you're only really earning around 5 percent, which is why saving on taxes is a huge return on investment (ROI). In fact, saving on taxes counteracts inflation and the fees.

Opportunity Costs

But it's not just direct costs like taxes that trip you up; there's also the opportunity cost, a fundamental concept when it comes to money. Any time you ask yourself what the next best option is with your money, you're thinking about opportunity cost, because money you spend in one place can't be spent anywhere else. For example, do I spend $750,000 on a boat or on a stock investment? I can't do both - so I need to choose.

Let's say I can put my money in the stock market and earn 10 percent annual return with high confidence. But I have another investment where I think I can get 12 percent instead. That makes my opportunity cost of the stock market investment 2 percent. While I don't have to write a check for that amount, it can be considered like a real cost.

And as I said before, this applies to time too—in fact, it's more important to understand this when you're deciding on where to spend time because you can earn back money, but you can't earn back time. What can you do with your time? You can exercise, you can take a nap, you can get some work done. You have to make trade-offs that maximize the return you get on your money and your time.

The concept and trade off with opportunity cost applies any time you have a scarce resource where you have to do one thing or another and not both.

Risk and Reward

Because money is hard to get back and time is impossible to get back, it's worth considering options before making an important decision.

Risk and return are fundamental to investing. Risk is your chance of injury or loss, while return is how much you get as a reward. While return is easy to measure—10 percent is the typical long-term average return from the stock market before taxes, fees, and inflation—risk is much harder to measure because it can be anything. It can be a theoretical threat to your finances or well-being, or it could be a real one.

Let's say you have a stock investment, and your $600,000 account has dropped to $450,000 in the last 6 months because the stock market is down, and that money is for the down payment of a house. To quit while you're ahead, you sell the investment; that way, you don't lose even more. But still, you lost money.

But if you don't need the cash and can wait out the stock market dip, what is the real impact to you of the drop from $600,000 to $450,000? Suppose the market recovers in the 6 months following the dip and every-thing goes back to $600,000. The dip was not really a loss after all. It was just a theoretical loss at the time you looked at it. It never materialized.

What do you think-does theoretical loss impact you more, or real loss? It may surprise you to learn that most human beings feel equally bad about both, and their actions demonstrate that.

According to the study The Origins of Stock Market Fluctuations produced by market research firm NBER in January of 2014, 85 percent of the movement in the stock market can be attributed to three things:

1. The actual productivity of the economy.
2. How much of the rewards of that economy go into people's pockets (wages, dividends, interest rates, taxes, inflation).
3. Risk aversion.

Of those 85 percent of market movements, a quarter of those were due to the first two trends, which are beyond anyone's control. The rest of the market losses were caused by reactions to bad news. Bad emotions caused the stock market to move; it wasn't some logical calculation based on earning per share or the yield on 10 Year Treasuring bonds. And the stock market is emotional about the future, since people want the future to be predictable when it isn't. Emotions change based on happy or sad news, and that changes how most people think about the future. It is these feelings that drive the market.

If you're trying to be logical about this, you will *not* have a good time.

Fear and Greed: Buying High, Selling Low

Related to the illogical nature of the market is the cycle of fear and greed. Here's how these work. You start off optimistic about making an investment. If that investment does well, you say to yourself that you made a great decision, and the longer it goes up, the more you attribute it to your own skill at investing. Then the investment starts to level off. You get anxious, and maybe consider selling it, but ultimately you see it as a blip. Then it starts to drop. Now you start to wonder if you did the right thing. But you don't want to miss out on the upside, so you wait for it to come back up.

It doesn't. Dropping continues and you realize you've lost most of the gains. Fear sets in. What should you do? There's more loss. Now it's too late to sell because you wouldn't make any money, so you hold it in the hopes that it will recover.

No recovery. *Crap.* It's probably just going to be a loss at this point. Now you're really in trouble.

Then it goes up a little. Oh wait! Might it come back? This was a shining star once upon a time. And it does come back a little more. Hope is restored! You might recover your money after all. More recovery. Now you're back at break-even. Oh thank God! Let's hold it longer and see if we can make money on this baby and ride it up!

And this cycle repeats again and again, depending on the types of investments.

This is a known cycle, but the problem with it is that when you're happiest about the investment, that's when you should sell, while when it's sinking and you want to turn it around, you should buy.

Buy low, sell high.

But the cycle of emotion makes you do the opposite—buying when the price is high, selling when you're afraid it will lose too much value. If you aren't careful, you'll fall for it every time.

But this behavior can be beaten. The truth is that time erases risk. Figure 27 shows an hourly trading price for the S&P 500 over a few days. It's all over the place. Figure 28 on the other hand shows the same S&P 500 over thirty years. Figure 27 is the cycle of fear and greed, a bunch of fluctuations that drive panicked behavior while Figure 28 is the beauty of compounding at work. It's the same fund - just two different time perspectives.

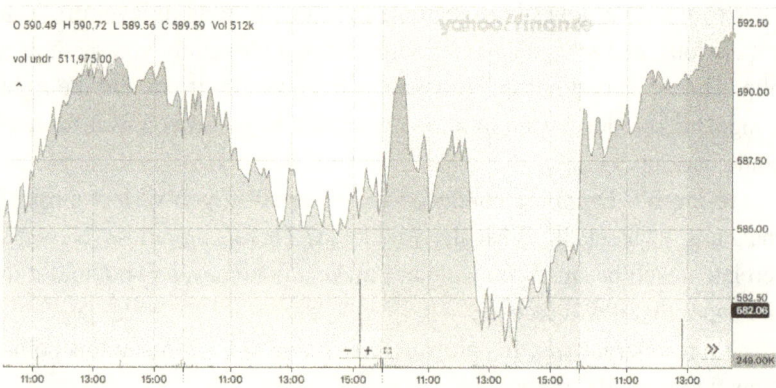

Figure 27 - minute-by-minute price of S&P 500 (SPY) over a few days (data source Yahoo! Finance)

Figure 28 - daily closing price of S&P 500 (SPY) over 32 years (Data source: www.macrotrends.net)

But what if you put all your money into the S&P 500 index in 1995 when a share cost $400, then forgot about it? Suppose you ignored all the news and hype for thirty years. Then in 2024 you decided to sell all your shares in the fund. You would make back *twelve times* your starting investment. The same peaks and valleys were there, but because you took thirty years, the risk disappeared. Time erases risk, and the more time you have, the better you do at smoothing out all the peaks and valleys. That's why the longer we can wait for passive income, the more risks you can take and the less you have to worry about it. This will help explain what comes next.

Passive Income Sources and Their Returns

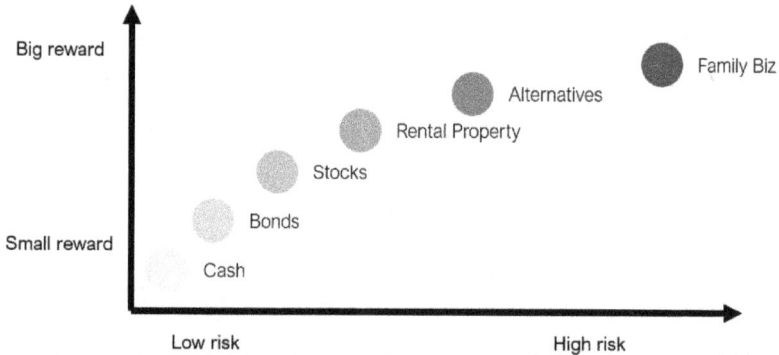

Figure 29 - examples of passive income options and how they are often related (source: ChatGPT, of all things, when I prompted it, I needed a list of common passive income sources and typical annual returns. I'm looking for data that is general, and I'm not making any financial decisions based on it. Provide typical annual returns for the following passive activities— rental property, cash, bonds, stocks, alternatives, and personal business. Your output will likely be similar to what's illustrated in the graphic.)

Investments in general are a tradeoff of risk and return. Figure 29 shows this tradeoff. Let's unpack it. In the lower left side of the chart we have passive income with small risk and small reward. As we move up and to the right, risk increases and thus investors get paid to take that risk by earning a higher reward.

Let's start with **cash** in the lower left corner. It's as simple as it gets: you put your cash in the bank, and it earns interest. At the writing of this book, 4 percent was common for high-yield checking accounts. Thanks to FDIC insurance, it's unlikely the cash in the account will go anywhere if you don't take it out so the risk of loss is low, and the returns are correspondingly small.

The next thing up and to the right a little is **bonds**. To understand how they work, think of a mortgage on your home. You're paying interest to the company that's servicing your loan. Someone can then buy a bond, which is when they buy the note that you're paying on, and they get interest every year. To illustrate, imagine the city of Austin, Texas, building a stadium and selling a bond, and large numbers of people buy these bonds. The return is 4 to 6 percent, which is typical. Cities don't normally default on stadiums, so it's not much of a risk.

But now, let's increase the risk by moving one more click up and to the right and look at **stocks**. A typical stock over thirty years is likely to return between 7 percent and 13 percent. In my own experience, my return has been about 9 or 10 percent after fees. When calculating this, don't forget to subtract the 4 percent for inflation and the 1 percent for your investment manager's fees. Not only will the returns on stocks fluctuate wildly, there is no guarantee that you'll even get your money back. With the increase in risk comes a higher reward, which means a better payout.

Another investment asset to consider is **rental properties**, which is one more click up and to the right from stocks. Rental properties generally return a little more than stocks but involve a *lot* more work. Because there's more to worry about, such as tenants not occupying the properties, tenants breaking things that require expensive repair, or tenants just not paying rent. But on the flipside, the US tax system rewards those who own real estate, so the returns are a bit more attractive relative to the time and effort you'll invest in the venture.

You can also invest in **small businesses**. It's not like investing in the stock market; think of it more along the lines of helping a local coffee shop buy an Italian espresso machine and you get a small cut of the profits. It's not so much investing in a market as investing in a business in your community. Risk can be high that you won't see a return on that investment—or it could go big. Buying into a small business is a type of Alternative, which is on the chart.

But the most important one here is your **family business**. Unlike the others, this investment isn't passive, and is likely the best one you'll ever have. We include it in this discussion to give you perspective. After taxes, the return you get from it likely greatly exceeds other passive investment options. But your business isn't a passive investment—it's an active investment. You know what the risks of that are, and they're huge. *Anything* can happen—lawsuits, pandemics, customer attrition, competitors, even theft. Plus the results aren't guaranteed; some years, you'll make 10 percent, other years you'll do extremely well at 50 percent, then next year you lose money. Even so, a well-run business is generally the highest returning investment the family has.

Speaking of which, how do you calculate the return on investment (ROI) for your business?

ROI of your Business

Calculating the ROI on their business is not straightforward, and no one's giving you a simple bank statement with your family business ROI on it. But you can calculate the ROI on your business and it's important to know this number when you consider your investment alternatives (remember opportunity cost?).

Here's how to calculate the ROI on your business for last year:

1. You look at how much you put into your business last year. You might think you didn't put anything in – and you're wrong. You left retained earnings in the business, and those retained earnings are shown on your balance sheet. If you look at retained earnings as of January 1 this year, you can see how much you left in the business at the end of last year, which is money that belonged to you. This is your investment.

2. Next, let's calculate your return. The return from your business is the net income (profit) plus your W-2 wage you've earned this year; you'll find the net income on your P&L and your W-2 income from your last pay stub of the year. Then do this math:

$$ROI \text{ on your business last year} = \frac{\text{net income from last year} + \text{W-2 wage last year}}{\text{retained earnings as of January 1 this year}}$$

Highlight that formula if you need to, or take a picture!

Choosing the Best Investment

Many families think there are better investments than a family business and they want to select the investment with the best ROI. However, that comes with a big problem—you never know which asset type will earn a bigger return on investment.

	Stocks	Cash	Bonds	Real Estate	Gold	Inflation
1930s	-0.9	1.0	4.0	-1.2	5.3	-2.0
1940s	8.5	0.5	2.5	8.1	-0.8	5.4
1950s	19.5	2.0	0.8	3.0	1.0	2.2
1960s	7.7	4.0	2.4	2.2	1.6	2.5
1970s	5.9	6.3	5.4	8.7	28.6	7.4
1980s	17.3	8.8	12.0	5.9	-2.5	5.1
1990s	18.0	4.8	7.4	2.7	-3.1	2.9
2000s	-1.0	2.7	6.3	4.0	14.1	2.6
2010s	13.4	0.6	4.1	3.8	3.4	1.8
2020s	11.9	1.9	-2.4	10.2	8.0	4.5

Table 5 - performance of various asset classes by decade (Source: pages.stern.nyu.edu/~adamodar/New_Home_Page/datafile/histretSP.html)

The economist Aswath Damodaran collected the data in Table 5, and it shows several passive investment types, with the inflation rate that year on the rightmost column. In the 1930s, stocks lost 0.9 percent; after all, they had hit their lowest point after 1929. Cash in the bank earned an interest rate of 1 percent. Bonds returned 4 percent. Gold returned 5.3 percent, making it the best investment in the 1930s. Inflation, however, was minus 2 percent, which meant that prices dropped in this period; given that this was the Great Depression. To protect your money in the 1930s, cash bonds and gold were the way to go. In the 1940s, however, stocks and real estate were the best option. In the 50s, it was stocks that outperformed.

Looking decade by decade, something different did better each decade, and it's impossible to predict what that will be. Trying to pick the best asset type is like trying to pick the best stock—you're going up against professionals who are also trying to pick the winner, and those experts have analysts helping them, which allows them to get the news before you do. In early 2025, Grok 3 estimated that 90 percent of all trades in the market were done by institutional investors (the professionals).

But you can beat the professionals, because they have a weakness: They have to show monthly or quarterly returns or they get fired or don't get paid. Regular people don't have that kind of pressure on them, so they can wait and see when institutional investors cannot.

How do you overcome this problem about selecting the right investments over time? It's not by finding the next hot stock tip, because the odds will always be against you. Instead, the key to overcoming this problem is *diversification.*

The Power of Diversification

	100% Stocks	100% Bonds	50/50 Portfolio
1930s	-0.90%	4.00%	2.80%
1940s	8.50%	2.50%	5.80%
1950s	19.50%	0.80%	10.50%
1960s	7.70%	2.40%	5.30%
1970s	5.90%	5.40%	6.10%
1980s	17.30%	12.00%	14.90%
1990s	18.10%	7.40%	12.90%
2000s	-1.00%	6.30%	3.70%
2010s	15.70%	4.20%	10.40%

Table 6 - annual returns by decade showing impact of diversification. Shaded cells indicate return did not keep up with inflation (source: Aswath Damodaran).

Table 6 shows that the math supports diversification too. According to Aswath Damodaran's data, going with stocks only or bonds only can cause losses due to the investment not keeping up with inflation, but simply splitting your portfolio 50/50 erases this problem entirely. Because picking good stocks or good bonds isn't always possible, picking half stocks and half bonds helps cover the weaknesses in either one. The result is an overall gain. You don't outperform the winner, but you don't lose either—you stay in the middle. The best part about this is that it doesn't involve complex research, just making sure that your assets are balanced in equal proportions.

This is a simple investment portfolio, and not recommended for anyone, but it's a powerful lesson. Note that in each decade, this simple portfolio beat inflation almost every decade. This kind of simple fifty-fifty asset allocation is something that anyone could do—no special investing software or statistics master's degree needed. But even with a simple and powerful portfolio like this, there are certain issues to watch out for—sins, if you will.

The Seven Deadly Sins of Passive Income (and Their Salvation)

First off, investing is not a **get-rich-quick scheme**. You're not trying to make a bet on picking the right answer that will solve all your financial problems. The odds are not in your favor when you do that.

Next, have a system. Bad investors don't have a system, instead working off of **unreliable emotion**—our second deadly passive income sin.

The third thing to worry about is **going along with the crowd**. Investing in something because it's trending is a recipe for disaster, so don't even bother. Don't make investments based on what you hear from a friend or in the news (or worse, on social media!). Also, the stock market is a zero-sum environment; if you win, someone else loses. If you lose, it's because someone took advantage of how you acted.

The fourth passive income sin is to **focus exclusively on short-term gains**. Don't put yourself in a situation where you need money within a short timeframe; if you need money in six months, you'll probably make bad decisions compared to if you have ten or twenty years to make the decision.

The fifth issue is **worrying about what you can't control**. You can control what's going on with yourself and your finances, so focus your energy there instead of on distant problems you can't solve like the economy.

The sixth issue is **taking the market personally**. Don't take the market personally when you have a loss. That said, you'll feel any loss, such as if the money you're trying to grow is for your kids' college. You can't help the feelings of hurt, but you can manage what you do next.

And the final issue is **thinking you know a lot**. You don't win through knowledge and intelligence in investing; in fact, such things will trick you. It's easy to make this mistake if your investments do well, especially early on. You may think you're great at picking investments when you just had a bit of good luck, luck that will run out. The key to winning at this is not relying on luck, but using a system.

Successful investors avoid these seven deadly sins. But if these are what not to do, what should be done instead?

First off, a good investor should have **emotional intelligence**. You have to be aware of your own failings, be able to regulate your emotions, motivate yourself to act, and have both empathy and social skills. Most things in life are about your emotional intelligence, not your book knowledge.

You also have to have **time and patience**. As I mentioned before, people looking only at the short term do not do well because they act out of panic. Making sure you have enough time, as well as being patient, will tilt things in your favor. On a related note, good investors **stay calm**. They don't panic at news or at losses. They are rational and they know how to deal with difficult emotions. They know about the cycle of fear and greed and how to spot it in themselves.

Fourth, when you don't know something, **admit that you don't know**. You'll avoid making decisions where you lack key information. Stay curious. Plowing ahead despite ignorance is leaving things to chance, and you don't want that.

Fifth, **understand any feelings of loss** you may have had. Whenever you've lost a loved one, it has impacted you emotionally and left you without any idea what to do going forward. You need to understand that history so that you can take the steps to keep those bad days from coming back. Everyone has a different story and different fears.

Here's an example from my own life: I walked away from a good, high-paying corporate job with nice benefits and decent security to start a business (this was before Firmstride), but I failed at it— it cost me around $250,000 in one year. How did my wife react? How did I react? That history is important because I need to know how to predict likely responses in the future to that kind of personal loss. My wife and I are aware of that loss from our past, and we talk about it so that we don't end up there again.

Moving on, successful investors have a **system**. Not a system for picking stocks or using statistics, but the kind of system for converting income from their business into passive income for securing the future.

Discipline Means Freedom . . . to Create Passive Income

Passive income is, I believe, largely the result of emotional intelligence, which you have to practice to get good at it. It's a hard road to walk and some people start out ahead of others. Passive income requires trading off some difficult concepts like living today and living in the future, and risk versus reward for things that are unknown.

This is where the power of **marriage** takes center stage. We're trading off money today with money in the future, and that requires making decisions about what we want in the future. When a husband and wife come together to make this decision collectively, the decision is better than when either makes the decision alone. That's because two people are coming together as one, which is a powerful way to make decisions about money.

Plus, spouses are great partners for each other when it comes to regulating fear and greed. When I feel proud of myself because I made a great investment, my wife is there to remind me of the times I lost a lot of money, and she does. It's not some put-down, some sitcom thing where the wife cuts down her dopey husband; she's just helping me regulate my emotions. This is what breaks me out of the cycle of fear and greed—and who better to help me than my wife?

Investing means behaving yourself, because misbehaving is expensive.

Morningstar Investment Category	10-Year Investment Return	10-Year Actual Return Achieved	Cost of Misbehaving
Allocation	6.3	5.9	-0.4
Alternative	0.6	-0.4	-1.0
International Equity	4.7	4.0	-0.7
Municipal Bond	2.8	1.4	-1.3
Nontraditional Equity	3.3	1.0	-2.3
Sector Equity	9.6	7.0	-2.6
Taxable Bond	2.2	1.2	-1.0
U.S. Equity	10.8	10.0	-0.8
Total	7.3	6.3	-1.1

Table 7 - misbehaving causes investors to surrender much of their potential gains (source: Morningstar Mind the Gap 2024 report)

Morningstar did an interesting study. On the left side of Table 7, there is a ten-year investment return across several investment categories. The average return over ten years was 7.3 percent; this is purely the mathematical return. However, actual investors achieved returns that were 1.1 percentage points less, putting the average return at about 6.3 percent. This is the real-dollars cost of the cycle of fear and greed.

If you can control yourself and behave, you won't have to surrender that 1.1 percent gain each year over time; in fact, you can beat people who can't control themselves. And we've already talked about the impact a small percentage can make over time.

Winning through Self-Control

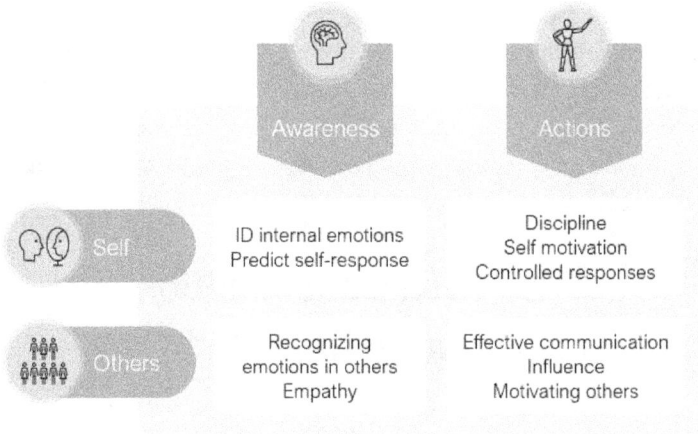

	Awareness	Actions
Self	ID internal emotions Predict self-response	Discipline Self motivation Controlled responses
Others	Recognizing emotions in others Empathy	Effective communication Influence Motivating others

Figure 30 - the four quadrants of emotional intelligence

To solve this issue, you have to have self control. And self control is an outcome from emotional intelligence. One of my favorite books that deals with this subject is Brandon Goleman's *Emotional Intelligence*, and he explains it through the four-part quadrant in Figure 30.

The two rows deal with yourself (top row) and others (bottom row). The two columns deal with awareness (left column) and your actions (right column).

Consider the top row in the table for "Self." The upper left quadrant is the set of skills to recognize and predict your own internal emotions. The box in the top row upper right corner is the skills for how to motivate yourself and control yourself once you have emotional responses.

The bottom row in the table is about others and is known as the external EQ skills. The left quadrant of this row is the set of skills to help you recognize and predict emotions in others. The box to the right of that is the skills to effectively motivate, influence and communicate with others. Regarding investments, the external EQ skills are relevant but not *as* applicable when it comes to self-control except when you start empathizing with others a little too much. This can create an unhelpful state called the fear of missing out (FOMO). It's when we see the world through another's eyes, feel what they feel, and think to ourselves, *I should do, see, and feel that, too*. Empathy devolves into envy quickly. This is why we must counterbalance with self-discipline. We are each running our own races; we're not simply starting the same race in different starting spots. I'd even say we're not all running our own races—we're playing different sports entirely! So let yourself focus on the investment outcomes *you* want and apply the requisite discipline necessary to achieve.

The Cash Consolidation Process, Revisited

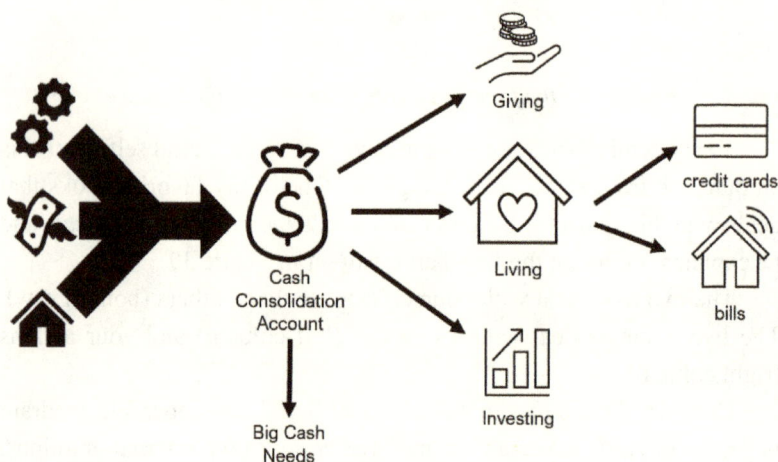

Figure 31 - Cash Consolidation Process is the ideal system for investing

Remember the Cash Consolidation Process? Of course you do. This is where the magic happens. This system helps you control your spending and solves the problem of investing for you because the system takes emotions out of the picture so you don't make poor decisions.

Remember, with this process, you put your money into your Cash Consolidation Account every month to save for your Big Cash Needs. After that, once you handle your living expenses and any philanthropy you might engage in, you put what's left into your investments. From here, you tell your spouse about how much is going into your investment account. Every month, you must talk with your spouse about the upcoming expenses for the next six months; this way, you're less likely to miss something and you keep your spouse engaged just enough that they know you have it covered.

And then once a year in November, you and your spouse sit down to do an annual review of all the investments. How are we doing? Are we on track off track or on track for what we need? What adjustments do we need to make in light of our situation? (If you already have an investment manager, you can ask that person to help you out with things that you and your spouse aren't sure about.)

Advice on Advisors

Putting a team together to guide you on your small business journey is so important (and complex) that this topic gets its own chapter, which is Chapter 10. But for now, while we're on the topic of passive income and investments, let's cover the essentials of an investment advisor. A good investment advisor:

- Helps you clarify your goals.
- Figures out how to help you achieve those goals through wise investing, and also figuring out asset allocation and asset location.
- Gets you to stick to your investment strategy once you've built it.
- Keeps you from doing something stupid when you get lots of ideas. You will want to do a lot of things, but your financial advisor is there to throw cold water on them if the ideas are unwise, no matter how emotionally invested you are in them. (In fact, before writing this book, I asked my financial

advisor if writing a book was a wise decision. What do you think he said?)

Now how much is a good advisor worth? According to investing firm Vanguard, a good advisor is worth about 4 percent per year.

- Half of that 4 percent is making you behave yourself.
- 1.2 of the 4 percent is figuring out how to take money out without costing you money on taxes.

How much should we put into the 401(k)? Should we use a Roth IRA? What about my brokerage account? That's how to withdraw money while managing your tax burden.

- Only 0.6 of the 4 percent of value is based on asset allocation, and
- 0.3 of the 4 percent is from figuring out how to save money on mutual funds and all the drag that comes with investing. Then they need to rebalance your funds for you again.

The biggest value your investment advisor brings is making you behave. You pay them 1 percent, but they're saving you 4 percent, but you won't see it because it's made of all the bad decisions you could have made **but didn't**.

Please do whatever it takes to keep a healthy relationship with your advisor. Let me remind you that every financial advisor is a for-profit business. Financial advisors make a lot of money by selling with fear, uncertainty, and doubt with authority and confidence. You want someone who knows what to do, not someone who makes you feel fearful or uncertain.

Think of what led you to select your previous or current investment advisor. Did someone else probably use and recommend their services? Maybe they've been in the family for a long time. Was it their confidence or credentials? Did they show you a lot of pretty charts that made it look like they could predict the future? Selecting the right advisor is challenging, and don't be surprised if you get with someone and then decide to change. I struggle with this, too.

So how do you form a healthy relationship with your financial advisor? You must understand how these advisors get paid. The old way was a commission charged for every transaction, but that was the wrong incentive because it didn't matter whether the investment was in your best interests or not. I still know a number of financial advisors that are stuck in this system because they either have old agreements or have clients who still want it. A typical transaction rate is 1 percent to 6 percent. Because they don't make any money after the trade, they have to keep doing trades in order to keep getting paid.

The more common, more modern way advisors get paid is a **retainer**. They charge a percentage based on how much they're investing for you. A typical going rate in 2025 is 1 percent for the first $1 million invested. And then as you invest more money, you pay less and less as a percentage on the whole overall thing. But the total dollars continue to increase as you invest more. Just to put this in perspective, let's say that you're investing $5 million and you're paying 0.75 percent for a meeting that you have once a year with your financial advisor. Your fee is about $40,000 for the year. The advisor doesn't charge you all that at once; you pay $1/12^{th}$ of that every month. And you didn't see it because your advisor just takes it out of your account (you gave them permission in the service agreement you signed).

The retainer approach is designed to create a great long-term relationship because the financial advisor wants to grow your assets just like you want to grow your assets. You're on the same team, and they're not incentivized to sell you the wrong thing or make the wrong decision.

But there's also the flat fee, where you pay someone to put together a plan for you. This is also common. Depending on how much money you're paying them, you will be sold services that you perceive as valuable.

Now you know why *I* use a retainer model at Firmstride; I want a long-term relationship and I don't want to have any weird incentives to make me want to sell you something. I want to have a clean relationship with you where I am in your corner.

Once you understand how your financial advisor is paid, you can understand how to be a great client. And to be a great client, you can't nitpick. I used to have a debate with my financial advisor about whether we had 6 percent of my investments in bonds or 7 percent. That's the wrong attitude; instead, I should have focused on the system. The system is, "I'm generating $50,000 a month that I put into a cash account that you invest for me, and I want you to put that money to work as soon as you get it as aggressively as you think I can handle with a 20-year horizon." That's a system.

Next, as the client, you define the outcomes. If your outcomes or your goals change, you need to tell your advisors straight away. "I'm planning on getting married. My risk profile has shifted." If you don't tell your financial advisor, that person will not know. And remember that their primary value is keeping you from doing something stupid with your money.

You must interact with your advisor as well. You don't want to call them up at some random hour because you freaked out about an election not going the way you hoped. You want to call them up after you've had time to plan, and you want some perspective. "Hey, I'm thinking about investing $150,000 to write a book. What do you think about that? Can you convince me that is a bad idea?" That's the type of interaction your investment advisor wants to have with you, not a panic about all your money draining away due to a sudden drop in asset prices. Healthy interactions will make you their favorite client.

Next, you have to be curious all the time. My financial advisor loves it when I ask him to teach me what led him to select certain investments for my portfolio. He puts a lot of time into his research and I always learn something new from him, plus he gets to show off all his work. Also, it's good to think of your investment advisor as one of your employees. They work for you, so if you have to fire them because they aren't performing, do it sooner rather than later.

Now, here's something you should probably talk about with your investment advisor as it pertains to your investments and passive income from them.

Asset Location

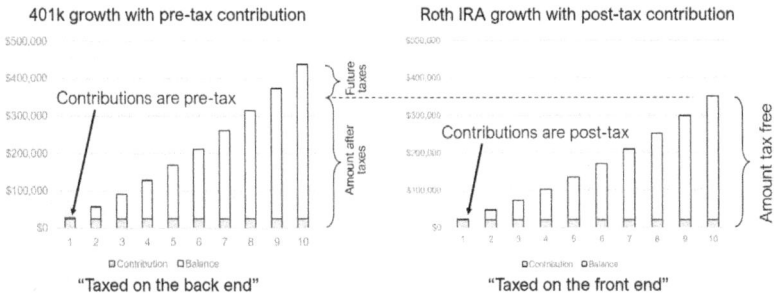

Figure 32 - traditional 410(k) versus Roth 401(k) if your average tax rate doesn't change over time, your net investment after taxes is the same.

Figuring out how to get money working for you in a way that works for your future is one of the fundamental jobs of an investment advisor (or financial planner).

It doesn't matter where the money is, what country it's in, or which bank has it. What matters is the type of account it's saved in, and the tax impact of the account. For example, Roth IRAs are different from traditional IRAs in that the Roth is taxed on the front end while the traditional IRA is taxed on the back end. 401(k)s can be traditional or Roth too.

The graph in Figure 32 contrasts a traditional 401(k) with a Roth 401(k). On the traditional 401(k) graph (on the left), I put in $22,000 every year. Over time, I end up with $450,000 at the end of the graph, but that's pre-tax. I have to pay taxes on all of it, which significantly reduces the amount I get to keep. With the Roth 401(k) graph on the right, however, the contributions are after taxes, thus the gray shaded box starts off slightly smaller with the Roth 401(k) than the traditional 401(k). However, when you get to twenty years with the Roth 401(k), there's no difference in your net pay. This is normal; in many cases 401(k)s and Roth 401(k)s mathematically yield the same amount **after** you pay taxes in the future years. However, the main pitfall is that your tax rate won't always stay the same for twenty years. When you're close to retirement, it can be quite different from when you started. Roth IRAs and Roth 401(k)s also have different estate planning impact compared to traditional 401(k)s or traditional IRAs. This is where your financial advisor can give helpful advice for your situation, preferences and assumptions.

But regardless of what happens, you don't need to choose one or the other because you could diversify by doing both.

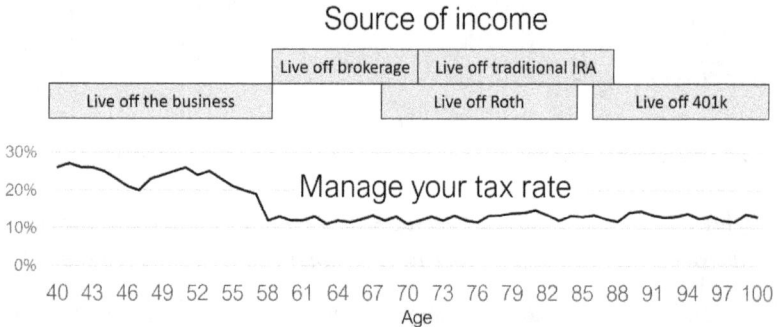

Source of income

	Live off brokerage	Live off traditional IRA	
Live off the business		Live off Roth	Live off 401k

Manage your tax rate

Figure 33 - an asset location plan looks at how you can withdrawal income in future years in a way that minimizes and manages taxes

Qualified retirement accounts aren't the only place to put investment assets. Your financial advisor will help you put together a full *asset location plan*, based on your age and your tax rate. Your asset location plan is the name for how assets are invested now with the goal of how to get to those assets when you are retired with the tax impact in mind.

A day may come when you don't want the business anymore, and you either sell the business or otherwise step down. When that day comes you will want options. Suppose since you've been investing for a long time, you decide to live off of your brokerage account because you aren't old enough to tap into your IRAs or 401(k) quite yet. Your tax rate drops because you need less income and have control over your withdrawals, and then when the brokerage account is all used up, you'll live off of your Roth IRA. After that, you'll live off of your traditional IRA, then you decide to tap into your 401(k). You don't need to figure this out—you're going to pay somebody to figure this out for you.

The next thing your investment advisor will figure out is your asset allocation. Inside each of the asset location accounts are investments that have to balance risk and return so that they're ready when you need them and they grow to meet your goals. Instead of guessing about the future, your investment advisor will run sophisticated software to look at best- and worst-case scenarios.

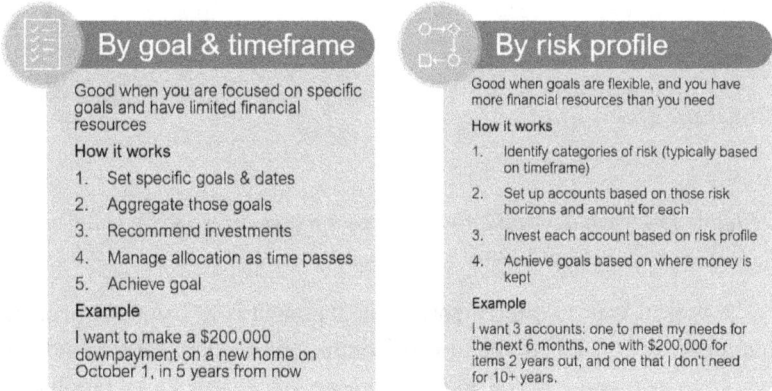

By goal & timeframe	By risk profile
Good when you are focused on specific goals and have limited financial resources	Good when goals are flexible, and you have more financial resources than you need
How it works	**How it works**
1. Set specific goals & dates 2. Aggregate those goals 3. Recommend investments 4. Manage allocation as time passes 5. Achieve goal	1. Identify categories of risk (typically based on timeframe) 2. Set up accounts based on those risk horizons and amount for each 3. Invest each account based on risk profile 4. Achieve goals based on where money is kept
Example	**Example**
I want to make a $200,000 downpayment on a new home on October 1, in 5 years from now	I want 3 accounts: one to meet my needs for the next 6 months, one with $200,000 for items 2 years out, and one that I don't need for 10+ years.

Figure 34 - two common approaches to asset allocation decisions

There's two main ways **diversification** can be done.

The first is to look at each of your specific **goals and their timeframe**. If you list out all your goals, what date you want them to be achieved, and how much money you need for each, your investment advisor can run all that through software to simulate what kind of portfolio would most likely achieve the outcomes you listed. The software will also figure out how to manage the allocation for each goal as you get closer to that goal's date so that the money doesn't disappear in the year you need it.

But as people get more sophisticated with their money, they move on to this second model—**investing by risk profile**. Because risk is tied so closely to time horizons (remember that time erases risk), the investment accounts can be divided by time. This approach works well when your goals are flexible and when you have enough money that you're not working with scarce resources.

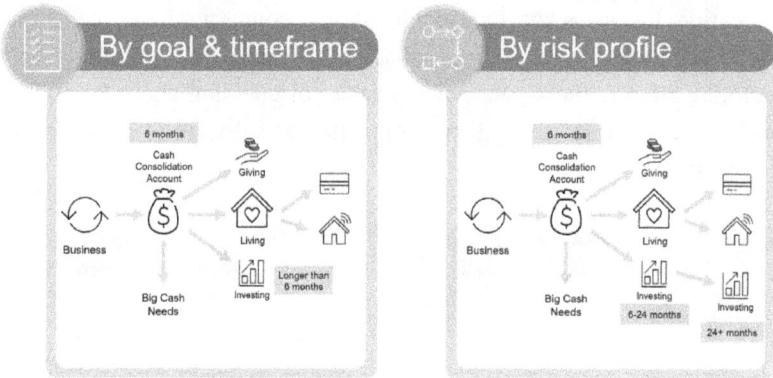

Figure 35 - Cash Consolidation Process handles investing by timeframe (risk) profile

A typical way to implemented this approach is to have one account that meets your needs in the next 6 months, one account for 6 months to two years out, and one for an indefinite period. If this looks familiar, it should, because it's the Cash Consolidation Process again.

When you start out, your accounts are likely to resemble the left side of Figure 35. You have your Cash Consolidation Account. It'll provide what you need for the upcoming six months, and it will also hold your emergency funds. Everything here is liquid; your cash is available immediately when you need it.

And then, if you're in the constrained system and you're planning for goals, you may have one investment account for an indefinite amount of time. It's like a 401(k). And you may have different types of accounts here, because you might want a brokerage, or a traditional IRA. You'll put in here whatever you can.

When you graduate to the risk profile method shown on the right side of Figure 35, you start out similar to the constrained method, with six months in your Cash Consolidation Account. But now, you've got a different account for six to twenty-four months, and this account, once it's fully funded and it has enough cash in it, will provide the funds for what you need for that 6 month to 24 month horizon. Whatever is left over goes into the infinite timeframe investment account where your investment advisor can make aggressive investments because there's no time pressure. The six to twenty-four months is to be invested much more conservatively because there is a specific need in a specific timeframe. For these kind of investments, investment managers may use things like bonds, CDs, money market accounts, which might return as much as 6 to 7 percent. With the time horizon approach you maximize returns and minimize risks while being prepared for all time horizons.

Now, the nice thing about the Cash Consolidation Process is you can start off with cash in one place, then migrate it over to another place. All you have to do is open another investment account, which your investment advisor will love because they make money based on how much you give them to manage.

Millions

Back to Austin and Liz, who were introduced to a financial coach, who helped Liz implement the Cash Consolidation Process. A repeatable, step-by-step procedure gave her visibility into where the money was flowing. With this control came insight into how much they were giving, spending, and saving each month, both on average and to be exact. Within weeks, Liz realized they were saving a *lot* more than they had originally estimated and so started to work more closely with their financial advisor on how to more effectively (and actively) invest that money. Instead of just "investing" for a "maybe someday" future, she and Austin planned a purpose for those savings.

Austin and Liz didn't fully understand the impact of what they had already saved over the years. While both Liz and Austin understood the concept of compounding, they had never calculated the future value of what they had already saved—or invested—and how much that was projected to be worth in the future. When their financial advisor ran the numbers and showed them a graph showing the probable value of the account year by year, Liz and Austin were stunned. The future value of their savings in ten years was on pace to be at least $15 **million**. The financial advisor showed an optimistic projection that could end as high as $29 million. This was more than they could have ever imagined.

The most meaningful subsequent change came when Austin and Liz realized the importance and impact that passive wealth could have in their life. By using the Cash Consolidation Process, they now had a way to easily funnel cash into their passive investments on a monthly basis instead of waiting for a big chunk. And making smaller regular contributions to savings is a smart way to put compounding to work. Austin and Liz's restaurants had a new purpose—to help the family generate passive income so they can turn around and use their blessings to bless other families.

Passive income for Austin and Liz made a big impact on their plans for the future. They are now considering starting a 501(c)3 so one day they can stop running the restaurants and do full-time ministry. They're also considering getting their adult kids involved with that charity so their legacy as a generous family can be firmly established beyond their time on this Earth—for generations in the future.

And don't forget about the lake house. They'll have enough money to buy five.

CHAPTER 7

PHILANTHROPY, THE TRUE WEALTH TEST

Husband and wife Chris and Teresa both worked stable corporate jobs while their children were young. But when Chris was laid off, he decided to restart fresh. In their region, the most promising venture with the most promising future was construction. Chris felt he knew enough about construction and project management so he started a business. There was the dream, but then there was the reality. It was rough. Long hours, longer sales cycles. Eventually, the business broke even. Chris, however, did not. He re-invested everything he could into the company, which meant no take-home pay. The family had to tread water, and it was Teresa alone doing the financial swimming. Some months, their heads dipped below the surface; Chris had to take on shark-level credit card debt to make ends meet (because they couldn't).

To the debt injury came the insult of withheld giving—meaning the money just wasn't there for their church and local charity that used to be when both Chris and Teresa were employed full time. During lean months of Chris's business, the family gave nothing. When months were flush with profit thanks to a job's completion (finally) and client payment (finally), they gave about 3 percent of their net. Even so, giving was not a priority but an obligation. Not first fruits but final leftovers. Chris and

Teresa felt as though they simply *had to* prioritize family expenses like the mortgage.

But eventually, the construction company transitioned out of *survive* stage into *thrive*. That meant no more additional consumer debt. No more my-savings-depleting. And no more charity-skimping; the couple began to give a consistent 4 percent of collective take-home pay each month (yes, Chris finally accepted a meager yet respectable salary).

Then better became best; Chris and Teresa learned about the Cash Consolidation Process and decided to use it to get their financial house in order. Now they had enough to plan ahead for the upcoming six months of expenses and could rely on the monthly amount they needed in their living expense account. The rest they could commit to investing in future passive income. They also learned to manage their taxes, including quarterly estimated tax payments and tax reduction strategies. Within a year, the family had become financially stable with quickly accumulating assets. Now what?

Giving Back, Giving More

Philanthropy is the act and the art of giving back, and it represents the pinnacle of wealth. When you've established stability in your life and have something of value, your perspective begins to shift. Instead of thinking, "We don't have enough—we need more," you start to feel, "We have plenty. We are so grateful. Let's show that gratitude by giving back."

Reaching this mindset is a beautiful milestone, perhaps the grandest of all for the small business owners. It allows you to focus on your purpose and make a greater impact on both your family and society. However, you don't need to wait for this shift in mindset to start giving. For some, the act of giving itself sparks this transformation.

More advanced givers take a different approach—they give off the top rather than giving only from their surplus. This is the method God calls us to in the Bible because He knows what is best for us regarding money. Giving off the top fosters trust and gratitude, which is the right response to God's blessings in our lives.

In many ways, giving is the ultimate measure of financial health. It demonstrates that you have control over your finances, with the right tools and processes in place to assign a purpose to every dollar you earn. Additionally, giving is often an indicator of spiritual health. It reflects trust in God, gratitude for the blessings He has provided, and a desire to give back to Him with an eternal return on investment (measured in "Kingdom Dollars," I like to say). This aligns with the ultimate goal of hearing Him say, "Well done, my good and faithful servant. You have been faithful over a little; I will put you in charge of many things. Come and share in your master's joy."

Furthermore, giving frees you from the bias and burden that come from hoarding wealth. It opens your heart and life to greater purpose, joy, and fulfillment. This happened to me and my wife, and it happens to the couples we know and counsel.

As another example, there's Laura and Sean. They attend a home-based church and the experience and community had a big impact on their faith and relationship with Jesus. They want to help more families start home-based churches and so they started volunteering time with the organization and tithing a percentage from their paycheck and draws by writing a monthly check.

When their business was just getting started, their donations were not a huge amount of money. As their business grew, they kept donating the same percentage off the top and soon they were able to donate substantial amounts in absolute dollars to support the church's growth.

Sean and Laura's donations were difficult to predict due to the nature of how they were giving—a percentage of their income—which was largely driven by the ups and downs of their business. The church's expenses were relatively steady. The difference between Laura and Sean's donations and how the church paid expenses created cash flow challenges for the church.

Laura and Sean decided to open a DAF to help solve this issue. That worked by allowing Laura and Sean to average out their donations by contributing more when business was booming and then continue to give from the DAF when business was slow. The church appreciated the constant and steady drip of donations because it made planning easier while

Laura and Sean received the same charitable deduction on their tax return. This was a win-win for everyone involved.

The family business grew and grew over the years and eventually Sean's business had more than 100 employees. Some of those employees had also joined the home-based churches and were being changed. Those employees were tithing too. Sean wanted to help stretch their dollars even further for starting home-based churches so he and Laura started a public 501(c)(3) nonprofit with the explicit purpose of helping grow home-based churches. They hired an attorney to help them form the charity and they invited certain friends to join their board.

Sean offered the employees of his business a match dollar-for-dollar if they donated to his charity. The board had a process for receiving those donations and selecting which regions and home churches would receive the funding. The home-based churches started growing faster as a result.

So now that Sean and Laura had a charity that was helping spread the home-based church idea they were passionate about, they wanted to find a way to make it last. Around the same time, Sean and Laura started to see that their interests were shifting and they started to realize they were financially independent. Sean was finding himself daydreaming about what life might be like if he didn't have to go into the business every day. He wanted to do more ministry and maybe become a deacon. So he approached the board of his charity and proposed that they hire him part time to work for the charity. He could travel to distant home-churches and provide training and ministry to struggling areas. The board agreed and Sean made plans to spend certain days working for the charity and fewer days working in the family business.

Eventually gravity took over and Sean decided to be a deacon full time. He sold the business and he and Laura were financially independent. They traveled and helped plant new churches and get them started. Along the way they discovered that they had a specific passion for marriage counseling. They started offering retreats for engaged couples through the charity while continuing to help plant and strengthen new home-based churches. Sean and Laura started to write a book for strengthening marriages within the church (a long-time dream for Sean). All the while the board continued to raise and manage the money to support the growth of home-based churches.

Sean and Laura realized that they wanted to leave a family legacy as home-based church planters. Now there were new challenges to solve to make things work beyond their direct involvement. They invited their kids to get more involved in the charity. At first it was in small ways— simply traveling to remote home churches to help out and donating their time and talents. As some of the kids started to get more involved by volunteering their time and seeing the impact they could make, their money soon followed.

Eventually Sean and Laura hope to invite one of their kids to join the charity's board. As that individual gets experience working in the charity they hope that individual can eventually take over as Chairman of the Board to carry on the mission. If that doesn't work out they may need to either find a person to play that role or promote one of the existing board members. Finding their replacement for the charity is no different than finding a new CEO of a business.

To provide long-term financial support for the charity Sean and Laura started, they have allocated a portion of their estate to the charity through a Charitable Remainder Uni-Trust (CRUT). This will allow them to provide substantial cash to the charity once they pass while allowing them to get the tax deduction while they are still alive. They hope that this funding plus the possibility of getting one of their kids to be the new Chairman of the Board to provide continuity beyond their lifetime with the mission they care about.

Meet David and Stacy

David and Stacy run a successful business that rents portable toilets and dumpsters. They view their business as a BaaM (Business as a Ministry) having helped many individuals down on their luck by providing meaningful work and support services that help them get back on their feet. In their personal life they also give financial support to families and provide community network connections to help them get back on their feet. They have a bank account that contains cash for that and it is their primary source of giving back.

As their desire to give more grew, they looked around for charities that could help with their mission. They found a few in the area but they didn't align enough with the family values and always seem to have a very high overhead cost. David and Stacy thought their approach was working pretty well and they wanted to invite others to contribute so they could grow their impact. David and Stacy decide to form a private foundation. They hired an attorney to set it up and they appointed a board from the employees in their business. The purpose of the charity was to provide financial grants to families and connect them to social services to get help for their needs. Families could apply for grants and the charity had a process for making a decision and providing oversight.

Stacy and David were busy with their business and raising their small children. The charity was essentially another company and functioned like another business—just not with a profit goal. Like any business it required constant oversight. While David and Stacy identified people to sit on the board, those individuals were not the right people to provide oversight of the processes or make decisions that the family felt were in line with the charity's mission. David and Stacy had to continuously get involved and it started to feel like they had created more work for themselves than they wanted. Over time the overhead of running the charity became a heavy burden and started to drain them.

David and Stacy didn't want to abandon the idea of helping marginalized families get back on their feet and they also no longer wanted to spend their Saturdays on their charity handling paperwork. They decided to take another look around to see if there might be another charity—already established—that was similar. After interviewing a few charities they did find one in their community that had formed since the last time they looked. That organization shared their values, was on a similar path of impact and had reasonable overhead costs. The family decided to close their charity and provide all the funds they had secured to the other charity. Because David and Stacy wanted to stay involved, David became a member of their board where he got to volunteer time with the families and use his experience to help guide the charity to make better grants to the families. He was also able to further his social and business network with like-minded individuals.

And let's not forget the star couple of this chapter—Chris and Teresa. How did things turn out for them? Let's go see.

Hope, Faith, and Giving More Than Ever Before

After Chris's construction project pipeline stabilized into a consistent flow, he and Teresa began to talk about their finances a *lot* more together. The first reason being, Chris now had the time in his day to do so. Only a few heart-to-heart conversations into this new normal and the couple realized something: they didn't need more, more, more. Their family's lifestyle, which granted them both far above average time with their growing children, brought them both contentment and happiness. They discovered they didn't need to worry about having enough money because they now had unshakable confidence in their present and their future financial well-being. One day on a walk, Chris told Teresa that he finally felt wealthy—he knew what it was like to have enough.

With this feeling came a change, particularly in Chris's heart. He felt called to deepen his faith, which in this context meant giving off the top of family income, not the bottom, the left-overs.

A specific experience changed Chris's approach to giving, for the better, forever. He felt called to make a big investment that would accelerate the business, and he decided to commit to it. The problem was that he didn't have the cash in the business, and the current business profits would not be enough to support the investment without putting family money into the business. He prayed about it and asked for wisdom from those he trusted. Ultimately, it seemed like the right thing to do—he felt called to do it even though he didn't know how the business would pay for it. So he and Teresa committed to the investment and prepared to move money out of their personal investments to cover the business expense.

Then a check showed up unexpectedly for the amount they needed. It turned out Chris had overpaid their tax bill; he had made an estimation mistake when his accountant sent him his draft tax return the prior year. Chris had forgotten to account for one of the tax mitigation strategies he had learned from his finance coach. That single tax mitigation strategy provided unexpected tax relief; the refund amount was what they needed for the business investment.

I bet you've heard other stories like this. These experiences are not random coincidences.

Chris's faith had never been deeper. This was a sign. And so he and Teresa began to give based on top-line revenue, not bottom-line profit, after all other expenses had whittled their take-home down.

This decision changed everything. Chris and Teresa's emotional state went from, *we'll be OK*, to, *we have been blessed, so we want to bless others. What more can we do?* Gratitude brings freedom. Chris and Teresa now have both.

CHAPTER 8

FINALLY "GET" HOW TAXES WORK

In 1980, Marie emigrated from Haiti to Texas to be with her family, who had also moved previously. Back in Haiti, Marie had worked as a chiropractor and alternative medicine healer. She brought her career with her, opening a small in-home massage and physical therapy business. Her business checking account balance stayed low during the early years. She tried to save, but she couldn't get much higher than $6,000 in the account balance, and sometimes, expenses cut that in half. She eventually moved into a studio with more space where she could see more clients every day.

In the year we start our story about Marie, her sole proprietorship business earned a profit of just over $49,000. This kind of money was unheard of back in her country of origin, and Marie began to feel anxious and afraid. What if she wasn't running her business properly? Would she be able to manage faster growth? What if she did something wrong? Haitian and American business law could not be more different (to say nothing of the culture). Maria's biggest fear, as you can probably imagine, was taxes. She knew she needed to file taxes each year but wasn't sure if she was doing it right. Every year, the bill was so high, and it *hurt*. She had no way to know how to reduce those taxes legally. She didn't even understand all the taxes she had to pay. And that's when we met.

When Marie learned about taxes, she learned that there are different tax codes and she could choose which one would be used to calculate her tax bill. The first big choice was about her business entity. She had never even thought before that she had a choice or had any idea how much that choice might matter. Marie was on track to earn $150,000 that year; it was time to be proactive about her tax decisions. With the help of her accountant Marie discovered that she would be better off if she chose to have her business income subject to taxes under Subchapter S instead of staying a sole proprietorship.

With the help of an attorney, Marie formed an LLC and elected to be taxed under Subchapter S, meaning she now had an LLC taxed as an S-corporation. This would give Marie the best tax advantages while also introducing a few new requirements to her business. For example, she now had to run payroll. Another example is that she had to file a separate tax return with a different deadline. While payroll was a new task for her to do each month, the S-corp designation didn't require her to pay Medicare and Social Security taxes (collectively that is called "FICA") on all the business income. She would have to pay those taxes on her personal W-2 payroll wages. Her accountant helped her comply with the tax code by identifying a market-reasonable wage. Because that wage was less than the total profit of the business, this saved quite a bit on those FICA taxes. Her accountant explained how under Subchapter S she could take a draw not subject to FICA taxes and that would keep her take-home pay at the similar level as before when she was a sole proprietor. Nice!

Of course this was all new to Marie, and her Firmstride coach took the time to explain how a dollar earned from a customer would flow through her credit card payment system, pay for her business expenses, get reported on her P&L, and then make its way to her tax return. She discovered how the balance sheet showed her the current balances in her bank accounts, the amount of the loans she had outstanding, and what was left over for her as the owner. She began to see how everything fit together.

You will, too.

Managing Your Tax Burden

An easy and effective way to grow your wealth is to pay less in taxes over the short and long term.

But tax mitigation is not enough. A successful family does more than just lower their taxes to keep more of their money—they manage the payment of their taxes in a smart way. This means planning appropriately for the payments and exercising their fundamental ability to select which tax code would be used to determine their taxes. They still need an accountant to know all the nuts and bolts of the IRS tax code but they develop a more fundamental understanding of how taxes work for and against their family system. There is a book by Robert Heinlein called *Stranger in a Strange Land* where a man from Mars comes to visit Earth. In the book the term "grok" is used to describe when you understand something so well that you grasp it intuitively. Wealthy business owners *grok* taxes, and if you want to improve your own finances, you should too.

An Introduction to Tax

Meet Bob.

Bob owns a car repair shop in California. His father started it in 1962, and Bob inherited it after his father's death. In its current state, it generates about $700,000 a year in net taxable profit (that accounts for the depreciation they can take).

As of this writing, Bob and his family live in California. They take a paycheck of $250,000 to use for living expenses, but because the cost of living is so high in the state of California *and* they want to live comfortably, they take out an additional $500,000 from the business, putting the total amount they use yearly at $750,000. On top of that, they own the building where the business operates.

Bob's business was founded as a C corporation—the only kind available in 1962 when his father created the business. They've separated the operations of their business from the assets to prevent liability from crossing over. This means they have the car repair shop in one business entity and the building in another. But apart from that basic piece of due diligence, things are not going so well.

They're behind on their mortgage payments. Even $750,000 in owner compensation is not enough for them to pay for their home *and* take vacations to Hawaii. A closer look at their finances reveals that they're paying $258,000 a year out of the company for taxes, and they're paying an additional $180,000 for personal taxes, bringing their total tax burden to $446,000 when both federal and state taxes are considered. And we haven't even considered the other local and city taxes they pay.

The problem for Bob is that he and his family have an effective tax rate of 55 percent, meaning that for every dollar they earn, they only get to keep 45 cents of it before their other taxes. So what's going on with Bob?

The number-one problem is that they've got to understand the types of taxes they're paying. They see the tax bill, but they don't understand how they all add up; all they know is that they don't have enough money to do anything because they don't fully understand where their money is going.

The other problem is that they're not doing anything to mitigate those taxes. By not dealing with their taxes effectively, they're giving up so much money and letting inflation beat them down further. To make matters worse, taxes aren't like investments; you're not going to get a return, or even improved services as your tax rates go up or down. The law requires you to pay them.

Thus they needed to understand the nature of their taxes.

The Taxes You Pay

Let's talk first about all the taxes you pay so that we can understand the relationship between them and then help you discover how to manage them.

There are different types of taxes and we'll start with the largest: **income** taxes, **consumption** taxes, **transaction** taxes, **tariff** taxes, and **wealth** taxes. The first and easiest one to understand is your personal taxes.

Income tax is a tax imposed on money that you earn. This includes things like your wages or your salary, bank interest, any profits from rent you collect on your real estate, and so on. If you have an S corp or a partnership, both the profits and the tax liability that comes with those profits pass through to you, unlike with a C corp where the company pays its own taxes. In this category is also payroll tax, instituted as a way to help people save for retirement through Social Security and Medicare.

Next come **consumption** taxes. These are taxes based on what you consume or what you buy. Sales taxes that you pay on items you buy are the most common example of this type of tax, but there are also other hidden consumption taxes separate from sales taxes, such as taxes for alcohol and gasoline. There are also excise taxes for things like gasoline or firearms.

Transaction taxes are applied when you exchange goods or properties of value; capital gains taxes are one type of tax that's like this. But it goes further; for example, if you're buying or selling a car, you're going to pay a car transfer tax in addition to the sales tax. When you're transferring property to a new owner, you pay a stamp tax, which is a tax to put an official stamp on the document to make the transfer official; oftentimes those stamps can be very expensive.

Tariffs are taxes on things imported into the US from other countries. When you hear politicians talk about creating taxes for certain countries to create incentives for jobs in the US, these tariffs get passed along to the consumer. Thus it's important to be aware of this kind of tax too, because it shows up in the final price of the product without being indicated on the receipt the way sales tax is. Tariffs have a complex impact on the economy short term and long term and are beyond the scope of this book to explore.

There is another type of tax that you pay called a **wealth** tax. It is a tax on the value of an asset or collection of assets. One example common in most states is your property tax. This is not a tax on income or consumption but a percentage of the value of your home (which is considered a personal asset). A similar type of tax in the United States is the Estate Tax, which is of great political interest right now because they were once the province of the ultra-wealthy but are now applied to more and more people since the government has been lowering the bar for it. Estate Tax is a tax your heirs have to pay upon inheriting your assets when you die, based on the fair market value, if the value is above a specific amount. The tax is currently 40 percent of the total value of your estate if your total estate value is larger than $13,990,000 per spouse (the threshold changes each year). Some states also charge their own Estate Tax that is added to the federal Estate Tax. Your heirs may have to pay both federal and state Estate Tax if your estate is above the threshold even if they don't have the cash on hand. This can result in a quick fire sale of estate assets to pay the tax bill. Life insurance is often used as a solution to this issue.

While this framework is useful for understanding the sorts of taxes you'd pay, it's not as useful for helping you manage your taxes. But what is a more useful framework? Let's look at who collects the taxes instead.

The Three Tax Collectors

In the United States, three main entities collect taxes: **local** governments, **state** governments, and the **federal** government.

With **local** government, the taxes collected are used for community service and community infrastructure. These projects are often visible and obvious, like local public parks, road maintenance, and bridge repair. It's also how public school systems are funded. The property taxes you pay largely go to the local authorities. Utilities and utility districts also join in, since water treatment plants are expensive to run but benefit the entire public.

One level up from local government is **state** government. State taxes are used to pay for larger infrastructure projects that local municipalities can't fund. These are things like major highways, the power grid, water distribution, and other services necessary for everywhere to maintain a modern standard of living. States collect their revenue through income taxes, sin taxes (e.g. cigarettes and alcohol), corporate taxes, gasoline taxes (much of what you pay at the pump goes toward highway mainte-nance), and most notably sales taxes. States like California and Nevada have high inheritance taxes, while other states have no sales taxes. Don't take too much comfort in that last one, though—your state will get your money from you in one way or another, whether it's through higher income taxes or higher sales taxes, because they want to maintain exist-ing infrastructure and build new stuff as well. On the other hand, low sales taxes often mean high corporate or personal taxes. When it comes to paying taxes, local and state taxes are sometimes combined.

Federal taxes are the biggest burden, and they are approved by Congress through the normal legislative process. These are the taxes collected by the Internal Revenue Service (IRS), and the IRS creates a process for paying federal taxes that works well for most people.

Now, when you hear people talk about "federal taxes," that's a bit broad, so let's focus on what is meant by this term. The first main focus of federal taxes is taxes on *earned* income. These are what you pay when you file your Form 1040 tax return. Taxes can be withheld from your paycheck, or you make quarterly estimated tax payments once your income gets above a certain amount because the withholdings through your paycheck won't cover your total tax bill. And if you don't pay enough of your tax bill throughout the year or pay the safe harbor amount (the minimum to avoid penalties), you could owe an underpayment penalty.

To incentivize saving for retirement, contributions to retirement plans such as 401(k)s are often made tax deductible. The 401(k) lowers your personal taxable income. If you consider a different type of contribution like a Roth 401(k), that is post-tax, you don't get the tax benefit when you contribute but when you take the money out.

The next thing to focus on is *corporate* taxes. If you're an S corp, a sole proprietorship, or a partnership, you probably do not pay this tax, as it's only for C corps. It's also one of the oldest taxes in the United States. Currently, as of the publishing of this book the tax rate on C-corps is 21 percent.

Changes were made to corporate taxes during the Obama administration. To pay for its signature Affordable Care Act, another 3.8 percent, known as the Net Investment Income tax (commonly called "NIIT" for short), was added as a tax on dividends from C-corps and other types of passive income. But while corporations aren't subject to this tax in the usual way (they still pay only the 21 percent), the tax is triggered when you get the money out of your C-corp and put it into your personal bank account because the money coming out of the business is a dividend. So while the corporation doesn't pay NIIT directly, anyone hoping to do something personally useful with the money has to pay that additional 3.8 percent.

We're not done yet. The federal government of course also collects taxes for Social Security and Medicare by deducting from your paycheck. They collect taxes from other countries through tariffs. They also charge excise taxes. All of this is to fund all organs of the federal government.

Federal taxes apply throughout the United States, whether you're in big-government California or a more tax-friendly state like Florida or Texas, or somewhere tiny and remote like Wyoming or Alaska. That said, federal funds that come from those taxes often flow down into states and municipalities.

How Federal Taxes Are Calculated

Now that we've covered the types of federal taxes, let's take a look at **how federal taxes are calculated** so that you can understand how different types of money are taxed.

Your biggest taxes will be on **active** income. Active income is generally going to be taxed using the federal tax brackets that you may have heard of. While you pay taxes on what you earn, any losses from active activities are deductible (which means you can subtract them).

The next type of tax to look at is **capital gains** taxes. These are common when you exchange goods or services between two people or two businesses where profit is made.

Finally, we look at **passive** income, which is taxed differently from active income since the most common form of passive income is investments, followed next in popularity by rent paid by tenants if you own an investment property. And rental properties in particular typically run at a tax loss because they're allowed to use depreciation. On top of that, a lot of rental businesses are not deductible against active income because passive income is limited in how you can deduct it from active income. That means a tax loss you have from a rental property cannot generally be subtracted from the income you gained in your W-2 or S-corp draw.

There is a fourth category you should note called the **non-passive** tax. It sits right in the middle between active income and passive income, which means it's subject to the usual tax tables like active income and doesn't have the same loss limitations as normal passive income. So if you have a non-passive loss, you can use that against your active gains while passive losses are currently limited to $3,000 a year. Non-passive income is also generally not subject to the 3.8 percent NIIT.

Now, we're about to begin thinking about **your** tax burden, how it's calculated, and why. But first, we would be remiss if we did not drill down into the dreaded FICA tax that Marie had to deal with.

Dishonorable Mention: FICA Tax

Also known as the self-employment tax, FICA is how Social Security and Medicare programs are funded; you can even see how much is saved up for you in your personal account on the Social Security website's web portal. The payout of Social Security is based not only on how much you've paid in, but how much you've paid in over the course of ten years (forty quarters).

Many times on your paycheck, you don't see FICA listed; instead, you see Social Security, Medicare, and something called FUTA, which refers to the federal unemployment tax (states have their own unemployment taxes as well.)

Social Security taxes are 6.2 percent, up to $168,000 as of 2024; if you're reading this book after 2024, the $168,000 figure has been adjusted upward for inflation. But once you reach that limit (whatever it may be that particular year), the tax stops; the next dollar you earn isn't taxed in that manner.

Medicare is different. With Medicare, the current rate is 1.45 percent, no matter how much you earn. Plus, when you earn over $200,000, you pay an additional tax of 0.9 percent, so if you're making $200,000 or more (filing Single, $250,000 if filing Married Filing Jointly), your Medicare tax is actually 1.54 percent.

As for the FICA tax, it works like so: half is paid by the employee of the company out of their paycheck, and half is paid by the company. The company gets to treat the FICA tax as a business expense, which means it's tax deductible; this means that if you're a pass-through entity, you're getting your personal tax rate applied to that as a discount. Let's say you're an average business. This means you may get a 22 percent discount or relief on your FICA taxes that you paid on behalf of your employee. Your employee, on the other hand, did not get any discount on that tax and had to pay the full amount of their half.

But you have to be careful with this because if you're the only employee of your business, you still have to pay the other 94 percent of the expense not paid by your business. Thus FICA taxes are still due even if you have a qualified plan like the 401(k). So let's say that you pay yourself a wage of $30,000 and you turn around and put $30,000 into your 401(k), which is a pre-tax contribution. Your total federal taxable income is zero—you won't owe any federal personal income tax and you won't owe any federal corporate tax. However, you will still owe the FICA tax on the original $30,000. That FICA tax has to be withheld from your paycheck by law, so you won't actually be putting $30,000 into your 401(k). It's going to be $29,000 and some change.

But now that we understand how those taxes work, are any of them optional, or at least the next best thing—have a possibility to be mitigated? Let's investigate.

Mitigatable Taxes

Let's start with **property** taxes, which are based on the fair market value of your property, including the land your building is on. How much control do you have over this value? Very little, but not zero.

Property taxes are determined based on the sale of similar homes nearby, not the list price. You can dispute the estimated value of your home and present your analysis to try to get an exception. You typically have to appear before a jury of your peers at the county to see if you deserve that exemption or deduction.

But exemption or not, you do not have any control over the tax rate itself; that's passed at the state or local level. The best you can do here is lobby for the candidates you think will lower your tax burden in this area. That's not exactly a quick impact.

By contrast, you have a lot of control over the **sales** tax you pay, because you can choose not to buy something, or you can wait for it to go on sale. In some states, there are tax-free weekends to allow people to buy school supplies and other necessities. Also, some items are taxed differently than others. For example, 100 percent pure orange juice may have no tax on it at all, but the more sugary orange juice may be taxed. Apart from health reasons, the prospect of saving on sales tax may motivate you to change what you eat or drink.

Another way you can control the sales tax you pay is when you're negotiating payment for a large purchase, such as a car. While you can't negotiate the tax away, you can negotiate the sale price down, and that affects the amount you pay in tax.

You can control **excise** taxes too, but in a different way. While you can't demand the federal government to stop taxing products from certain countries, you can shop around to see where you can get the best deal on a product, reducing the amount you spend overall (remember, excise taxes are built into the price, so they won't show up on a receipt the way sales tax does.)

As for **personal** or **corporate income** taxes, you have a lot more control here. As usual, you can't control the tax rate, but you can get deductions and credits. In effect, you're negotiating how much you're being charged.

Inheritance taxes are also a tax you have little control over. The federal government will charge what they're going to charge, and you can't do anything about that. But "hard to control" does not mean "impossible to control"; there are strategies you can use to mitigate the tax, but it's nothing illegal—just strategies to move your money in ways that reduce the amount of taxes you pay.

Let's turn from theory to practice now. Earlier, we took a look at Bob, but an important thing to remember is that Bob is not an average taxpayer. He lives in California, which has one of the highest state tax rates in the country, thus he is not a good example of "average."

Therefore, let's consider a more average family. This is a husband and wife with no dependents and a fairly average business. The business is taxed as an S corp, making it a pass-through entity that sticks the family with both the profits of the business and the accompanying tax liability.

This business is doing well, with an income of $750,000 a year. The husband and wife pay themselves $250,000 a year in wages as a couple. The combined business profits and W-2 wages comes to $1 million. They live in a house worth $1 million and are happy living there. They spend $20,000 a month on various things—groceries, gas, eating out at restaurants, vacations, clothing, and the like. Let's also assume that they're maxing out their 401(k), and that they are under fifty years old. They live in an average city.

In terms of their taxes, let's look at their property taxes first (which cover their local taxes). They live in a $1 million home in an average state in an average city, so they'll pay $8,900 in property taxes for the year, which is close to 1 percent of their total income of $1 million.

Now let's look at their state taxes. They're paying a couple of state taxes, not just one. First off, they're paying their state income tax, which is $71,200 in this average state of the union. Second, they're paying sales tax based on the food they eat and the gas they use while driving around; this amount comes out to about 3 percent of their income (they also pay $300 in excise taxes.)

At the federal level, they will pay $223,700 in taxes from their pass-through entity and their W-2. They're also paying an additional $9,200 in federal FICA taxes for Social Security and Medicare—another 1 percent taken. Taken together with other federal taxes, the bill comes out to $346,400, which is about a 35 percent rate. That means that for every dollar they made, they paid 35 cents to various federal entities.

Now two things should be noted with this situation. One of the most common things to look at is the federal income tax rate. If you're making between $500,000 and $1 million, you want your tax rate to be in the low twenties. When you make more than $1 million a year, however, it's hard to keep your federal income tax rate in the low twenties like that; you'll float up to the mid-twenties and you'll float up there quickly. Another thing you should note is that their total taxes represented 35 percent of their income, but only 22 percent of that was paid via their tax return. Add in the state tax and it becomes 29 percent; the rest is from the other taxes we mentioned, taxes that are paid through consumption.

Alright now, that example reminds us how much ground we've covered so far in this chapter, and we've also begun to view income and its obvious relationship with and impact on different tax burdens. Let's drill down into the details.

How Income Gets Reported for Tax Purposes

Let's dive into the kinds of income that get reported. The best one to start with is the most straightforward of them all, the W-2.

The Wage

Wage income is subject to progressively higher taxation based on how large the earned wage is; you likely hear of these increasing tax rate levels as "tax brackets." They range in 2024 from 10 percent to 37 percent. Income from wages is considered active income because you earn it by actively working; you don't just receive it for nothing. The next thing about wages is that you never have a loss with them because if you lost money by working and giving money back instead of getting a paycheck, why would you do it?

The S Corp

LLCs taxed as S corps are examples of active income. Their income (i.e. profits) are taxed under Subchapter S which uses the same progressive tax rate for the portion of the personal federal tax as your wage. And if you take the wage you earned via your paycheck and add that to the profit that you earned in your LLC S corp, you are on your way to calculating your total taxable income. If you have a loss in your S corp, you can use that to offset your wage with certain potential limitations. S corps report their taxes on Form 1120-S and that tax liability is passed to the owners to pay. The report given to the owners so they know how much to include on their household tax return is called Schedule K-1 (usually shortened to just "K-1").

The C Corp

If your business is taxed as a C corp, the business itself pays its own taxes under Subchapter C tax code. The taxes are calculated and reported on Form 1120.

C corps are subject to double taxation because the corporation pays the first tax and then when the owners take the profits out (called a *dividend*), they get taxed again on a household level. They also get to pay the Net Investment Income tax (NIIT) and some people count this as a third tax while others lump that into the capital gains tax on the dividend. That's at least two taxes as a C corp and one tax as a S corp, hence why C corps are said to cause "double taxation."

You might think that the double taxation from having a C corp would increase your taxes, and while that is typically the case, it's not always true. It depends on how much money you make, and that's because when you take money out of a corporation taxed as a C corp, you're paying capital gains on the dividend. These capital gains taxes can be 20 percent, 15 percent, or nothing at all, depending on how much money you make that year. You also have to pay the 3.8 percent NIIT. The sum total of all the C corp taxes might be less than the taxes due if the business were an S corp. In addition, S and C corps can provide different benefits, which one could argue is also a form of income.

C corp income is not treated as ordinary active income; instead, it's subject to the corporate tax rate, which is the 21 percent flat tax rate I mentioned earlier. C corps can also have losses and those are handled by the corporation, which is responsible for its own taxes.

Bank Interest

Another common form of income is bank interest. You didn't have to earn the interest by the sweat of your brow so it is considered passive income.

Rental Income

Rental income is passive unless you do short-term rentals (7 days or less) or you qualify to be a Real Estate professional. When it's passive income a loss can be used to offset other capital gains, say from a stock sale or bank interest. For example let's say your stocks did really well (profits from stock sales are considered passive income) and your rental properties are running at a tax loss. Everything is considered passive income, so they can offset one another; this works in your favor.

But when assessing any of your taxes, you have to do what you would do with any large bureaucracy: Fill out a ton of forms. **Correctly**.

Essential Tax Worksheets

Every single one of these types of taxes has a different worksheet for calculating and doing the math to comply with the respective tax codes. These worksheets walk you through the process of calculating your tax step by step with no steps skipped. We call these worksheets *tax returns*. Because of the complexity of all these taxes, and the types of assets and transactions and all the things that you do in your families and your businesses, there are likely many pages in your tax return. That same tax return and worksheets that you use are also used by 165 million other families so they have to handle a lot of different and unique scenarios.

The federal tax return Form 1040 is the most important of your tax returns because it is the primary driver of both your federal taxes and possibly your state taxes as well. A lot of people get their tax return draft back from their accountant and feel overwhelmed by it because it's probably more than a hundred pages. But it's not as bad as you might think. Thus the key thing to do is verify that your tax return is correct because if you don't, you're setting yourself up for a lot of trouble down the line.

Regarding verification, an important thing to remember is that if your tax return is wrong, your accountant is not responsible, you are; after all, it's your signature at the bottom to which you are agreeing:

187

I declare that I have examined this return and accompanying schedules and statements, and to the best of my knowledge and belief, they are true, correct, and complete.

Reviewing your tax return is not as difficult as you might think and can probably be done in under 30 minutes. And reviewing your tax return is likely to catch errors—especially after you read the section later in this chapter about how to review your tax return. Most of the time my experience is that tax return errors are in your favor, not the IRS. This means that you are likely to actually save money by taking the time to review your tax return.

Filing as an S corp

Let's demystify this a bit. The tax return you file will depend on what tax code you have selected to use for calculating the taxes on your business. This goes back to how you structured your entities. What type of tax code you selected drives what tax returns need to be filed and what rolls up to your personal tax return. If you are an S corp (which means you selected to have your business taxed under Subchapter S), it doesn't matter if you call yourself a corporation or an LLC. You're going to take your P&L and your balance sheet and reconcile them so that you know your P&L is correct. Your accountant (unless you are filling out your business tax return yourself) is going to fill out the IRS Form 1120-S. Again, it doesn't matter if you're a corporation or an LLC, whether you're an "Inc." or an "LLC". What matters is you have selected to file under Subchapter S by selecting to be taxed as an S corp. Form 1120-S is really simple, closely resembling your P&L and balance sheet. The reason Form 1120-S doesn't exactly match the format of your P&L and balance sheet is that over 5 million businesses filed Form 1120-S in 2023 and the IRS wants all the P&Ls and balance sheet information in the same format—their format. So if you can read your P&L and your balance sheet, you can review your Form 1120-S tax return. It takes about the same amount of time.

While there are other worksheets relating to international income, the main one you need to worry about is Form 1120-S if you have an S corp. The profit and loss is on page one, and your balance sheet is on Schedule L. When you file that form with the IRS, it will be identified with your Employer Identification Number, or EIN. This is like a Social Security number for businesses. There's also a Schedule K-1 that's included in 1120-S. This is a summary of the taxes and reports everything to all of the business's owners. Each owner of the business must be given their K-1, wherever they are located. The IRS also gets a copy of all the issued K-1s.

Form 1120-S is due March 15—one month before April 15 so that you have enough time to send all the K-1s out to the owners.

Filing as a C Corp

When filing as a C corp, you again start with a reconciled P&L and balance sheet. C corps file Form 1120 (no S this time.)

C corps are not pass-through entities. They do not issue Schedule K-1 forms to inform the owners of their tax liability because the tax is paid by the company itself. Page one of Form 1120 has the P&L, and the Schedule L on Form 1120 is the balance sheet. Now if anyone takes money out of the C corp that's an owner (a shareholder), that shareholder is given Form 1099-DIV ("DIV" is for dividend).

Filing as a Partnership

C corps and S corps aren't the only type of business you can have. Another common type of business is the partnership. In this case, the partnership files Form 1065 instead of Form 1120-S, but it looks almost exactly the same as Form 1120-S, with the P&L on page 1 and the balance sheet on Schedule L.

The main difference here is that you have to distribute a lot more Schedule K-1 forms, since partnerships typically have more owners than S corps do. Each recipient of the K-1 will put it on their tax return (Form 1040) when filing.

Filing as a Sole Proprietorship

With a sole proprietorship, you report the P&L for the business on your personal Form 1040. Everything is on you—it is inseparable from you. All the tax liability is on you personally. There's nothing else to file. How the money is made doesn't matter—it's all reported on Schedule C of your Form 1040.

Filing a Personal Tax Return

When you get your draft tax return from your tax preparer or from tax planning software (TurboTax, H&R Block, TaxAct, FreeTaxUSA, Tax-Slayer, eFile.com, etc), there are going to be a lot of pages. The IRS is like grade school in that they want to see all your work for full credit.

But odds are good that you only need to review 2 pages.

You need to find Form 1040. This is your personal tax return. Let's walk through the logic and how it works.

Page 1 of Form 1040 is all your personal information. This includes your name, your address, your social security number, your filing status and the list of your dependents. This information takes up half of the first page. Not scary.

The next section is your income. Everything you earned. There's a place to report your wages, your business profits if you're a pass-through entity and all the interest you earned on your bank account. Maybe you sold some stock and made a pretty profit—that goes on there too. It's every source of income you can think of. And some you probably haven't thought of.

The next thing you get to do from that income is you get to make some adjustments that subtract some things, such as contributions to your IRA, to your Health Savings Account, and even the portion of the self-employment tax that you pay as a business owner. So adjustments are just the things that the government wants to incentivize us to do more of. And so if you take all your income and you subtract those adjustments, what we get is your adjusted gross income, or AGI.

But the deductions don't stop there. Did you give to charity? Did you have a lot of medical expenses? Did you buy a home? Because your home mortgage interest is also a deduction you can claim. All of those deductions are collected together and reported as a total. If you want to see them broken out, look for Schedule A. You get to take the largest deduction possible—either the sum of your itemized list or some other minimum (called the standard deduction). When your list of items is more than the standard deduction and you use that number because it's bigger; it's called "itemizing."

In the Tax Cut Jobs Act in 2017, the government decided it wanted to reward those people that ran a pass-through business. This is because small businesses tend to be pass-through entities and small businesses are so good for the economy. Therefore, we deduct a few things related to owning a pass-through business. So now if you take your adjusted gross income and you take away all those deductions, we end up with your total taxable income.

This brings us to the end of page 1. All the hard stuff is done. The rest of the tax return is basically the outputs from all those page 1 inputs. Again—not scary.

After we figure out your taxable income, we calculate your actual tax bill at the top of page 2 in a section called "Taxes and Credits." We put your total income through the progressive tax schedule (with all those tax brackets), adding up the numbers of each of the brackets that you filled up. After you do all that, you have your initial total tax. But we're not done yet.

Now you may get some tax credits. For example, the government wants to lower the cost of having children, so they give you a tax credit for that. A tax credit is when you take how much you owe in taxes, then deduct from that amount. This is different from deductions, which affect your income before the tax is calculated. There are additional credits for buying electric cars, using childcare services, and other things; you'll find that the tax code often represents the political mood of the country, because the government incentivizes behaviors by affecting how much tax you pay.

So now page 2 of Form 1040 shows your total tax. But is that how much you need to now pay? No—because you've already paid some of that bill throughout the year. You paid some of that tax bill out of your paycheck. And you may have made quarterly payments as well. So we add up everything we've already paid and then what's left is the balance due on the total. Some people have overpaid their taxes and get a refund—that is, they're *getting* money from the IRS or the state government. Other people have to pay out. Either way, you have to true-up and pay the total amount. Then you get to sign the bottom of the return and send it in electrically or on paper.

So the logic of taxes is not complicated. What's complicated is that the different types of income are all calculated differently and subject to all these crazy rules, like loss limitations and carry forward limitations and several other things. That's why the tax return is complicated, but taxes themselves are not. You simply take your income, subtract some things to get your total income, calculate your total taxes, get some credits, figure out how much you've already paid, find out what you owe, pay it, and you're done. That's possibly the shortest summary of IRS Form 1040 ever written.

So now you understand the basics of what taxes look like. But what about who's going to be helping you?

The Tax Preparer

There are multiple types of service professionals who will fill out your personal and business tax returns for you. The most common are Certified Public Accountants (CPAs) and Enrolled Agents (EAs). At minimum, you pay these professionals to take all your tax-related documents, go through them, find the numbers, put them in the tax software, and double check to make sure that the numbers were entered correctly. You are not paying your tax preparer to make sure your taxes are correct; that's **your** job. You are the one signing your tax return at the end (or giving your tax preparer your permission to file electronically on your behalf), so what's important is that you understand that you have a critical role to make sure that the numbers on your tax return are right. Typically your tax preparer offers more services than just filing taxes, so we'll just call them your accountant from here on.

If you take the approach that you and your accountant are on the same team trying to accomplish the same goal (i.e. file your tax return on time with correct numbers), it will likely change your expectations and how you interact with them as a member of your team. Like other members of your team, you pay them for their services and to perform a certain set of important tasks.

Working with your accountant is however a bit different than managing your other employees. Let's unpack this further. The first thing is to understand that your accountant has many clients that are paying them to complete similar tasks. So you're not the only person they are worried about. Second, there are deadlines throughout the year that you need to hit. Filing taxes is not a one-and-done project. If you think of your tax filings as a series of small projects with deadlines that span the entire calendar year, things will go far better for everyone.

Let me tell you what a calendar might look like. First off, it starts before the calendar year is over, usually in November. What you want to do here is schedule an end-of-year meeting with your accountant to review how to end the year well. Many accountants will reach out to you to schedule this, but you can really impress them if you reach out to them first. It's usually a one hour meeting, and the agenda includes a review of how the year is going with a rough prediction of where things are likely to end up. Where do you think you will end the year with your business profit? What do we think we need to do for the January 15 estimated quarterly tax payment? What tax strategies will you change or add for the coming tax year? That's the minimum of what you'll cover in your November meeting.

The next major milestone in your tax calendar is around February. At this time, you file a request for a deadline extension on your tax returns. Even if you want to get your tax return done by March and April, you should file an extension because it relieves the pressure on your accountant. Extensions do not increase your chances of audit. I understand that you may want to file in March for your business tax return and April for your personal tax return—to get it all over with—but oftentimes from a stress management standpoint and the emotional impact of taxes, what you really want to know is how much cash you need to set aside money to pay in April (called the "true-up"). Because you have to pay up in April—even if you have a deadline extension—it's simply often better for all parties to request the deadline extension and focus on estimating how much cash you need for the April true-up. If you request an extension and happen to get the tax return done early, that's great—you can file it at any time before the final deadline in September and/or October.

If you and your accountant think you overpaid your taxes throughout the year and you'll be getting a refund, you can still file the extension and then work hard to get it done as quickly as possible to get your money back.

The other element that you want to consider is whether or not you need your previous year's tax return done for some formality. Let's say you're getting ready to buy a building and the bank asks you for your previous year's tax returns so they can see if you're eligible for a loan; you'll want your tax return done so it doesn't hold anything up.

The next big milestones for your tax year come in April. In April, you have to make your estimated tax payment for the first quarter, so even if you filed an extension, you still owe the first quarter's estimated tax in April in addition to the prior year's "true up." To get all this sorted out, collaborate with your accountant. For successful business owners April tax payments are a non-trivial amount of cash, so you may need to plan ahead.

Most accountants go on a long vacation in late April and early May to get their sanity back. This is the quietest month of the year from an accountant's workload perspective. They just finished a bunch of tax returns working late nights and weekends. They need a break and don't be surprised if it's longer than two days.

The next touch point is June. On June 15, you make the next quarterly estimated tax payment. June is smack in the middle of Q2—and your estimated tax payment due June 15 is for Q2. I have no idea why the IRS does it this way, they just do.

June is more than just your quarterly estimated tax payment. In mid-June you're going to create your own document to track what tax forms and what tax documents you will give to your accountant in time to file by the extension deadline. You would think that your accountant is going to give you this list, and they might, but many accountants don't do that and they just say "Send me everything." Their tax software may not track what forms you need to provide in order to do your tax return—so be proactive and help your accountant out. A good place to start is with last year's list. If you create a document list and you track that in the first year, it becomes the starting point for next year's taxes. You create the list of documents you need in June. And then what you do is send it to your accountant and say "Here's the list of documents I think I need to collect. Are you aware of any others?" They will start to love you.

Now in July, you're gonna get all the documents uploaded to the shared file folder your accountant has set up for you. The reason for this is most people don't get it done in July; instead, they get it done closer to the final September and October deadlines. If you get it done early, that means your accountant will work on your tax returns first because they have a queue and you've given them everything they need.

After July, the next touch point is the month of August. At that point, you want the first draft of your tax return to be done. You should there-fore remind your accountant that you uploaded all the necessary files in July—just like you said you would—then ask when you can expect to see the first draft of your business tax return. They'll probably tell you they'll have it in early August, maybe early September at the latest. That's when you'd want the first draft. And once you have the first draft, do not take a week to return it. Even if your accountant says it's okay to review it for a week, don't do that. Do it within a day if you can. Be fast.

You want to be fast because your accountant is going to respond to you as fast as you respond to them. The best way to get a fast response from your accountant is to always respond to them faster than they respond to you. In August you get your draft business tax return, then review it that day and send it back the next. Maybe if you're with a coach-ing service, you would ask your coach to review it, then you get it back to your accountant fast.

Next will be your personal tax return in September. Again, you would ask your accountant in July when you can expect a draft. Then, they'll get you the draft. If they go a day past that, you send them an email asking about the draft that was promised. When they get you their personal return, you get them a response within two days. Personal returns take longer to review since there's so much more to look at.

Tips for Talking with Your Accountant

My first tip for you is that when you meet with your accountant in November for an end of year tax plan, take notes and send the notes in an email to them. Remember, you and your accountant are on the same team. Lead by being a servant. Second, as I mentioned earlier, you should always try to respond faster than their other clients. Most professional service providers will respond in kind, and they'll respond to their best clients first. Next, create that professional document checklist and send it to your accountant to review. It'll look professional and they'll know you're serious.

Save your meeting notes and send it in follow-up emails. For example, after the November meeting, when you send the documents, attach your November notes and any appropriate documents. If you're sharing a file folder with your accountant, you would just send them a link to those documents. Every time you send an email to your accountant, include a link to your business entity diagram. Accountants have many clients, they may have forgotten what they were doing with your specific taxes. Send them the entity diagram in every email to remind them.

Just having the entity diagram and providing it to them in every single email is going to differentiate you. Even if you have a basic question, send them a link to your entity diagram—in fact, just keep sending it until they're sick of it. They will thank you for that.

Next, always meet the deadlines you promise. If you want your accountant to meet your deadlines, you better meet your own commitments. If you say to your accountant you're gonna have all the files uploaded by July 31, you better have them all done unless somebody has not provided it to you, in which case you would point that out so you get half credit for following through.

Next, use clear file names. Use a structure where the form number is at the beginning, then the tax year, and then the description. For example you might name the file "Form W-2—Nick payroll 2024." That way, they know exactly what it is by looking at the file name; they don't have to open it.

When you review your accountant's work, keep in mind that your accountant will likely be proud of the work they did. They've gone through a lot of education. They've paid a lot of money for software, and they've spent a lot of time putting together your tax return. Treat that return with the respect that it deserves. Give them a professional report back with your questions and comments.

Sometimes mistakes are made on your tax return. It may be your fault or your accountant's fault. But you only have control over yourself, so here's what you can do to avoid common mistakes.

Frequent Tax Filing Mistakes

The first thing to understand is that you are ultimately responsible for the state of your tax return, since you're the one signing it and paying the bill.

The most common reason that people file a tax return with a mistake on it is that they forget to tell their accountant something. When that happens, the accountant didn't make a mistake, you did. So the way to prevent that is to be organized and know enough about tax returns to catch errors.

You've got a document inventory. You've got a business entity diagram. You've got your notes from your November tax meeting. The most helpful and effective way to avoid errors of omission is to be organized. The nice thing about this is that once you're organized one year, it's drop dead easy to reuse those same organization documents the next year, especially because chances are your tax situation doesn't change too much year over year. So by starting with the previous year's templates, even the data in those templates, you can reduce the overhead of being organized to something you can do during your monthly Saturday morning financial routine.

The next most common error is typos on your tax return. This is not common if you're staying with the same accountant year over year because their software remembers your tax return from the previous year and lets them import your family information to the current year. This error is most common when you change accountants. You'll have to recheck the Social Security numbers, the address spelling, the spelling of your business, your EIN, and everything else. If you didn't have the problem last year and you stayed with the same accountant, odds are that you won't face this issue. But if you change accountants, you'll have to double-check all of your information to make sure it's still straight.

The next mistake is an error in categorization. Unlike the previous errors, this one is an error your accountant makes in logic. For example, let's say that they miscategorize your rental property if you operate your business out of it. Something like that is a little known fact about the tax return, and many accountants don't think to check if your income is categorized the best way. The only way you catch an error like this is if you know enough about the tax personality of your business and you know where to look on the tax return to verify it is correctly designated.

That said, when you're reviewing your tax returns, you do not need to check any math because all of that is done through software. You also do not need to check if the right forms were attached, and you don't need to learn the rules about whether Schedule A gets attached or Schedule D or any of that stuff, because your accountant's software handles all that. All of the forms and all the worksheets are filled out in the software.

Your accountant is going to send you a personal tax return draft that is very long. It will have many pages and all the required forms, schedules and statements. There are some pages that your account can choose whether to provide you or not. Many accountants don't want the tax package to be any longer than it absolutely needs to be—so they select to keep those out. You may want those worksheets and optional forms. Your accountant should be happy to provide everything to you including all the worksheets upon request - after all, every page belongs to you. It's especially helpful to get all the optional pages if you know you are going to use a different tax preparer next year.

Marie's Tax Education

Let's return to Marie, who decided on the advice of her accountant to change her business entity from sole proprietorship to an LLC taxed as an S-corporation. It was soon after this that Marie started to learn about tax strategies. The lightbulb of her business brain was already on, but this education proved to be a floodlight.

When Marie first learned about transforming into an S-corp from her accountant, she got curious about the new tax return she would be filing. She learned that there exist different tax codes—codes for personal income, codes for S-corps, codes for other types of businesses, and even codes for charities. Each code explained the IRS perspective of money. Her view of money had been pretty simple—it's what was in the bank or in her purse. But that different perspective of money allowed her to see how taxes worked—and how to save money on taxes without giving up cash from her bank account.

For example, Marie learned about depreciation and how that applies to an S-corp. This was totally different from what she had experienced as a sole proprietorship. She discovered that some of her business equipment could be depreciated over time, a way to reduce taxable income each year with an expense as the equipment wore out and became obsolete. Using depreciation, Marie could spread out the tax hit of the expense of the equipment rather than one large expense upfront when the equipment was purchased. She would save on taxes while still using the asset. Her perspective as a sole proprietorship had been that equipment was basically a cash expense to the business, complete with the big upfront hit. Depreciation became an important factor in Marie's decision to buy better equipment to attract new customers. She started to plan her new equipment purchases with the tax savings in mind.

Marie saw other ways that the tax view of money was different from her cash view. One of the biggest impacts came when she learned how to unlock new tax saving options using an Accountable Plan, which further takes advantage of the tax versus cash perspective of income.

Marie implemented the Accountable Plan at the advice of her accountant and this allowed her to feel better about running additional expenses. Now she knew with confidence she could deduct her monthly mobile phone bill, part of her home office, part of her home internet and the mileage she was driving for the few remaining home-bound clients. She also started to use an HSA to get a tax deduction on part of her medical expenses. Her Accountable Plan became an important part of her regular routine. The tax-savings created an incentive for her to be more organized in her personal checking account and personal credit cards so that she could identify all of the business expenses she had paid with her personal credit card. It was like she was getting paid to get herself organized.

Paying taxes had always been a stressful thing to Marie. It seemed large and so random. She couldn't understand what caused taxes to go up or down nor how taxes even worked. Now that she had learned more about taxes, she started to understand how to control and estimate them. With that came a clear understanding of how to pay them. When Marie figured that out, she changed her withholdings in her paycheck and started to use her quarterly estimated tax payments to control how much she paid the IRS in advance of the deadlines. She wanted to keep her cash in her business working for her, not provide an interest-free loan to the government.

Marie is naturally a competitive, honest, numbers-driven person. She loves looking at her profit and loss report each week to see how her new marketing ideas are working out or how many of her clients are using her new treatment equipment. Once Marie learned how taxes work—and the different perspective that the IRS takes compared to her cash perspective—it became a game. And the game was to reduce her taxes as much as possible by playing by the rules. The challenge was that the rules of the game are not easy to understand because they are contained in 6,871 pages (over 22 million words) of tax code.

But there is one report that showed Marie how well she is playing the game—her personal tax return. The rules of the game are long and complex but the personal tax return is her report card. Her personal tax return shows line by line how well she is playing the game.

Can I reduce my taxable income here while keeping my cash income over there? Can I increase my deductions over there?

If you want to know how well you're playing the game, learn to read your personal tax return. Not only will you know intuitively how to save on taxes, you'll have something to look forward to in April.

CHAPTER 9

SCROOGE-MAXED TAX STRATEGIES

Did you originally pick up this book to learn how to save on taxes? That's true for most people who read this. Well, it's been quite a journey to get to this point, this point where we're finally talking about taxes, specifically how to reduce them. Why? No; *why not?* Saving money on taxes is not a simple checkbox on the tax return. Tax mitigation involves understanding multiple areas of money including entity structures, applicable tax laws, and financial statement ins-and-outs. You need all these tools (and a whole lot more) to accomplish the seemingly simple goal of saving on taxes. Yes, tax savings is an outcome—not an input. My point is: When you do things well and have your business organized, you can save money on taxes. In fact, you probably will, and maybe a *lot*. So, let's jump in to learning about tax strategies. And as usual, let's learn through story.

Meet Steve and Brenda. This couple owns a heating, ventilation, and cooling (HVAC) company. Steve has been running this business for over fifteen years since purchasing it from the original founder. The couple live in Ohio where they're raising their three children, who range in age from eleven to sixteen. While Brenda occasionally helps with the business, her primary focus is caring for the family.

Steve's HVAC business operates as an LLC taxed as an S corp. Last year, the company generated $3.2 million in sales, resulting in a $650,000 taxable profit after depreciation. Steve paid himself a W-2 salary of $3,800 per week, totaling $197,600 annually. The business employs nine full-time staff and two part-time staff, offering benefits such as a 401(k) with a match and access to discounted family health insurance through a group program. Steve also personally owns the building where the business is located. He also recently purchased a property down the street for $5,000, intending to use it in the future for parking the company's trucks if—and when—they expand.

Now, given all that, here is a snapshot of Steve and Brenda's 2023 tax situation:

Form 1040 (Personal Taxes)

- Box 1: Taxable W-2 wages: $197,000
- Box 8: Taxable business income: $650,000
- Box 10: Less adjustments from health insurance: $(7,600)
- Box 11: Adjusted Gross Income ("AGI"): $840,000
- Box 12: Less standard or itemized deductions: $(27,700)
- Box 13: Less QBI Deduction: $(130,000)
- Box 15: Total taxable income: $682,300
- Box 16: Federal individual income tax: $182,594

Other Taxes

- Ohio state taxes: $26,416
- Social Security + Medicare withheld via paycheck ("FICA"): $12,798

Totals

- Grand total individual + FICA + state taxes: $221,808
- Average federal tax rate (individual + FICA / AGI): 23.3%
- Average state tax rate: 3.1%
- Total average tax rate: 26.4%

This year, 2024, Steve's business grew over 2023. By October 2024, Steve knew he would reach a new record and estimated they would end around $3.5 million in sales, with profits nearing $700,000. That's not all that happened in 2024. Another business in town expressed strong interest in that property Steve had purchased it for the future because he saw a bargain, and he decided to sell it because they offered so much—he sold it for $185,000! He had only paid $5,000 for that property a few years back. What a return for doing nothing with the property! Before the end of 2024 with this new money he had been blessed with, Steve decided to make some improvements to the shop, including an addition (a new room for tool storage) and a new HVAC system, ironically.

Every year in the past, Steve relied on an accountant to handle his books and file his tax return. Typically, he received a draft of his completed tax return, signed it after looking at how much he owed and moved on. He'd known and trusted his accountant for years. The accountant had never proactively offered advice on reducing taxes, focusing instead on filing and answering occasional bookkeeping questions. But this year Steve knew he had made a lot of money and wanted to do whatever he could (legally) to reduce that upcoming tax bill.

Everything changed when Steve attended a Firmstride tax strategy webinar. He was so impressed, he hired us immediately afterward. It was late in the year when his family engaged with us so we first got to work developing a tax plan he could implement before the end of the year. The plan paid for itself in the first year, and Steve was able to continue using the strategies he learned in subsequent years. Table 8 outlines how that critical first year with Firmstride turned out thanks to our expertise.

Description	2023	2024
Form 1040 Box 9: sum of taxable wages + profit from business	$847,600	$677,539
Form 1040 Box 16: Federal individual income tax	$182,594	$118,175
Ohio state taxes	$26,416	$20,574
FICA via paycheck	$12,798	$8,453
Grand total individual + FICA + state taxes	$221,808	$147,202
Net take-home cash to owner after taxes*	**$625,792**	**$937,198**

Average federal tax rate (individual + FICA)	23.3%	18.7%
Average state tax rate	3.1%	3.1%
Total average tax rate	26.4%	21.7%
Net savings on taxes from strategies compared to baseline (no strategies employed)	$0	$131,689

Table 8 - financial impact of working with Firmstride to employ tax strategies

*Note that net take-home cash is a way to look at how much money the family added to their personal assets after paying taxes. This includes their W-2 wages, all the profit from the business, 401(k) matches, cash proceeds from asset sales (e.g. the property sale proceeds) and home rental income.

I'd like to draw your attention to these three key observations:

- **The average tax rate dropped from 26.4 percent to 21.7 percent despite increased income.** Steve and Brenda can continue to repeat many of the tax strategies they learned in future years to reduce their tax drag as much as possible.
- **Taxable wages and profit from the business dropped.** This is one of the ideal outcomes from tax strategies. Because you pay taxes on wages and profit from your business, if you earn less in *taxable income* and *taxable wages* (notice I didn't say *take-home cash income*) you pay less in taxes. So understand that . . .
- **Take-home cash is not the same as taxable income.** By shifting taxable income to the most efficient tax code, Steve and Brenda benefited overall and kept more cash.

The rest of this chapter is dedicated to explaining tax strategies and how to deploy them. At the end, we'll review what, exactly, Steve and Brenda did to achieve that $131,689 savings in just one year.

How to Treat Taxes Like Ebenezer Scrooge

OK, I would like to start this next section by describing what this chapter is *not* going to cover.

This chapter is *NOT* about how to avoid paying taxes. That would be *tax evasion.* It is a crime—a felony resulting in a prison sentence if the amount of taxes you "avoided" paying is substantial ($3,000 or more). Anyone who tries to tell you about a loophole where you don't have to file or pay taxes is going to get you in trouble.

This chapter is also *NOT* about how to disguise your income and so trick the government into thinking you owe less money or have suffered losses and thus get a tax benefit. That would be referred to as *tax fraud,* and is also a crime. Anyone pitching you ways to hide your money is also going to get you investigated by the IRS.

So what is this chapter about? What *are* these strategies for? The title refers to "Scrooge-maxing," which is of course based on the miserly approach of Ebenzer Scrooge to money, which was to pay as little of it as possible and not a penny more. Repurpose this mindset to taxes and what does that mean? It means **we want to pay as little tax as legally possible and not a penny more.**

That said, these Scrooge-maxing tax strategies are not secret tax codes I've cracked (though I will admit that some tax codes are not well understood by accountants). These are methods that we've found and used, I and Firmstride's clients.

This helpful guide will show the **forty** different strategies we will discuss—to Scrooge-max your taxes owed. They are organized alphabetically.

1031 Exchange

A 1031 Exchange allows you to, in effect, swap one investment real estate for another. You can defer capital gains taxes that you would normally incur from selling one investment property by investing the proceeds of that sale in the purchase of a "like-kind" investment property, within a specific timeline. This strategy only makes sense for those selling real estate at a profit. A 1031 Exchange is in reference to the tax form you complete when you do the exchange. This strategy can have a high one-time benefit for the ROI because it defers capital gains (opposed to you having to pay that and then use the proceeds to invest) and it's difficult to repeat this every year unless you buy and sell a lot of real estate. A 1031 Exchange is a way to keep leverage in your investments so that you can put more of your profits to work in the next investment instead of surrendering that capital to the IRS.

However, there are caveats with this kind of exchange. It *must* be an investment property that is sold *and* bought, and the new property must be what's referred to as a "like-kind" property. There can't be a change in the entity name on the new property, and a qualified intermediary has to handle the transaction. There's a 45 day window to identify the property, and a 180 day window from the sale to complete the exchange. And this has to be reported to the IRS. Because of these requirements, this has more of a chance of IRS scrutiny than some others.

To implement this tax strategy you must find and engage with a Qualified Intermediary. This is a third-party who can hold the real estate proceeds according to IRS regulations. You'll also want to work with an experienced real estate professional and your accountant. 1031 Exchanges are not rare among people that like to make real estate investments.

199A (QBI) Deduction

A Qualified Business Income (QBI) deduction, or a 199A deduction, is fairly straightforward. You get to deduct up to 20% of your business profits from your personal taxes so long as you have a pass-through entity making profit. This is a nice benefit designed to save money on taxes for small business owners so it makes sense for pretty much everyone that owns a business. This deduction has low risk of scrutiny because you're just using the deduction for what it was designed. The deadline for this is April 15th.

The maximum QBI deduction (as of the latest published version of this book) was 20% of QBI. If your tax return indicates you got the 20%

then there is no need to dive into this further - you're got as much deduction as you could. If you run a pass-through entity and you earned less than 20% then it is likely worth your time to figure out what limited the QBI deduction because you might be able to change it by simply providing a note to the IRS in your tax return. This is not always the case but is worth looking into. How do you know if you got the full 20%? Go to your personal tax return package and look for Form 8995-A. On Form 8995-A compare the sum of Box 3 (all columns) to Box 16. If they add up to the same then you got the full 20% and you can move on. If you instead have Form 8995 in your personal tax return then compare Box 5 of Form 8995 to Box 15 - if they are the same then you got the full 20%. If they are not the same then it is unlikely you can do much about it and you can see what caused the limitation. In either of these cases if the numbers don't match you can see how the calculation worked out to see where you were limited.

The magic of using the QBI deduction tax strategy is in understanding how it works. There are certain thresholds and limitations that can unlock additional tax savings if you understand how it works. Many accountants know that the QBI deduction exists and few actually know all the limitations and how to set things up to maximize your savings by maximizing your deduction. You may need to work this out on your own. One of the best ways I've found to work the QBI deduction calculation to maximize your benefit is to manually walk through the IRS Form 8995-A line-by-line (Form 8995 is the simpler, shorter form designed for taxpayers with straightforward QBI situations and is less useful for identifying aggregation opportunities described in the next paragraph). You may find Form 8995-A in the monster PDF your accountant gave you with your Form 1040 or you may need to download it. The steps in this form are not complex and you'll see certain calculations that say something like "take the greater of *this* UNLESS that is *true* then take zero." If you understand how to modify your wage (often to get over those thresholds) you can unlock more savings. You can walk through the form by hand to try different scenarios or interact with an AI bot to ask it to help you identify if you are hitting any QBI deduction thresholds. Make sure to understand the security issues with sharing any personal information in an AI prompt before you try this.

Another excellent QBI deduction technique that many accountants overlook is called aggregation. You must use form 8995-A to do this technique - and this is why we recommend using that form over the simplified version, Form 8995. QBI aggregation refers to the process of grouping multiple businesses together for purposes of maximizing the QBI deduction. Businesses must have common ownership (which is common for family-owned businesses) and meet additional criteria. Doing aggregation is optional and not typically handled by the expensive tax-prep software packages. The best part is that aggregation can be useful to overcome some of the limitations and thresholds that would otherwise limit the value of the deduction. If your QBI deduction was not 20 percent of your pass-through business income, make sure to figure out why this turned out to be the case to see if you can make an aggregation change to get more deduction. Talk to your accountant for help but be prepared that they may not know much about aggregation rules and you may have to research it yourself.

280A Home Rental (The "Augusta Rule")

Under Section 280A, or what's colloquially known as the "Augusta Rule," you can rent out your home, if it's your primary residence, for a total of fourteen days out of the year (deadline is December 31st) completely tax free. Yes, the rent you receive for those 14 days is not taxed. The home has to be your primary residence, and the rental rate has to be market-appropriate, but it's simple to set up and maintain, applies at pretty much any income level, won't likely incur the IRS's scrutiny, and has a more moderate return on investment.

You could rent your home to anyone for fourteen days. But why not rent it to your business? This has a multiplier effect on the savings because you reduce the profit of your business. And when you have less profit you pay less in taxes.

The Augusta Rule is directly written into the tax code and you can look it up and read it for yourself using the internet. Many business owners find that they can implement this strategy themself though it does help to find a qualified company that can help you determine the fair market price for your home's rental fee. To implement this tax strategy you'll want to draw up a lease agreement between you (as the homeowner) and you (as the business owner). You'll also want to keep documentation on the 14 days you rented your home and why.

There are multiple ways your accountant could report this on your tax return. Some may list it in Part I of Schedule E and leave the column blank and others may just include it on your business tax return and not even report it on your personal return. Just ask them to explain how they reported it and make sure you are not paying any taxes on it (including NIIT).

401(k)

This is probably the one everybody knows about. A 401(k) is a retirement plan that's popular because it lets you make *pre-tax* contributions. A full 401(k) plan is of moderate complexity to set up and maintain. These plans are very common and there are many providers in the market that could help you. You will also need a financial advisor to help manage the investments. Because there are multiple professionals involved with helping you set up, administer, and manage a 401(k) plan, the plan overall tends to be expensive when you add up the costs of all the people involved. While it does offer a nice tax benefit to the owner who participates (and spouse too), the tax savings are usually offset by the cost of administration for the program so the net of offering a 401(k) is not actually a financial savings. This makes the 401(k) strategy less of a net tax-savings strategy than a strategy to attract and retain employees.

If your business income is under $500,000 there are other qualified plans that might be a better fit for your situation. Talk with your investment advisor to explore options.

A 401(k) plan does have a high level of scrutiny, but it's not by the IRS. The third party administrator does the annual compliance work including documentation, timely notices to participants, compliance testing, and annual required form submissions. Your investment advisor running the plan will also be involved.

These contributions need to be made before the end of the year, December 31st, and you need both a Third Party Administrator (TPA) to administer the plan and a qualified financial advisor to make the investment decisions. If you want to learn more you can talk with your financial advisor.

Accountable Plan

An accountable plan is for reimbursing expenses you pay out of pocket that are legitimate tax deductible business expenses. It's simple to set up and maintain, applies to pretty much all businesses, and actually helps avoid IRS scrutiny. The only downside is that the return on investment is on the lower end of the scale. On the other hand, having an accountable plan will help you stay organized and can be a useful chunk of work if you wish to pay your kids or spouse under that tax strategy.

You will be implementing this tax strategy yourself under your accountant's watch and guidance. Ultimately your accountant decides what is a legitimate tax-deductible business expense and what is not.

Backdoor Roth

Roth IRAs are great investment account options with a catch; you can't make more than a certain amount, and if you own your own business and are making more than $150,000 to $250,000 a year, then you can't contribute to a Roth IRA. A "Backdoor Roth" is a way to get around that, by contributing to a more traditional plan, and then rolling over those contributions into a Roth IRA. It's fairly simple to implement, and although the ROI is on the lower end of the scale, it can be useful to anyone who can't contribute conventionally to a Roth IRA. The best part is that you end up with a Roth IRA down the road worth some money.

To actually implement this, you just need a qualified retirement plan that allows for this kind of rollover. That's pretty much it. The maintenance is simple, the risk of IRS scrutiny low, and all you have to do is make sure it's done before you file your tax return.

Backdoor Roth goes by other names like "MegaRoth," "Two-Step Roth" or "Roth Ladder." You should talk with your 401(k) Plan Administrator if you want to learn more about whether your plan already has this feature. You can also work with them to add it if you want. You can also discuss this in depth with your financial advisor as they often help to implement these programs.

Bonus Depreciation and Section 179 Deductions

As a business owner, you're factoring in asset depreciation into your taxes (and if you're not, you absolutely should be). Using both Section 179 rules and bonus depreciation, you can expense the full purchase price of some of your equipment, if it qualifies. Bonus depreciation lets you take that further. The amount depends on the year you purchase the asset. It's fairly simple to implement and your accountant should be the one to help you. The rules around combining Section 179 and bonus depreciation varies state by state.

There are a few requirements to take advantage of these options. First, the asset has to be tangible. Then, it has to be bought by the business and in use more than 50 percent of the time by the business. And lastly, the asset cannot have been purchased from a relative. It's moderately complex to maintain depreciation schedules because you are required to track depreciation asset-by-asset (likely a monster spreadsheet or tax-planning software), but carries a low likelihood of scrutiny from the IRS because depreciation is written into the tax code, and the deadline for utilizing this is when you file your taxes because depreciation is a number on a line on your tax return. Your accountant can help you maximize Section 179 and bonus depreciation.

Business Entity Selection

This is, simply, how your business is set up. Is it an S-corp? A partnership? A C-Corp? The fact that we had had an entire chapter about this topic should indicate how crucial this is to your financial flourishing. The ROI on this is high, and this may be the most crucial action you take in handling taxes. This is the best way to decide under which tax code you want your income taxed.

There is a moderate amount of scrutiny from the IRS this can bring, and while it is more complex to set up than some options here, once you have selected the type of entity, it's fairly easy to maintain. If you are considering this as a tax strategy make sure to read Chapter 3 and then consult with qualified professionals (accountant and attorney) before making the final decision.

C-Corp Conversion

This is where you convert a business that has previously elected to be taxed under Subchapter C (a c-corp) to a different tax code (like Subchapter S). While this kind of conversion can apply to a business at any income level, it is fairly complex to implement. It can have a high ROI over time and may have a one-time tax bill when you do the conversion.

This does require a positive balance in equity in the c-corp, and you do have to file several forms with the IRS. It also comes with a moderate risk of scrutiny from the IRS. But this has to be completed by no later than two months and fifteen days from the beginning of the entity's tax year. You may be able to do it later than that and before you file taxes - talk with your accountant.

If you want to change your entity from one tax code to another, make sure you work with a qualified accountant and attorney who has been down the path before. This tax strategy is among the more complex to execute short term and there are many trade-offs to consider. You will also want to make sure you have a clear understanding of your equity situation before and after the conversion so that you can manage the transition properly.

Cash Balance Plan

This is an employer-sponsored defined benefit retirement plan that combines elements of both traditional pensions and 401(k)s. Contributions to the plan are treated as an expense to the business and are thus tax deductible. Account balances for each eligible individual grows two ways: one, by annual contributions that are usually a percentage of salary or a flat amount, and two, by interest credit, which is a guaranteed annual interest rate. Then when you take a distribution of funds when eligible, the income is taxed at your then-ordinary income rates.

This kind of plan operates a lot like a 401(k) from a tax perspective except it allows significantly higher contributions. For a cash balance plan, typically both the owner and all employees need to be eligible, and thus are most commonly deployed when you and your spouse are the only employees of your business.

What's needed to set up a Cash Balance Plan? First, you need to retain a Third-Party Administrator (TPA) to facilitate the plan because these plans are subject to Employee Retirement Income Security Act (ERISA) rules, like providing benefits equitably and following funding requirements. The TPA will handle the annual actuarial certification, manage the documentation for the plan (including annual disclosure statements), and report the plan to the IRS. As such, while this isn't the most complicated thing on this list to maintain, it isn't simple to administer either. The cost for these plans can be high and can provide significant tax savings.

Overall level of scrutiny for this strategy is very high - mostly done by your TPA. And thus there are low odds of scrutiny by the IRS unless you try to bend the rules or don't maintain proper documentation. The deadline to implement this is based on when your business tax return is due (typically March or April unless you request an extension).

This strategy makes the most sense for higher levels of total household income, those making above $500,000 a year is where this really shines. It has a high ROI compared to other tax strategies, and absolutely has some complexity (and cost) to implement because of compliance requirements.

Charitable Remainder Unitrust (CRUT) and Charitable Remainder Annuity Trust (CRAT)

These are both a type of irrevocable trust that allows donors to contribute assets, receive a payout as income over a specific period, usually for life or a set number of years. This payout is a fixed percentage for a Charitable Remainder Unitrust (CRUT), and is a fixed dollar amount, regardless of the trust's value, for a Charitable Remainder Annuity Trust (CRAT). At the end of the term, the remaining assets are then transferred to one or more designated charitable organizations.

Why do I have this listed here in the chapter on taxes? Well, the donor can receive immediate tax benefits, including a charitable tax deduction, while the charity benefits from the remainder of the trust assets. This really only applies for the people making a lot of money, over $2 million per year, and it is one of the more complex things to implement. But the ROI is also high.

To implement one of these trusts, one needs to have the proper documentation, and you also need to have assets to put into the trust. There isn't a deadline, and it's less complex to maintain than it is to set up, but it does bear a fairly high risk of scrutiny from the IRS. If you decide to utilize this strategy, make sure you are working with a professional that has done this before and double-check all the paperwork yourself. This is the kind of tax strategy that is expensive to set up because it requires the help of a specialized and experienced legal professional.

Conservation Easement

This is where you donate some of your rights to land that is deemed valuable and worth protecting. While this does mean you can't do certain things with the land, you get some fairly impressive tax benefits.

The catch is you need to own eligible land, and have the proper legal documentation for the easement. It's fairly simple to maintain, but it also comes with a high risk of scrutiny from the IRS. This strategy is specifically on the "watch list" by the IRS. To execute this strategy you will need an attorney that specializes in easements, a certified land appraiser, your accountant and a land trust. This is a complex strategy to execute and can provide a high ROI.

To get the tax deduction in any specific year you must make the donation and have all the paperwork done by December 31st.

Cost Segregation

This is a strategy where you create a custom front-loaded depreciation schedule for real estate, one that's more detailed than a standard depreciation schedule. Here's how it works. Buildings as a whole are depreciated over 27.5 or thirty-nine years. But you don't have to do this—you can break a building up into the components it's made of (plumbing, electrical, roof, foundation, windows, doors, etc)—and put each of those separately onto their own depreciation schedule. Because some of those items have shorter depreciation schedules (e.g. carpeting has a five-year schedule), while the sum total of the depreciation is the same, because some of the items depreciate faster, you tend to end up with a depreciation schedule that is front loaded.

The way you get this custom depreciation for your unique building is you buy an engineering study from a qualified company. Because these studies are not cheap, the building has to be worth enough—and have enough depreciation left—to justify the expense of the study. Once the study is done you provide the depreciation schedule to your accountant and they include it on your tax return. This strategy doesn't increase the total amount you can depreciate from your real estate, it just front-loads the depreciation so that you can take advantage of cash flow from tax reduction. To determine if this strategy makes sense you need to make certain assumptions about your tax rate today compared to the future and the time-value of money. You also want to consider if having cash today is more important and impactful than having that same cash in the future (e.g. you could use it to invest in your business).

This strategy can be used on its own and it is often coupled with the grouping election strategy if you own and operate your business out of the building that you own (known as a Self-Rental).

You obviously need to own real estate to utilize this strategy and it needs to be done by the time you file taxes so your accountant knows how much to include. Make sure you start working with the engineering company early enough so that they have time to complete the analysis before your accountant needs to file. Make sure to save all the documentation from the engineering company.

Defined Benefit Plan

This is an employer-sponsored retirement plan that provides a good ol' fashioned pension—a guaranteed monthly pay amount or lump sum—to employees upon retirement. The amount is typically based on factors like salary and years of service. Like the Cash Balance Plan, it's for more of the higher levels of income, those making more than $1 million a year. It has a moderate ROI compared to other options here, and it's about middle complexity to implement. This strategy is not as common as a Cash Balance Plan because it costs more to implement and maintain. There are also other risks with this strategy as the plan must be funded to guarantee the payment to the employees. This can get tricky if your business fluctuates between profitable and unprofitable year-to-year. Make sure to review the Cash Balance Plan strategy to learn more about the complex compliance requirements.

Like with a Cash Balance Plan, you need to have a plan sponsor (a Third Party Administrator, or "TPA"). The plan also has to be compliant with ERISA and the IRS guidelines, and you'll have to submit to non-discrimination testing. You will have to get an annual actuarial certification, and will also have to have extensive documentation for this (all handled by the TPA). This strategy has a high scrutiny rating because of all the compliance work the TPA must perform. If the TPA doesn't do all the requirement compliance work and submit all the required annual forms, this could invite IRS scrutiny.

Donor Advised Fund (DAF)

A Donor Advised Fund (DAF) is an account that holds and grows charitable assets earmarked for a 501(c)(3) organization. The benefit of a DAF is that it removes the pressure of the end-of-year donation deadline to get yourself a tax deduction on charitable giving. With a DAF, you simply donate the money to your own DAF account and you get the full tax deduction that year, even if you haven't yet given the money to a 501(c)(3) non-profit organization. Once the money is in your DAF you can invest it and the growth is tax free. But the money can only come out by giving it to a 501(c)(3) organization. And you get no tax deduction when the money comes out.

A DAF essentially gives you time to pick the right 501(c)(3) non-profit organization without the pressure of the 12/31 deadline and grow your charitable dollars in the meantime. A DAF is especially useful if you have a bumper year and want to make a significant charitable donation, but haven't yet selected the specific recipient 501(c)(3) organization or you want to spread your donation over time.

A DAF is simple to set up and is a high personal tax ROI strategy because it's basically on your tax return and is treated as a big donation to charity. Most institutions that will set up and manage your DAF will charge an annual fee of at least 1 percent. One drawback to a DAF is that once the money is in the account (which means you got the tax deduction), it must come out to a 501(c)(3) organization. And you don't get the deduction for giving the money to a 501(c)(3) on the backend because you already got the deduction. So if you like to give cash to people in need or make donations to non-501(c)(3) organizations then you want to avoid using a DAF. Another common approach is to have a DAF for your 501(c)(3) donations and a dedicated checking account for cash or non-501 gifts.

For some families, a DAF is more convenient than starting a full-fledged charity or foundation. A DAF generally makes sense when you have at least $50,000 that you want to give to 501(c)(3) organizations (one time or per year) or you want to start giving "grants" to 501(c)(3) organizations without the overhead of a foundation or starting your own non-profit.

A DAF account naturally has a very low risk of scrutiny from the IRS, and also is fairly simple to maintain in comparison to some of the other options listed here. They are common and are supported by all the big investment companies and banks (and you know how conservative they can be). All you have to do is set up the DAF account (often can be done online in a few minutes) then transfer money, and the deadline to do so is December 31st to get the tax deduction that year. You can likely get more information about DAFs from your financial advisor.

Grouping Election

Under Internal Revenue Code (IRC) Section 469, the process of combining multiple business or rental activities for tax purposes is called a "grouping election." A grouping election treats multiple businesses or rental activities as a single activity for tax purposes, potentially avoiding passive activity loss limitations. It's moderately complex to understand and amazingly simple to implement once you know how. The ROI can be very significant especially if you combine this strategy with a cost segregation study.

To be eligible, you need to own a building in one entity from which you operate a business (as a separate entity) and the two must be considered one economic unit. The same household must have ownership of the operating business and the building, and the grouping must be done the year the building was put into service. There are exceptions to this rule—generally triggered if you are doing a big restructure project of your entities. This is complex and you will need to work with your accountant closely to see if you qualify. And if you do—the savings on your taxes for a few years can be very significant. This is one of the tax strategies that few know about—and few people can figure out how to execute properly and on time. It must be done by your accountant as part of your tax filing.

One of the bigger challenges with this tax strategy is that it is relatively not well understood by accountants. Grouping businesses together is not a common thing and accountants often view it with skepticism due to lack of understanding. There is not a tax form out there for making a grouping election so accountants don't get really asked about it. Grouping elections are sometimes best understood by accountants that work with commercial real estate companies that separate property management from building holdings. Seeking out a consultation with an accountant with that speciality may help you research the strategy to see if it might apply to you. Frequently clients of Firmstride have us get involved to work with accountants to do the proper form preparation for this strategy.

Non-Profit (501(c)(3))

A 501(c)(3) is a tax election for an entity (typically a corporation) that can collect money for giving to other organizations while providing tax benefits to donors. 501(c)(3)s can be either public charities (so that other people can donate) or private charities (only funded by the family). Private 501(c)(3) organizations are typically called "family foundations."

Running a 501(c)(3) has unique and special compliance regulations. All charities have strict funding, operating and governance regulations. Public 501(c)(3) organizations are less likely to get audited than private 501(c)(3) organizations.

To set up, you need an organizational structure that fits a 501(c)(3) non-profit, governing documents for the 501(c)(3), IRS recognition forms, and a Board of Directors. It's complex to maintain, and can provide multi-generational impact of the family's wealth to social causes the family cares about. If you start a private or public 501(c)(3) you can also draw a salary so this can provide an option for your energy after you exit your business. If you decide to set up a 501(c)(3) make sure to engage an attorney with that specific kind of expertise and experience.

Pay Your Kids

As it turns out, you can also pay your own children via payroll, essentially federal income tax free. It's simple to implement and maintain because it's just like having another other employee. There is no tax law about the age of the kids that you can pay but courts have generally ruled that the child should be at least seven years old. Your child can work for the family business at any age without violating child-employment laws. The requirements are that the child must perform legitimate work for the business and must be paid a market-reasonable wage. Appropriate work could be sweeping the floors, taking care of the business landscape (mowing the grass), helping enter receipts, prepare holiday gifts for your clients, etc. And you can't pay them $1,000/hour for that work either—the wage must be reasonable. You'll want to pay them less in wages than the standard deduction to make this strategy as tax-efficient as possible. Children under 19 are also generally exempt from social security and Medicare (though you will still be required to withhold that from their pay when you run payroll). If you are an S corp and you pay your kids out of that business entity you'll want to work with your accountant to get the FICA taxes back. The deadline to do this is December 31.

While it's best to run this tax strategy by your accountant before you execute it, you aren't required to review people you want to hire with your accountant. It's good to talk with your accountant about how you plan to establish a fair market wage for your child so that there aren't surprises during tax filing.

Profit-Sharing Plan

A Profit-Sharing Plan is a retirement plan where employers contribute a portion of their profits to the employees' retirement accounts, typically based on the company's earnings. This is different from a 401(k) plan because employees are not required to contribute. The earnings can vest over time and while this strategy can provide tax savings, it is best when the primary purpose is employee retention. Setting up the plan requires a Third Party Administrator (TPA) because the plan must comply with ERISA and other IRS regulations. After creating the plan you establish a trust that will hold the money for your employees. This is fairly complex to implement and maintain, and is best suited for those making between $500,000 and $2 million per year. Its ROI is more moderate compared to the other items on this list - profit sharing plans are typically primarily used for employee retention instead of tax savings.

There is another form of "profit sharing" that can sometimes be called by the same name. This is when you create a bonus plan for your employees based on the profits of the company. Incenting employees to make small every-day decisions in their work to improve company profitability is generally a very good thing. Some people call this "profit sharing" and this is implemented by adding the amount of the bonus to your W-2 wages at the end of the year. There are many clever and useful strategies for how to structure these kinds of bonus programs that share profits with employees and you can hire compensation consultants or talk with your Firmstride coach about models which may work most effectively for your unique business.

Qualified Small Business Stock (QSBS)

If you meet an interesting list of criteria you may be able to avoid the capital gains tax on the profit from the sale of your business in the future. You have to plan ahead carefully. The requirements are:

1. The business must be a corporation taxed as a c-corp.
2. The corporation must be a "qualified small business". To quality, the business must have had less than $50 million in gross assets (so you don't get to subtract liabilities). This also includes the amount of capital raised by selling stock (if that happened).
3. You must have received the stock directly from the company (not bought it from another shareholder). This means you are basically a founder.
4. You must hold the stock for at least 5 years.
5. The company must be engaged in a qualified trade or business (go online to find the list of what is excluded)
6. The company must actively use at least 80% of assets in the qualified business.
7. The proceeds of the stock sale are below the exclusion limit.

Utilizing this option is open to pretty much any income level, though it is of moderate complexity to implement. However, this strategy boasts very high ROI if you can implement it properly and all the criteria are met when you sell your company. You should work with a qualified attorney if you think this strategy applies to your situation.

Qualified Opportunity Zone (QOZ)

Certain communities have been identified where investing in real estate may grant you deferrals or reduction on capital gains taxes from the sale of some other asset (like your business). If you have the ability to invest in real estate in a Qualified Opportunity Zone (QOZ), this may earn you preferential treatment.

Remember that QOZs exist for profit sake so you are investing in a company that is using your money to earn a profit. Therefore they will typically pay a dividend. And then if they sell the whole property, you may earn a return on your investment (plus get your initial investment back). Those dividends and returns are tax free. So not only can this strategy help you reduce capital gains from some asset sale, the returns are also tax free.

However, since these zones are set aside for preferential tax treatment, there is a higher risk of IRS scrutiny into those that invest. To use this tax strategy you will need access to a QOZ fund and will also likely have to meet certain holding period requirements (QOZs are all different so the requirements are different). Talk with your financial advisor to find a fund that looks interesting to you and your situation. If you plan to defer capital gains through a QOZ, there are requirements for how fast you have to invest.

At the time of the authoring of this book, the QOZ benefits for deferring capital gains in the initial investment are set to expire as part of the Tax Cut Jobs Act of 2017. Make sure to find out if those tax benefits have been extended if you plan to use this strategy. The QOZ dividend and return gains are written into the tax code in a more permanent way so they are likely to stay in effect.

Qualified Settlement Fund (QSF)

A Qualified Settlement Fund (QSF) is a type of trust for litigation attorneys that defers taxes on settlements. It is moderately complex to implement because of the documentation requirements that this introduces into the court process, and only really an option for those making more than $2 million per year in taxable income, but it has a very high ROI to make up for that and can provide significant value to litigation attorneys that face the challenge of managing their personal and business cash flow during the unknown ups and downs that come from practicing litigation law.

A QSF requires a fund administrator and is only available to litigation attorneys. The administrator gets paid a fee and the implementation of a QSF is complex arising out of the operational impact to the law firm.

Real Estate Investment Trust (REIT)

A Real Estate Investment Trust (REIT) is a company that owns or finances income-producing real estate, and allows investors to earn a share of the income through dividends without directly buying or managing the properties themselves. It's moderately easy to implement because you are buying stock in an investment. This is a great way to get the tax benefits of real estate and add real estate to your investment portfolio, without actually directly owning and managing real property.

There's no deadline to take advantage of a REIT and you should talk with your investment advisor to see if it makes sense for your situation as a part of your portfolio. You typically have to qualify to buy into a REIT because it is for accredited investors, and may have a fairly large minimum buy-in.

Real Estate Professional Status (REPS)

This is an IRS designation where you use tax losses in real estate to directly offset the income you earn from actively operating a business. It's moderately complex to implement because you have to prove you meet the IRS criteria, which may involve time tracking. But anyone otherwise can use this strategy—even those that are not Realtors®.

The ROI is moderately high on this strategy for those that have passive income losses from real estate because REPS converts those losses from passive income (where losses are typically limited) to non-passive income (where losses are not limited).

Each year you can qualify for REPS if you meet the criteria. Make sure to inform your accountant about this if you think you qualify so they know how to properly reflect your status when they draft your tax return. Because REPS requires appropriate documentation, make sure you get a smartphone app or have a way to keep records to produce evidence in the event of an audit.

Roll-Over for Business Startups (ROBS)

A Roll-Over for Business Startup (ROBS) is where you take a loan from your 401(k) to invest in starting a new business. It's for aspiring entrepreneurs with significant retirement savings in their 401(k) who want to start a business without taking a loan or venture capital. This can be especially useful for buying a franchise or experienced business operators with high confidence their business will return a profit. ROBS requires setting up a C-corp with a qualified retirement plan (usually a 401(k)) that allows employees and the owner to contribute. The owner rolls over their existing 401(k) into the new company's 401(k) and then buys stock in the new company. The new 401(k) now owns shares of the business and the company can use the funds from the sale to fund operations. There are many rules and regulations to follow and it can make sense to work with a ROBS provider to ensure everything is set up correctly.

This is a complex tax strategy, with a high potential ROI. This strategy is high risk so you will want to consult with your investment manager, your accountant, your attorney and likely hire a ROBS Provider for additional compliance with IRS regulations.

Savings Incentive Match Plan for Employees (SIMPLE) IRA

A SIMPLE IRA is a retirement savings plan for small businesses that allows both employers and employees to contribute to individual accounts with a match. This offers tax advantages and requires less administrative work than other qualified retirement plans. It's still not simple, despite its name, to implement, while still being more simple to implement in comparison to other qualified plans, and it possesses a moderate tax savings ROI because contributions to the plan are treated as a deductible tax expense.

To quality for a SIMPLE IRA you must have less than 100 employees in your business and no other retirement plans in place. Your business must match the employee contributions, and there has to be documentation about the plan. And this must be in place by January 30th.

Self-Directed IRA

An IRA is a way to make a post-tax contribution and buy investments that grow tax free. When you sell the investments and take out the cash (once you are old enough), the withdrawal is tax-free. Most people buy stocks, mutual funds, and ETFs in their IRA. But suppose you wanted to buy something different for your IRA, perhaps equity in a local car wash or a rental property. How could you do that? You would set up a self-directed IRA. A self-directed IRA is when you manage your own IRA investments with your own IRA money.

A self-directed IRA requires a third party custodian of the IRA, and they have to offer the investment type you want (and that type of investment needs to be permitted by the IRS). You can't engage in any prohibited transactions, and must fulfill ongoing compliance. This does bear a moderate risk of scrutiny—especially if you are a rule-bender. And you'll pay a management fee to the custodian to ensure you follow the IRS rules and file the appropriate paperwork. The ROI for this tax strategy can be quite high—especially if your investments grow large and you are able to avoid taxes when you sell.

Self-Rental

Renting your own building to your own business is a way to reduce your Net Investment Income Tax (NIIT), and it's very simple to implement. It also bears a low risk of scrutiny, and is easy to repeat. You need to both a) own the building you're renting, and b) operate a business out of it. And the deadline is April 15. You can tell that you are implementing this strategy correctly when Schedule E Box 1b(A) is set to 7. Many accountants miss this fact and mark your building in Box 1b(A) as "4" (which means the property is type "Commercial"). But this means you pay NIIT—which is unnecessary. Changing Box 1b(A) to Self-Rental (which is "7") will immediately reduce your taxes if you qualify. Make sure to check with your accountant that you qualify.

Simplified Employee Pension (SEP)

A Simplified Employee Pension (SEP) allows you to make tax-deductible contributions to your employees' individual retirement accounts (IRAs). Contributions must be uniform: for example, if you decide to contribute 10% of your own compensation, you must also contribute 10% of each eligible employee's compensation. This is why SEPs are popular among business owners where they are the only employee (or their spouse is also employed). Once you hire your first W-2 employee that meets the eligibility criteria, you must include them in the plan, contributing the same percentage for them as you do for yourself. The eligibility requirements for employees to participate are age 21+, worked for you in 3 of the last 5 years, and earned at least $750 (this adjusts each year). This means you can continue to contribute to your SEP IRA until 3 years after you hire your first W-2 employee and then in the third year you must either stop contributing or move to a different kind of qualified plan.

When you contribute to the SEP on behalf of the employee you may contribute up to 25 percent of their wage or $66,000, whichever is less.

SEP IRA contributions are paid as a business expense, so they are tax deductible. SEP IRAs are simple to set up (often online at your favorite investment brokerage) and you have unlimited investment options. This plan is an effective tax strategy for pretty much any size business and is a good place to start when you are a small business and make enough profit to set aside money in a qualified plan. The next step after a SEP is often some kind of 401(k) plan.

SEP IRAs have very low levels of scrutiny, and are very simple to maintain. They are very common. All you need to do is set up the SEP account by April 15th and make the contribution. You can talk with your financial advisor about SEPs to see if they are right for your situation.

Sole Proprietorship to S Corp

This is a one-time tax benefit when you convert from a sole proprietorship to an S-corp. It's moderately complex to implement, seeing as you're changing your business entity, but it's an option available to any income level, and boasts a moderate ROI. It's worth mentioning that this tax strategy will actually reduce your chances of audit because sole proprietorships tend to overstate their deductions while entities taxed under Subchapter S tend to be more organized. Under an S corp you are required to run payroll. Sole Proprietorships that have a profit north of $100,000 will generally benefit from making an election to be taxed under Subchapter S.

Electing to be taxed under Subchapter S of the tax code is one example where you are explicitly making the decision to be taxed under one tax code over another. You want to make this change when it benefits you from a tax and legal perspective (Sole Proprietorships pass all the legal risk to the owner while an LLC with S corp tax status provides protection). To make this decision you should consult with your attorney and your accountant. Recognize that they have different perspectives (one legal and the other tax) so their answers will be from the perspective of their respective discipline. And while they are both trying to help you discover the answer, the right answer for your situation may not be what either of them says—but a combination of both. This is the perfect area to engage with a professional services firm like Firmstride. Make sure to review Chapter 3 on business entities before starting any discussions so you have context and background on entities and how they are taxed.

Solo 401(k)

A Solo 401(k) is a 401(k) plan for small business owners and their spouse without a lot of the excess compliance that comes with a traditional 401(k).

This qualified plan requires that your business has an Employer Identification Number, is profitable, and is run by you alone (though your spouse is allowed to participate). This has a low risk of scrutiny by the IRS, and low maintenance complexity, and the deadline to implement it is December 31st. Talk with your financial advisor about this to see if it makes sense for your situation.

Special Needs Trust (SNT)

A Special Needs Trust is where you set aside money for the future of a special needs child, without impacting the child's current Social Security and Medicare benefit eligibility. It's moderately complex to set up, and can be important for the wellbeing of your child. There are multiple approaches to SNTs and you will want to find a qualified attorney to help you figure out what is best for your specific family situation. This is less of a tax strategy than a way to take care of the future needs of your family. We include it in this list because it can have a significant impact on your children.

Spousal Lifetime Access Trust (SLAT)

A Spousal Lifetime Access Trust (SLAT) is a type of irrevocable trust where one spouse sets up and gifts assets to the trust for the benefit of the other, allowing the beneficiary spouse to access the trust's income while reducing estate tax exposure for both spouses combined. The benefit also impacts the lifetime gift tax exemption, which can reduce estate taxes.

This strategy is highly complex to implement, and works best for those with high net worths that are worried about the Estate Tax. Setting up a SLAT requires a specialized attorney.

State and Local Tax (SALT) deduction

This is where you can claim state and local taxes as a business expense, which means those taxes are tax deductible. This is simple to implement, and likely applies to any business but there are a few caveats.

First, the state in which you live and work must offer a SALT deduction. You also need a pass-through entity. Some states also require forms to be filed by certain deadlines that vary state by state, and you will likely also have to pay your personal state taxes from the business account. Talk with your accountant about this to make sure you get this deduction if you qualify.

Tax Loss Harvest

A tax loss harvest occurs when you sell investments at a loss at year-end to offset capital gains from earlier in the year. Because investments are a type of passive income and passive losses can offset passive gains (passive losses are limited in how much they can offset active gains), selling an investment at a loss will reduce taxes overall when you have investment gains elsewhere. Your financial advisor implements this strategy by selecting and selling investments at a loss. You may have to request them to do that around the end of the calendar year. This strategy requires two things. First, you need passive income assets (usually stocks) that have lost value; second, you need to have had prior trades in the tax year with gains. And the deadline for this is December 31st. If you reach out to your investment advisor (early December is recommended) you can talk with them further to see if this strategy might benefit your specific situation.

Wages

Your wage has a lot to do with your taxes. Getting your wage in the right zone is an important tax strategy and one that is easy to maintain. Similar argument applies to your spouse's wage, if you pay them out of your business.

If you are an S corp, you are required to pay yourself a market wage. This is typically difficult to pin down and the number you choose has a large effect on your taxes. In general, if your business is taxed under Subchapter S, you will want to pay yourself as low a wage as you can. If your business is taxed under Subchapter C, you will want to do the opposite and pay yourself as much as possible. S corp owners want to pay themselves as little as possible to reduce FICA taxes. C corp owners want to pay themselves as much as possible to avoid double taxation that comes from the 23 percent corporate tax and NIIT on dividends.

What makes this tax strategy so complex for S corps is the QBI deduction. With the thresholds and phase-outs, picking your final wage can be a complex tradeoff between FICA taxes and the QBI deduction. There are a few general patterns that I have seen over the years for S corps.

1. If you run a business taxed as an S corp where you have other employees earning a W-2 salary, reducing your FICA taxes will be the dominant factor on how to pick your wage. This means going as low with your wage as you can. And paying your spouse is generally a good idea especially if your spouse can contribute to a 401(k).

2. If you run a business taxed as an S corp where you are the only employee, your QBI deduction is likely to be limited by your wage and not your profits, so the ideal wage is 2/7^{ths} of your anticipated profits. You can true-up as you get closer to the end of the year. This is a handy rule of thumb that maximizes your QBI deduction most of the time.

No matter what, you should confirm with your accountant what you are thinking and get their perspective and opinion. They may even be willing to do an analysis for you if they have the right tools. Firmstride runs a wage analysis standard for our clients to optimize this tradeoff.

If you have concerns about your wage, you can also contact a wage consulting company and buy a study. Often these companies will interview you or have you complete an online questionnaire about what tasks you are responsible for, how you spend your time and where you live. The value of these services is the documentation they give you that you have in your hip pocket if you are concerned about an audit.

Next Steps & Free Downloads

First, bookmark, highlight, or otherwise make a way to remind yourself which of these tax mitigation strategies popped off the page for you. If any of them seem like they could apply to your unique situation, talk with the recommended expert for each.

Second, download and fill out the **Tax Estimator**, located at firmstride.us/tax-estimator. You can enter your income and wage assumptions for the year and the spreadsheet will run the numbers to roughly estimate your minimum quarterly estimated tax payment (Safe Harbor) and April true-up payment so that you avoid tax penalties. This tool is not highly accurate and it will get you in the ballpark to help you confirm the numbers your accountant gave you. This will also help you get ahead of taxes by helping you plan what you might expect.

Third, go through our **Business Tax Return Document Checklist**, located at firmstride.us/business-return-document-checklist. This document helps you keep track of what you need to collect to send to your CPA to prepare your business tax return. Not personal, but your business.

Finally, download and fill in the **Year Over Year Tax Comparison** sheet once your taxes are filed, located at firmstride.us/tax-comparison. This spreadsheet will capture the most critical boxes from your tax return and calculate your key performance indicators each year so you can compare your year over year tax performance and identify trends in what you pay to the IRS.

Fewer Taxes Now, More Wealth Later (and also Now)

And now we find our way back to Steve, Brenda, and their HVAC business to see how they achieved that six-figure tax savings. Their basic strategy was to shift taxable income to the tax code that let them pay the least amount in taxes.

Strategy Employed	Savings	Why It Worked
Lower Steve's W-2 to a market-reasonable wage of $80,000	$19,554	Reduces FICA, federal and state taxes by more than the foregone savings of the QBI deduction.
Max out Steve's traditional 401(k) contribution of $30,500 (he is over 50 years old)	$12,487	Reduces taxable wages for Steve and tax on business profit because the match is a business expense and lowers taxable profit while putting the match into Steve's account.
Pay Brenda a market-reasonable wage of $33,685 and max out her 401(k) contribution ($30,500)	$5,890	Nearly all of Brenda's wage is not taxable because it goes to her 401(k). Also reduces taxes on business more than foregone savings of the QBI deduction. Match is a business expense and lowers taxable business profit while putting the match into Brenda's account.
Qualified Opportunity Zone	$42,840	Defer or eliminate capital gains from property sale depending on how long they stay in.
Ohio Pass-Through Entity tax deduction	$7,348	Ohio allows businesses to pay their state taxes as a business expense, which makes it tax-deductible on the federal level.
Pay each of their 3 kids a reasonable wage for actual work done ($14,000 each)	$12,309	Kids file their own tax return (still dependents on Steve and Brenda's return) and take standard deduction, thus owing no federal taxes. Parents make each kid open a Roth IRA and contribute $6,000.
Rent home 14 days at $2,600 per day	$10,024	Steve used their home for 14 days of legitimate work purposes instead of renting local rooms. This rent payment from his business is tax free for him personally.

Grouping election and cost segregation study	$17,508	Moved the building from personal ownership to disregarded LLC that Steve rents to his HVAC operating company. He made a grouping election and bought a cost-segregation study to get a custom depreciation schedule including the remodel. Cost segregation study reports $60,000 of new depreciation in first year due to remodel.
Donor Advised Fund contribution of $30,000	$3,730	Family decided to give more out of gratitude for the abundant year and tax savings. Instead of selecting a charity and making an end-of-year donation they put the money into a Donor Advised Fund so that they could give it when they felt called. DAF is now invested in the stock market and multiplying.
Total	$131,689	Of this total savings, at least $70,513 is expected to repeat next year and all years going forward.

Table 9 - tax strategies and their outcomes

If you can save a few points on your taxes with annual tax strategies like Steve and Brenda, you too can make a big impact on your long-term wealth.

CHAPTER 10

MAKE (THE RIGHT) SMART PEOPLE DO ALL THIS FOR YOU

A shley loves jewelry. It was her hobby from before she could ever remember. As she grew up, so did her jewelry. What started as a fun girlhood activity spun out of control—in a good way. As Ashley grew into an adult, all of her friends wanted custom pieces made by her and had been willing to pay, and pay a lot. So Ashley opened her own online story—thanks to Etsy and eBay—and is now *killing* it. She quit her job earning $90,000 a year as an insurance underwriter when she earned as much from her jewelry business as her underwriting job. And her jewelry business has continued to grow. After a short two-year sprint, her brand was popular enough that she had to hire helpers to produce even more pieces using her original designs.

There's something you should know about Ashley's mental point of origin as an entrepreneur. A few things, actually. Ashley grew up in a family where her dad was a dentist. He had his own practice and the family did well financially. Ashley's dad had an accountant named Gregg; he was a friend of the family, and Ashley's dad used to trade services with him. Ashley's dad was a great dentist but not as great a businessman. Thank goodness for Gregg, who kept the business finances from flying off the rails. Ashley remembers Gregg and his family coming over for Thanksgiving each year, and she even became fast friends with Gregg's kids (now adults like her). So when Ashley started earning real money in her jewelry business, she turned to Gregg, who was still practicing and delighted to help.

Ashley had never worked with a business as large as her custom jewelry company had become. She was new to finance, and the amount of money going through the business felt scary. Thank goodness she had Gregg by her side. He made things so easy. He handled payroll for the helpers Ashley had hired; she just had to report their hours to him every two weeks. He took care of the bills and the online payments for her online stores. Ashley could log in to the bank's website any time and see the balance of the accounts—but she never needed to do that. Any time Ashley had an important decision that she thought might impact the money side of the business, she knew she could talk with Gregg and he would be there in a heartbeat to help. Ashley didn't need to know anything about financial reports—that was Gregg's department. If she ever had a question, she knew Gregg would help.

To make things easy on her, Gregg had set up a special checking account where Ashley and her husband banked. She or her husband could take money out at will to cover her family living expenses. She took as much as she needed, and it always worked out. She knew Gregg ran payroll every two weeks (because her team always got paid). She didn't receive a paycheck because Gregg had explained it would be easier to just use that special bank account—he was paying her FICA taxes - so they were good.

Ashley liked not being distracted by finances because she could put her energy into the part of the business she was best at—designing beautiful jewelry and ensuring the quality that her customers had come to expect. And frankly, she was a little uncomfortable with the money side because she didn't understand it.

Ashley trusted Gregg and was never concerned about his actions. She was also never worried about someone in Gregg's company stealing from her. Everything was going well. Gregg was a life-saver. He made everything so easy.

Too easy.

Ashley always had a nagging feeling around tax time that she was paying a lot in taxes for the amount the business was earning. She hired a consultant to look over her tax return and business finances and give some pointers. It was supposed to be a meeting that included Gregg, but the tax strategist requested a private meeting with Ashley instead. What he said shook her pretty hard.

"It looks like your accountant is handling your business properly and has done excellent work on your returns. We didn't find any outright errors on your tax return. But we're confused about some things that we see. Are you aware of how much you're paying yourself in your wage?"

"No," Ashley said. "I just take money out of the account each month when we need it."

"Are you aware that you have receivables that are nearly forty percent of your total sales?"

"What are receivables? Is that good or bad?"

"Are you aware that you have $600,000 in equity and are holding nearly forty-two months of cash in the business?"

"What's equity?" asked Ashley.

"Are you aware that your sales are flat compared to last year but you've nearly doubled employee wages?"

"No. What's the impact of that?"

There was a pause on the other end.

"Are you the owner of the business?"

Gulp.

Ashley's story is an extreme example of a common situation—a business grows so quickly that the owner doesn't have time to develop their business and financial acumen to keep up (or they don't want to). This gap in skillset is often covered by the team that supports the owner—the accountant, the attorney, etc. This is especially true when the advisors want to be helpful and save the owner from feeling stress and pain—but this is not what happens because they rob the owner of the incentive to learn and grow. Without this development the owner gets dragged along, holding on for dear life, while the big decisions—the ones that shape the future of the business and the wealth of the family—are being made by the advisors. And the owner may not even know it. While the advisors will typically do their best to make the right decisions, they are ultimately not the ones who have to live with the consequences.

Hiring the Right People (Who Aren't You)

You must hire the right people to do it all correctly for you—*the first time*. Tax accounting, payroll, legal compliance, and everything else should **not** be in your hands because, frankly, you have better things to do than to try to teach yourself from scratch and risk **not** doing it right the first time (or second or third or fourth). Taxes and law are critical to get straight from the get-go, so whoever you hire also has to be the best for the job, not merely someone close at hand whom you know well (that said, do find people you can trust. It helps a lot. I'll show you how).

Think of building a team of advisors this way. You, the business owner, are a lot like a quarterback in American football. But quarterbacks can't carry a team all on their own; they need other types of players to win the game. Your job is to delegate crucial tasks to these key players; you tell them what direction to go and you call the plays, and they figure out how to do it. And you should make sure everything is done right. Your job is not to abdicate responsibility but to wield it.

When looking over someone's work, the point isn't to micromanage; instead, you should see if a given course of action will get you into trouble. Lawsuits, audits, or even fines are not something you want. You have to be competent enough to review anything your team does so you can know what success looks like and hold your team accountable to it.

You can hire people and expect competence, and you should. But as competent as they are, they can't know what's right for you, because they can't read your mind. This book is here to help you self-train so you know what options make sense. You need to be capable enough to check their work. If you're building a structure, you know you need a two-car garage and a foundation at least as wide as the home. But you don't need to know where the pipes are supposed to come out of the foundation; you just know you need plumbing.

Competent advisors are one of the most important things you can have. Without them, you won't be able to take care of yourself, your business, or your family (if you have one.) You need to understand the roles you need to fill on your advisor team, how to find them, how to evaluate them, and when to swap them out. We'll also talk about how to balance delegation and decision making with your advisors so that you can become their favorite client.

An important thing to note is that reviewing advisors happens all throughout the time you work with them, not just at the first step. There's no point where you go, "This advisor's good," and leave it at that; instead, you review all throughout your work with them. You have to know when they're doing well and when they aren't cutting it. There's never a time you can take your hands off the wheel.

Your advisors are there to assist you in not only building your mastery but in implementing the work that you need to get done to make the business profitable, sustainable, and smooth-operational. So, who all do you need?

Mission-Critical Advisors to Hire

The job of your **accountant** is to make sure you play by the rules laid down by the tax code. They make sure you file your taxes on time and in a way that is complete and legally compliant.

The job of your **attorney** is to ensure legal compliance. If you get sued (and you will; it's part of the cost of doing business), they will provide the services you will need. They also have your back.

Insurance sellers are there to help you manage risk. They'll help you understand the tactics and the strategies that you can employ to keep life's surprises from becoming financial catastrophes. And sometimes they'll sell you an insurance policy to do that.

Your **investment advisor** is there to help you build long term passive wealth. They build investment portfolios and try to make you behave, as indiscipline with money has ruined many.

And your **banker** is there to help you manage your cash and use it to grow.

All of these advisors must work together. They must not only be experts in their fields, but they have to work together with experts in other fields to produce the results you want. The most powerful strategy is to integrate the disciplines of wealth so that you and your family can achieve more than is possible working alone or in a single discipline; as the saying goes, two heads are better than one.

A great advisor is the same as a great employee in many ways. Such advisors know how to do their tasks. They communicate effectively with you, not only with quick responses to emails, but also by seeing things from your perspective and communicating in a way you can relate to. Such a quality elevates an advisor from good to great.

Great advisors can also integrate other aspects of business oversight. If you have an advisor on your team that only stays in their lane and won't consider different perspectives, then that advisor is not a good fit. In fact, this is the opposite of a great advisor because successful wealth strategies bring the disciplines together to maximize the benefits not only to you and your company but to your family as well. That's how you do effective entity structures, estate planning, investment management and know how much risk to take on. All of those things are tied together, and they rely on multiple disciplines. They are most effective when they're put together into a holistic plan. This is likely why you often want to bring things together—you know everything is related. So you need advisors who go beyond their expertise and play well with others.

Your ideal advisor team would have clients that are bigger and more successful than you, as it establishes their credibility in a way that doesn't depend on opinion. Once you've established this about them, see if they can foresee problems that you might run into and help you contain those risks right now.

Another element is **trustworthiness**. Does this seem like someone who will do the work correctly or take shortcuts? This is especially important because they'll be handling your money and helping you with complex decisions about your future, and you can't just hand all of that over to just anyone. You and your spouse (if you have one) should have a good rapport with whoever you hire to look after your money.

You need this team to be stable; this way, you don't have to explain yourself to new people every time. In fact, you want an advisor team that not only knows you, your business, and your structure well, you also want one that can work in all the gray areas you're not sure of or still discovering.

And you need a team that knows how to adjust what they do to fit changing circumstances. If you don't have that, then you will have unnecessary stress in your life. Over the course of most family businesses, you'll face multiple changes in tax codes as political winds change directions, new court cases get passed that establish new precedents and new investment options become available.

And lastly, you need an advisor that charges a reasonable price (this does not mean going for the cheapest option.) Advisors are businesses. They have to make a living, and so do you. Affordability is a good metric to use, but don't be afraid to pay more for quality.

Why Your Current Advisors May Not Be the Best

When you put your current team together (that is, the advisory roles you've already hired for), you most likely did not know what you needed or what to look for. Just as likely, you took whatever options were available to you at the time. For example, you may have started your business focused on your main area of concern, seeking a foothold in whatever market you're pursuing. Then you hit a legal hurdle and realize that you need an attorney. Since you wanted to get back to your business, you went through a short list of friends, including people from your church, colleagues you had been introduced to, and people you had met at the park. You called one of them, and they offered to help like good friends do. Then you just kept going with that person, not realizing that you had outgrown their abilities and that there might be far better candidates available. However, you've been working with these people for a while, and you now fear that changing may create problems you don't want to deal with or it might be too much work.

Just as easily, you didn't know what a "good advisor" was supposed to be. It's nice to have a benchmark of what's expected among advisors so that when you evaluate them, it's not just a vague sense of whether or not you like them. You want specific things that tell you if they're doing a good job or not.

What does the ideal advisor team look like? How do you know when you've got a good one? Let's explore those topics in depth.

The Accountant

Almost any business that makes more than $200,000 per year probably either has an accountant or desperately needs one. As your operation grows, your needs change too—and this is especially true when it comes to taxes. Your accountant's number one job is filing your taxes on time and in a way that is correct and compliant with the tax code.

People who are allowed to file your tax return can be a Certified Public Accountant (CPA) or Enrolled Agent (EA)—two different roles with different skill sets and backgrounds. CPAs have an accounting or finance degree and have passed the state requirements, which allows them to have their certification. An EA has gone through training on tax code, how to prepare tax returns and has passed a test certifying their knowledge. CPAs are certified by individual states while an EA is a federal-level designation. An EA is allowed to prepare tax returns and represent you in an IRS audit. However, an EA is not authorized to prepare a state-approved audit or provide certain reports that are used for official documentation of audits. A CPA is certified to do all of the work of an EA plus the official audits. Often, CPAs specialize in a given area of finance.

Quite a few CPAs don't prepare tax returns. They work inside other companies that may be publicly traded or may have very sophisticated accounting needs. Maybe your accountant is a CPA or maybe they are an EA. But no matter what kind of accountant you're working with, they have a team supporting them.

Some accounting firms are full service firms which may offer services in addition to tax return preparation so that you can just work with one firm instead of several. Some accounting firms offer bookkeeping services where they'll process your receipts and keep your books accurate every month. Others may offer controller services, which oversee accounts payable and receivables and do the appropriate approvals on those. Sometimes, they'll do bill pay on your behalf, and may even run payroll.

Your accountant can also help you implement correct accounting procedures. If everyone used a different accounting system, preparing tax returns would be more difficult than it already is.

A common misconception about accountants is that they are there to help you save on taxes. Let me burst your bubble—they're not. In fact, their exams do not contain any questions on how to help a client save on taxes. CPAs and EAs do not provide that service to you; the only thing they're required to do is make sure you follow the tax rules. Many people get frustrated at their accountants because those accountants aren't proactively helping them pay less in taxes, but they don't realize that accountants aren't meant to do that. While full service firms may offer tax mitigation strategies, most CPAs or EAs you hire aren't going to do this.

The other thing you need to know is that accountants do not have a fiduciary duty to you. That means that they don't have to do what's in your best interest; they have to make sure you comply with the tax code. It's even implied in the name "Certified Public Accountant"—they do what's in the broader public's interest, not their client's interest. If they did what was in their client's interest, it would be tempting to help everyone cheat on their taxes.

But this independence isn't an obstacle; in fact, it's a benefit. You can run things by your accountant knowing that they don't have to say yes to everything. They won't give you the answer you want to hear, instead giving you an answer that complies with the tax code.

Another thing to remember is that "accountant" does not equal "bookkeeper." While you can pay an accountant for bookkeeping services, it's not directly within the scope of their practice unless they choose to explicitly offer bookkeeping services. If you want your accountant to monitor your receivables and payables, you need to put those jobs into your service agreement with the accountant and they'll likely charge you a little extra for the work.

But just as your accountant is not your bookkeeper, your accountant is not your CFO. For example, let's say you want to buy a business down the street and you ask your accountant whether you should take a loan or come up with some other financing arrangement. The thing is, your accountant doesn't know where to find the best rates, whether a SBA loan would be too much work or which approach you should take-any more than you do. Your accountant probably does interact with a lot of business owners and they may be able to share what others are doing. You see this with things like QuickBooks. If you ask your accountant a question about QuickBooks, that implies that you think they know because Quick-Books is a thing that accountants use, but the only reason your accountant knows about QuickBooks is because they use the advanced features. And secondly, they talk to other clients that probably have the same question. They've probably seen that question before and thus they can help you. Otherwise there's no reason to believe that they would know any more about how your bookkeeping software works than you do.

If you want to ask your accountant a question like "What are the possible depreciation schedules for depreciating my work truck" your accountant will know all the details.

The last thing about accountants that people don't realize is that they charge for their time, but it's not always obvious. Maybe they charge based on the number of entities that you have; the number of business entities is a pretty good proxy to how complicated your situation is which probably has a lot to do with how much time they'll have to spend with your tax returns. Some accountants charge by the number of tax returns that they will need to prepare for you. There are different actual implementations of how they bill by time, but CPAs and EAs are limited on how many hours are in the day, so therefore they'll charge for the time that they spend on your case.

But how do you know your accountant is doing a good job? Let's take a look at these four criteria.

"Technical" Expertise

This is about how well they complete your tax return. Have they done it correctly? This is a harder question to answer than you think, because the only true way to know your tax return was prepared properly is to get audited, and no one wants an audit. A better way to do this is by finding other people that know how to review tax returns and ask them to look over either your current or previous year's tax returns to see how completely they've been filled out and how all the information is being displayed. That will give you a better picture of how your accountant is doing.

The second reason it's difficult to know how well your accountant is doing is that there's a lot of gray areas on the tax returns. In fact, if you gave the same documents to two different accountants, with the exact same background information, they would likely prepare tax returns that look slightly different. They should come to the same final number, but the way that the data is displayed in the tax return may be different. Some fields require you to use a statement, while other times they're in a form, and sometimes an accountant can decide where they want to put that data. It's really difficult to check a tax return with a casual glance. And as for the nature of these errors, actual tax-related mistakes are rare. Much more likely is you not providing the right information. Either you omitted something or something wasn't clear to the accountant, thus a lot of mistakes on the tax return are actually not your accountant's fault; instead, you didn't give them the right information, or you didn't give them enough information.

However, technical ability isn't the only thing to worry about here. The other question you must ask is one of the most basic—how well matched are you with your accountant? You might think that tax codes are black and white and that your accountant's knowledge of it is the only thing that matters, but that's not the case. A lot of the tax code is a gray zone, so you need to have an accountant that can understand your needs and can interpret the tax code in a way that fits with what you want.

I had a client one time who was very risk averse and did not feel comfortable interacting with the IRS, fearing an audit. They avoided gray area deductions because they felt such deductions were risky, even if their business might be eligible for them. Their accountant was okay with them taking the deductions, but the client didn't feel comfortable. And so the accountant needed to adjust their style. And even though they would typically take those tax deductions for other clients, it would be inappropriate to do so for this particular client. Thus my client paid a little bit more to the IRS in taxes because they didn't get as many deductions, and the accountant had to adjust their style in order to meet the risk profile my client had.

Here's another example that illustrates the opposite. I had a client that was interested in paying the least amount of tax possible. That is all they cared about, and they had a very large tax bill that was a couple of hundred thousand dollars a year. And so they worked with their accountant, and we discussed a tax strategy that we knew historically would increase their chances of an audit. My client was very comfortable with that high risk of audit because they knew that the strategy was legal. The accountant also knew it was legal and wasn't comfortable with the high probability of an audit. The accountant either had to fire my client or accept his level of risk tolerance and implement the strategy. The accountant decided that he would rather keep my client and so he implemented the strategy. My client didn't get audited in the end.

It's generally best to seek an accountant that matches up with your level of comfort on issues of risk so that there is a natural fit.

Effective Communication

Your accountant needs to be one of the most important advisors that communicates well with you, and that's because they have to be willing to take the time needed to explain things to you since they are not responsible for the final correctness of your tax return. You might be surprised by this, but if you read the service agreement of your account it actually says that they are not responsible and some do not warrant the accuracy of your tax return—that's on you. And so you must have an accountant that's comfortable explaining things to you in a way that you can follow because if there's a penalty on your tax return due to an error it goes to you, not your accountant.

I had an accountant a while back that was very good at tax strategies, and I loved how thorough his answers were. But I'm the kind of guy that's very impatient and I feel strongly that the advisors I retain answer me within 2 business days. Unfortunately, he couldn't respond to me in less than a week. It drove me crazy—I couldn't handle waiting that long for the answers I wanted. He was just not a good fit for me because he had a different style. So I moved on to someone that fit my style and desires better. This new accountant would often respond to me within 24 hours via text. It was a much better experience for me and I was much happier.

Collaboration (With You)

Your accountant needs to be highly collaborative. Your accountant will explain how your decisions affect your tax obligations. They'll know a little bit about other disciplines but when you come to a decision that goes across disciplines, where you have a legal perspective, a tax perspective and a risk perspective, you'll need your accountant to play their role and stay in their lane. That means they may need to collaborate with your other advisors and bring their unique perspective. They will need to listen carefully and participate in looking at the situation from multiple angles. This means possibly taking input from other advisors and adjusting their views on the fly. Especially when you get into topics like entity designs, estate planning, life insurance—these kinds of topics span across disciplines and there are often trade-offs between competing priorities. Your accountant is one of the most important people that has to play their role.

I've worked with many clients over the years, and I find that they generally do not correctly understand their relationship with their accountant because they view their accountant as a person responsible for their taxes. And this is not true—as stated many times before. You are responsible for your own taxes. I find that a flipped perspective yields a more effective outcome for the business owner. The flipped perspective is that you, the business owner, own your tax responsibilities, while your accountant is a team member you pay, who uses the information you provided, to accurately prepare your tax return and guide you through the tax code. Here's an example to illustrate a flipped perspective. Suppose you are frustrated that your accountant didn't provide you with a list of documents to collect for preparing your taxes. You could look at **the** situation differently - it is your job to provide your accountant with the documentation that they need to do their job effectively—so you should get organized, make the list (which you verify with them), and provide the documents quickly, completely and on time. By taking responsibility for your part, they can take responsibility for their part. With this mentality, you empower your accountant to take better care of you. I've found this servant-leader perspective is more likely to get the outcomes you need.

Let's say you're having a period of rapid growth. If your business doubles in size over the next two years, does your accountant's knowledge double in the same way? Doubtful. What you need at this point is an accountant who has been there and done that. When you're looking at an accountant, don't make your decision in terms of where you are today, but in terms of where you'll be in the next two to five years. If you do that, you'll have someone who can help you get things in place today that will carry you forward for the next couple of years.

Fair Pricing

And the last thing that we need out of an accountant is that their price is fair. Per return, you'll likely be paying $1,000 to $1,500. If they're providing additional services like bookkeeping or quarterly meetings with you to review your financials, then it's going to be more. If you have one business return and one personal return, and you're paying your accountant $15,000, then you're paying too much.

If you have the same two returns and you're paying your accountant just $500 that's also out of line. You want to stay away from accountants that charge either way too much or way too little because they're possible red flags about future problems. It's generally best to find and retain an accountant that charges for the fair market value of the services they deliver. If they're overcharging you, then you need to understand why they're doing that. Are they providing some service that you're not taking advantage of or do they have some expertise that you haven't tapped into? If your accountant's charging too little, then that's a sign that they may not be a long term viable business or they're trying to "make it up in volume" and you may not get the personalized attention you desire. So look at spending between $1,000 and $1,500 per entity. If you have questions about that, talk to your Firmstride coach to see if they can give you some benchmarks of how much they think you should be paying for your region or area.

Now let's take a look at your accountant behind the scenes and give you some perspective on their world so that you know how to interact with them and get the most out of their services.

If your accountant is a small firm where they are the only employee, they probably are managing about three to five hundred clients, and that's about all they can handle. If your accountant works for a bigger firm, they'll have a support staff and they have people helping them be more efficient. They might manage as many as 1,000 to 2,000 clients. If that's the case, you may not be remembered unless you're in that top tier of clients. If you're in the top fifty percent (based on the fees you pay), you'll get the most attention, and if you're in the top twenty percent you'll get even more attention. But if you're in the bottom fifty percent, you're competing for attention, and that's a difficult spot to be in. So you need to know how big the firm is, and if it's a big firm, meaning they've got more than fifty employees, then you might need to know if the person that is your accountant is a partner or not. If they're a partner, which means that they're an owner of the firm, that means they'll have a higher level of authority, which means they'll have people working underneath them. If they're not a partner yet, that does not mean they wouldn't be a great accountant for you-it means that they're an employee with a partner above them.

The next thing to know is that your tax return is not prepared in TurboTax. It is not filled out by hand, and it is not done in Excel. It's done in very expensive accounting software—it may cost upwards of $100,000 every year. They don't just buy it once. In addition to a very sophisticated package that creates tax returns, your accountant has access to supporting people to help them interpret tax code and make decisions. They probably have access to an actual tax attorney plus other accountants within their professional network they can run things by. They may even have a direct line into the comptroller's office of your state. No matter what you think about that, your accountant is going to be using very sophisticated software to prepare your tax return. Any errors won't be math errors or even tax code errors, it will likely be errors of omission—that is, information *you* failed to provide or things your accountant didn't interpret correctly that you told them.

But now, let's move on to a different kind of expert—the attorney.

The Attorney

An attorney is an important part of your team because they're going to help you understand the legal work and the legal risks that you face in your family because of the issues regarding your business. Attorneys are licensed by state, which lets them practice in that state, and they can receive additional licenses or can be board-certified for complex and niche areas of law. Law is such a broad topic that there's not any one attorney that can handle all of it. As a result, a lot of attorneys work together inside a single company called a limited liability partnership (LLP) where they can pass work to each other and can represent clients in bigger, more sophisticated pieces of law than they could if they worked on their own.

An attorney is a very specialized resource, and as a result they have a group of people that support them when they work with clients. The most common one that you may run across and interact with is a paralegal. A paralegal is not an attorney, but they know a lot about the procedures, methods, and workflows that are important for practicing law. Many attorneys also have people in the back office that help them with paperwork, scheduling, keeping track of deadlines with the courts and things like that.

Oftentimes, attorneys subscribe to very expensive services which give them access to legal document templates, state by state and issue by issue so that they can very quickly create documents like wills, operating agreements, or other important documents.

The attorney has four basic roles as they work with you. The first one is to just provide advice, which means to listen to you, understand the situation and try to come up with solutions that are in your best interests.

The second thing they do is draft legal documents. You might think that attorneys spend their whole day doing that, but in truth most attorneys spend most of their day talking to people trying to give them verbal advice. Behind the scenes they're oftentimes taking notes and writing down the advice that they gave you so that they can keep track of it. Now when you have a specific case where you have court dates and things like that, the attorney is tracking all those dates. They're submitting all the paperwork that the courts require. And then they're representing you in the legal proceedings.

The third thing they do is represent you in negotiations in conversations with other people and the like.

Finally, attorneys make sure you're compliant with the laws that apply to your business. For example there may be things you have to do as part of your employment law in your state; your attorney will oversee that and make sure that you stay within legal bounds.

The Disciplines of Law

The discipline of law is very diverse. Each one of these topics requires extensive training and experience, so it's very likely that the attorney that you're working with is going to be a specialist in one (or a couple) of these areas. Let's walk through them in general so that you have some idea about what the different kinds of attorneys are so that when you have a need in one of these areas you know where to go.

The first is a **general business law** attorney. These are folks that know a lot about entity design, contracts, and basic employment law. They'll also know about mergers and acquisitions. So it's general business law.

Family law will include things like estate planning, divorces, small claims court, and other things like that—general family practice. They would also be able to help with things like adoption or custody issues with children.

The next is **estate law**. I mentioned earlier that family law often includes some basic estate planning, but estate law is such a complex topic that there are specialists devoted exclusively to it, and some of those specialists are only experts in certain states. And some of those states are very complicated—for example, California.

An attorney that is certified to practice estate law in California will likely only practice there and they may not even live in California, yet all they do is work with clients from that state. Other complicated states include New York and Illinois. Those are places that have very unique and complex laws and the attorneys for those states will tend to be specialists.

The next one to mention is **employment law**. Attorneys in this practice area understand contracts with employees and may represent employees in lawsuits or represent the business. If you should be sued for something like sexual harassment or discrimination, that falls under the domain of employment law.

Next is **intellectual property law**. This is when you have created something that is unique that you wish to copyright, patent, or trademark, and you wish to have an attorney help you navigate that process and help you maybe even defend those patents against someone that infringes upon them.

Next is **litigation law**. These are attorneys that either work in property or health, where they are extremely adept at the court system and they know how to work within those parameters to help achieve outcomes for the people they represent.

Next is **real estate law**. This is going to be around contracts and property rights. It also covers working with cities and zoning and things like that.

And the last one is **personal injury law**, which is often related to litigation, but personal injury is specifically when you've been injured as a result of someone else's negligence and you're going to sue them in court.

So there's a lot of things that attorneys can do, and it's unlikely that one person will practice in more than one of these areas, though it is possible. Most attorneys work for a firm that can practice in multiple parts of these areas of law. And so that gives you a one stop shop to get all of your legal needs met, which can be extremely helpful.

Now as a business owner, you may not need help all of the time in all these different parts of law. It's recommended to have a working relationship with a general business law attorney. And it's likely that you'll also have a family law attorney. Sometimes business law attorneys are comfortable practicing in family law and sometimes vice versa. If you need an attorney on speed dial, the one you want most is likely a business attorney.

This is all well and good, but how do we know our attorney is even doing a good job?

Actual Competence

Good attorneys demonstrate a strong understanding of the law and provide sound legal advice based on your specific situation. When you explain your situation to them, they have to know what issues are at hand to help guide you to a solution.

Once you've explained your situation to them, they have to be able to offer a clear strategy for handling your legal matter, outlining possible outcomes and the steps needed to achieve your goals. It's not enough to point out where the problems are; they have to show you options for how to address them, even if the solutions don't create an ideal outcome.

When implementing the agreed-upon solution, the attorney must be thorough in their work, with careful reviews of documents, contracts, and legal filings for accuracy. Getting the documentation right is crucial to any legal matter, as not filing something correctly can mean the difference between closing a deal, getting sued, or winning a case.

Demystifying Communication

How well does your attorney communicate? Can this attorney explain legal concepts and strategies in a way that you can understand and apply to your situation? The law is complicated, and you have to be able to trust your attorney to guide you through it all.

When you have questions, is your attorney available in a reasonable timeframe? Do they respond promptly to your inquiries? A good attorney must be a responsive attorney; all that legal knowledge is no good if they can't help you when you need them to.

Playing Well with Others

How well does your attorney work with other advisors in your network? Do they listen and then provide their legal perspective? Many attorneys understand the complexity of wealth-related topics and they may naturally bring taxes and risk into the discussion. Sometimes they might not be correct or the tax code has changed, and they need to be open to hearing other perspectives so that they can correctly advise you.

Proactiveness

And does your attorney mention problems to you before they spiral out of control?

You want a situation where an attorney that performs well in at least three of the areas we just covered; if not, it's time to find a new attorney, because the current one isn't serving your purpose. But how would you do that?

Attorney Fees

Attorneys are like accountants in that they are a limited resource that provides direct interaction with clients and so they're going to charge by time. Attorneys can charge a variety of different ways—either by the hour, which is very common, or by the topic. For example, forming an entity might be a fixed price at one firm, because they believe this kind of work tends to take about the same amount of time, and by the hour at another firm, because they find that they spend inconsistent amounts of time with their clients. So while they might appear different on the surface, they both are basically charging for the time.

The cost of hiring an attorney varies significantly depending on the practice area of law and the firm's structure. Specialized fields like intellectual property or corporate mergers often command higher fees due to the expertise required—think patent lawyers navigating complex technical filings or dealmakers orchestrating high-stakes acquisitions. These attorneys may bill at premium rates because their knowledge is niche and their decisions carry substantial financial weight. Similarly, large firms with multiple disciplines, such as litigation, tax, and real estate under one roof, tend to charge more. Their overhead supports a broader range of services, and clients pay for the convenience of accessing diverse expertise without shopping around. Smaller firms or general practitioners, by contrast, might offer lower rates for routine matters like wills or basic contracts, where the legal terrain is less intricate.

Criteria for Selecting a New Attorney

Before we talk about what criteria to use, let's talk about **how** we would find them first. A tried-and-true method is referrals—ask your family, your other advisors, other professionals in your field, etc., what attorneys they use; they may be able to point you in the right direction.

You can also look online, through legal directories such as Avvo, Martindale-Hubbell, or the American Bar Association's lawyer referral service, to find attorneys who specialize in the area of law you need.

Once you have a possible candidate, you can hold a consultation meeting. Many attorneys offer free or low-cost consultations to discuss your case and determine if they are a good fit.

Once you have a possible attorney in front of you, it's time to evaluate them. Do they:

- Have directly applicable prior experience?
- Match the expertise you seek?
- Work well with your schedule?
- Communicate the way you want and update frequently?
- Make their prices clear?
- Have a clear engagement process?

If they get all or nearly all of this right, then you have someone you can likely work with for years to come. Remember that you're hiring for the long term, so be careful who you choose to work with at this step.

But of course, once you bring that person on, all the services they provide have to be paid for. This is where bankers come in.

Banker

Your banker is there to help you with cash and all the products they can sell related to that. Products include loans, lines of credit, and accounts. Any time that you need to get a hold of cash for your business, your banker should be the first to come to mind.

Now this is not a perfect model but it is helpful at predicting the behavior of banks and the outcomes. There are three general categories of banks—local, regional and national.

Local Banks

A local bank is one based in your town. They're going to be very focused on knowing the people in the community and supporting the businesses that make the community thrive. Decisions are made at that bank because it's locally owned, and they're going to be generally active in the community to build their business. And in addition, because it's a bank, it will have some products that are useful for cash control and for loans. However they'll be limited because they don't have the deep pockets of the national banks. They may also have a limited staff and IT budget, so they may not have the fancy whiz-bang smartphone app.

Local banks generally have somewhere between a hundred million and five billion dollars under their management. There may be multiple branches in your town. These banks have certain advantages that you may want to take advantage of as a business owner.

Regional Banks

As banks grow, they go from being local to expanding to become regional in nature. That means they could span multiple states, or maybe they're in a tri-state region, or they tend to focus on a region like the southwest or the northwest or something like that. But they've got a region where they do business. By now they've established a corporate office, and they'll still have a focus on personal relationships. Inside your town's branch, the big decisions are now consolidated into a corporate office. The big decisions include the products, policies, and systems the branches will use.

Regional banks will have more product options than a local bank, and because they're larger and they can negotiate with the federal government from a stronger position, they'll have slightly better rates on things like accounts. They'll also have a richer and deeper set of products for business owners. A lot of these banks have IT budgets that are large, but they still don't look like the big banks in the US. They're obviously a lot further along than the smaller local banks and they're generally managing somewhere between five billion and two hundred billion dollars of assets.

National Banks

If a regional bank continues to grow because they're successful they could make it to the national level. And when they get to the national level, they'll have branches everywhere because they're not closing down the branches that they had when they started. And they'll focus instead on differentiating themselves. Their focus will be efficiency, standardization and working at scale. They're going to start to use policy to guide decisions—and you're unlikely to get exceptions. They implement the systems to support those policies so that branches can comply and stay within the policies that they want.

They also focus on national level initiatives. For example, the housing market might be desirable in a certain region, or interest rates may be high, and so they'll focus on offerings that will appeal to the region or their national market. They might still run regional promotions, but they won't do as much locally because they're trying to gain efficiency through scale. They'll have sophisticated IT budgets integrating with all of the tools that you could imagine. They probably have their own little smartphone app that's fully featured, and they have at least two hundred billion dollars or more in assets. To put this in perspective, if you look at some of the big banks out there like Chase, the last time I checked they had two trillion dollars of cash assets under their management. You better believe they'll have a great IT budget and a full-scale system. But the products are not going to be customized to your little business, and you can forget about exceptions to the policies that you as a business owner might want.

What Bankers Can Actually Do (For You)

All of these institutions will have bankers. These bankers can do a variety of things for you and they'll have different capabilities based upon what kind of bank they work for. A local bank will be focused on helping to grow the community and the businesses within their community and to grow their business. They act like entrepreneurs. They meet with you, find out about your business's needs and figure out how they can win your business by helping you. Decisions are made locally at these banks by a person you may know or have met. If you are meeting with a vice president of a local bank, this means he/she controls enough of the branch's decisions to have earned that title. That's what you get in a small bank—a local feel and a local experience. These kinds of banks often offer unique and creative solutions to your cash needs because they're not bound by onerous corporate policies. They can make decisions locally and hand-hold things. So when your application needs to be submitted, they can handhold it and get a fast answer, whereas if you submit an application for a private loan to a large national bank you might be waiting a long time. Also because these bankers are locally connected to the network of business owners, they probably know a lot of other business owners in the area. They may even know your local mayor or city council.

But Is the Bank Doing a Good Job?

How do you know if your banker's doing a good job for you?

Does the banker you're working with understand your business and what you need? If you want a warm relationship where you don't have to explain yourself every time, your local bank is probably best. They may even refer people to your business. If that's the case then your local bank will have a deeper understanding of your business needs and will relate to you better as an entrepreneur. Also, it's easier to map products to what you need at the local or regional level. While their options are likely fewer, they'll know you better and thus give you the best deal with the options they have. A national bank will have more sophisticated products and they'll have much less direct knowledge of you or other businesses like yours. And the banker that you're working with may not even know all the products or may not have the experience to map your needs to the right products.

Your local bank will be slightly more expensive, and the interest rates won't be as nice either. Big national banks will give you better rates and they'll likely cost less, but you won't get the same level of service. So you have to take into account all these factors when you're evaluating if bankers are doing a good job or not.

As you can imagine, at the local and regional level you'll get a lot more support and a lot more love than you will at the national level. It's great when you have a banker that regularly checks in. I used to have a regional banker when I was at another firm when I was a partner. And that regional banker checked in with me about once a quarter. He was learning to play golf, and he loved to take me to play. And we would have a lovely lunch and talk about our kids and how business was going. He was the president of a regional bank that served the Texas and Louisiana area and I referred so many people to him, it was insane.

And then the last thing is how quickly you can get resolution to your problems and get solutions. Banks will have different timelines with which they work. A local bank will probably make a fast decision. A regional bank needs to fly it up through corporate so you may have to wait a little while. And the national bank, if you're within the policy it might be instantaneous. You might be able to even do it on the website. If you're outside of their standard policy it's gonna take a lot longer or just may not even be possible.

All right, so you have money—what'll you do with it? Here is where the investment advisor comes in.

Investment Advisor

Your investment advisor is there to help you create passive income. "Investment advisor" is a generic term for a number of different types of roles that you might or might not have on your advisor team.

In general when we say "investment advisors" we mean two different classes of advisors: a financial planner or an investment manager.

A financial planner is a person that has very broad experience and knowledge about personal finance. You could say their knowledge is broad, but not deep. By contrast, an investment manager has financial experience in one specific deep domain, which is around passive income.

Oftentimes a sort of a financial planner wishes to get certification so that they can differentiate themselves to their clients and in the marketplace. And the best place to get certification when you are a financial planner is the Certified Financial Planner Institute. This is not managed by a state or the government; it's a private company that people can take a test for and show that they've gone through the correct amount of education, and also show that they've had some time under the wings of an experienced advisor. If they pass the test and meet all the criteria, they can use the logo and the mark Certified Financial Planner® or CFP®.

Those people will have broad and shallow experience with investments, real estate, estate planning, and bank accounts, among other things. But it's going to be shallow—as opposed to an investment manager, who will specialize in one specific domain—investing. Now the financial planner knows a little bit about that domain, but the investment manager will have deeper knowledge of investments and how to generate passive income.

Investment managers that want certification will work towards Chartered Financial Analyst® (CFA®). Now I know CFA looks a lot like CFP but they are totally different. CFP usually takes one and a half to two years to earn. CFP doesn't require a college education, but it does require knowledge and practice. Oftentimes people become CFPs to help people with their general finances. On the other hand, the CFA designation is equivalent to a master's degree in investing. It takes multiple years of college with a very challenging exam. It's a high standard that tests for deep knowledge in one domain.

Now certified, investment managers can be called by many different names—investment manager is one common term; another term might be portfolio manager. You may hear "investment advisor." You may also hear "wealth advisor" or "wealth manager." Those are all terms that are reserved for people that do deep and thorough analysis on passive income and making investments.

Many investment managers are not employed by general financial services firms whereas financial planners are easy to come by in your community. An investment manager typically is going to work either in a family office for a very high net worth family, work at a hedge fund, or work for some kind of a trust or state organization that requires very sophisticated investment knowledge.

An investment manager may also practice individually, which means that they will work with people that have a lot of money that want to invest. And a financial planner generally isn't going to have a minimum to engage with them; in fact, they like clients that are just getting started and that are going to grow. Whereas an investment manager is going to typically have minimums that you have to produce in order to work with them. For example, they may require that you move a million dollars into their oversight before they will work with you.

So let's look at what these two advisors can do for you and when to engage them and add them to your team.

Financial Planners and Investment Managers

A **financial planner** is generally valuable all the time as you grow and develop wealth. They're going to look at broad financial planning topics like debt, saving, investing, estate planning, and cash management. They're going to be very good at helping you identify your goals and figure out how to make those goals possible through a combination of paying off debt, saving, and investing.

Some financial planning firms are small. This means there will be a small support staff and they will offer broad-based planning - everything from debt reduction to life insurance. Other financial planning firms are larger and the planners have direct access to other team members that have specific domain expertise. You may have a personal preference for what kind of experience you prefer and what you think you need.

An **investment manager,** on the other hand, will focus on investing. They want to understand how the money that they're investing fits into your bigger plan, and they want to see this plan so they know how to help you best. Many times, if you go to an investment manager and you don't have a financial plan of any kind, they'll send you to a financial planner to get a plan and then you come back to actually do the investing. An investment manager also has some things that they can do for you that a financial planner cannot. An investment manager can put together a very sophisticated custom-to-you portfolio of investments. A financial planner will typically buy investment portfolio models from other companies, or they develop it in house if their firm is big enough. Typically the investment models presented by a financial advisor will be simple relative to the work by an investment manager. For example, financial planners will promote a portfolio of stocks, bonds, mutual funds, exchange traded funds (ETFs)—things that you would typically be able to buy in the market.

An investment manager's portfolio will likely be different. While they do have access to all the same options as the financial planner, they also have access to more approaches. Their investment recommendation will also be more customized to your personal situation. Their investment approach will likely consider things like your business and your real estate. They won't be forced to use specific portfolio models and know how to tweak for your needs.

Just because an investment manager can create a more tailored investment strategy does not mean it will perform better. It might or it might not.

Investment managers also have access to different types of investments that a financial planner is unlikely to offer. An investment manager may be able to get you into private equity deals in your local community. They may be able to get you into opportunity zones that you wouldn't be able to enter otherwise. An investment manager can likely integrate non-traditional investments that a financial planner wouldn't know how to accommodate. For example I knew an investment manager that created a completely well-balanced custom investment portfolio for a client that only wanted to invest in women-owned businesses. A financial planner using a standard set of portfolio options would not be able to create such options.

How to Know If Yours Is Doing a Good Job

Financial services is a for-profit industry. Therefore, they should be doing what you pay them for; so then, how do you pay them, and what for?

The number-one most-common way these professionals used to get paid has been going out of style—charging a commission for every transaction. When my dad started investing (and taught me everything he could), commissions were standard. This is the wrong incentive because financial advisors who charge a commission want to do more transactions to make more money—whether or not it's in your best interest. A typical transaction rate is between 1 percent and 6 percent. Since they don't earn anything after the transaction, they have to keep making trades to keep getting paid!

The next method is a retainer, currently the most common approach. Instead of a flat monthly fee, the professional advisor charges you a percentage of what they are looking after. That way, they make more money as your investments grow. My own advisor, for example, charges 1 percent for the first million. As you invest more, the percentage on the total goes down, but the total dollar amount you pay will still go up. To put it in perspective, if you invest $5 million at 0.75 percent per year for one meeting with your advisor, that's $40,000 annually—paid monthly in twelfths. It can be expensive (some advisors even charge more, like 1.5 percent), but this kind of arrangement aligns your advisor's incentives with yours because they get paid when your assets grow!

Finally, there's the flat fee approach. "I just need a plan, but I'll handle my own investments," you might tell them, or you might pay someone an hourly rate (for example, $500 per hour) to create a financial plan. Many advisors do this, aiming to earn around $10,000 a year from a client by charging for services that you find valuable. They're just not involved in day-to-day management.

Now, are they actually doing what you're paying them for? Well, let me ask you. Does your Financial Planner/Investment Manager:

- Make you stick to the plans and strategies you agreed upon?
- Help you figure out how your investments impact your taxes long term?
- Help you select the detailed investments so that you can balance out risk over time?
- Tailor strategies to your specific financial goals?
- Report your progress toward your family goals?
- Watch your portfolio to see if it is performing in line with the benchmarks you want and adjust as needed?
- Rebalance your portfolio on some regular cadence?

We want a *yes* for each of these, obviously. And does this advisor?

- Provide consistent updates on your financial plan, your portfolio's performance, and any changes in strategy?
- Make themselves available in a reasonable timeframe and respond quickly to your inquiries?
- Explain things in a way that you can understand and relate to?

And there's more.

- Does this advisor work well with your others, so that any course of action is in line with what you've decided elsewhere?

- Does this advisor anticipate and suggest financial strategies, not just react to changes in the market or your situation?

Again, we want a *yes* to both. But there are things you can do to make your financial planner or investment manager's life easier. You can . . .

- Define your financial goals and objectives so that your advisor can develop a strategy tailored to your needs.
- Have your financial documents, such as tax returns, bank statements, investment account details, and any other relevant information on hand, and well-organized.
- Share all relevant information with your advisor, including any financial concerns or changes in your financial situation, as well as any major life events, good or bad. The more they know, the better they can help you.
- Make an effort to follow through when your advisor tells you something to do or think about. Advisors appreciate clients who take their advice seriously and act on it.
- Show up on time for meetings and be mindful of their time constraints.
- Understand that financial planning is a long-term process, and results take time. Avoid expecting immediate or unrealistic returns. Trust your advisor's expertise and be patient with the strategies they implement. Regularly evaluate progress, but understand that not everything will change overnight.
- Stay informed about financial topics relevant to your situation. A knowledgeable client is easier to work with and can engage in more meaningful discussions.
- Introduce friends, family, or colleagues. Advisors appreciate clients who help grow their practice.

The last one, of course, assumes you're happy with what they do. And if you've vetted them well, then you are more likely to stay happy.

Bringing It All Together: The Davis Family Story

Sometimes, all it takes is one more addition to your team to create synergy that empowers everyone to do what they do best. That was the case for the Davis family with Firmstride.

The Davis family operates a digital marketing company in the United States. Over the years, they built significant wealth, owning their primary residence, a vacation home, and condos in various exotic locations. Their business was stable, producing about $1.2 million per year in total taxable income. They lived a steady lifestyle which required far less than $1.2 million to support. So they had a lot of excess. While they had some investments, they primarily held the excess as cash.

They had an advisory team that included a CPA, an investment advisor managing their employees' 401(k), an estate planning lawyer, an insurance broker, and a personal assistant. But they weren't sure if these professionals were doing a good job or how to get them to work together effectively. In the prior year, their adjusted gross income was $1.3 million (profits from the business plus their W-2 wage), and they paid $292,620 in federal and state taxes.

When Firmstride first started working with the Davis family, they were like many of our clients—on autopilot, without clear financial direction or purpose. The family hadn't started out with money. As their business grew, so did their income, and with it, their sense of being out of control. They had hired professional advisors to help, but each one focused on their own area of expertise. No one was tying everything together into a comprehensive strategy for the benefit of the family.

They had two main issues. First, their finances felt overly complicated and unpredictable, and no one had taken the time to explain things in a way the family could fully understand. It's not that they were incapable of understanding, just that none of their advisors had taken the time. Second, they lacked an integrated financial plan. While their advisors provided guidance in their respective fields, it was often unclear whether the advice they received was truly in their overall best interest or just relevant to that advisor's area of focus. As a result, they didn't know if they were on track to achieve their overall family financial goals.

The most unsettling part was that they knew that they didn't know. As one family member put it,

> Before we started working with Firmstride, we were on autopilot. All our personal and household bills were automatically paid each month, including credit cards. We weren't really paying attention to how we were spending or investing. None of our advisors were asking about the other members of the team—they were just focused on their specific area. And none of them were considering a long-term vision for our family.

The first step we took together working with them was to analyze the details of their financial situation. We reviewed their business entities, tax returns, insurance coverages, investments, bank accounts, trust, will, and charitable giving patterns. We also looked at how they organized financial documents, managed passwords, and handled cash flow from their business.

Next, we interviewed the family about their goals, hopes and dreams—what really mattered to them. They shared that philanthropy and giving back were central to their long-term vision. During that very first onboarding meeting, we asked, "A year from now, when you think about your family finances, what phrase would you use to describe a feeling of overwhelming success?" One spouse responded, "Having an approach to family finances with both a short-term system and long-term vision." The other said, "Finally have organization and direction." Perfect. They came to the exact right place.

With that in mind, Firmstride developed a written plan that brought everything together—business entity structure, tax strategy, passive income investments, philanthropy, cash management, banking, insurance, and estate planning. One family member later said of this,

> The plan Firmstride delivered was wonderful because it provided a step-by-step process for working with our entire advisory team. It helped us understand what to ask and ensured we were asking the right questions to get the answers we needed.

Now that they had a clear plan, we worked with them to implement the right strategies to meet their goals. The main concerns we helped them address were reducing their tax burden, converting business cash flow into wealth-building assets, gaining a deeper understanding of their finances so they could better interact with their advisors, and developing a comprehensive vision that took all aspects of their wealth into account.

Of course, it would have been ideal to set up this foundation twenty years earlier when they started their business, but at the time, they didn't know where to turn for help. Now, we focused on prioritizing initiatives based on urgency and importance. One spouse continued running the business while the other took charge of managing financial initiatives, working with advisors, implementing the financial plan, and leading weekly check-ins with me, their family financial coach.

Weekly Firmstride check-in meetings were key. These meetings kept things moving, answered questions, and ensured the family's advisors were executing the strategies correctly. The family also had direct access to me, their coach, outside of those meetings for additional questions or concerns, just in time as they came up.

With Firmstride guidance, the Davis family successfully implemented several key projects. They restructured business entities for tax efficiency and asset protection, employed tax mitigation strategies to reduce their tax liability both short-term and long-term, resolved past tax issues and refiled previous returns to reclaim funds, and established a streamlined cash management system to improve control over cash flowing out of the business. They also reviewed and re-engaged with their financial advisor, attorney, and accountant, while creating a family digital library with a password manager for key documents (something we teach all Firmstride clients to do). The family developed an accountable plan to ensure compliance for business expenses paid by the family, invested in new passive income opportunities, and designed a charitable giving strategy to extend their philanthropy. One family member reported, reflecting on our time together,

> I loved the weekly meetings . . . I felt like I had a cheerleader in my corner, helping me navigate everything. My coach

encouraged me spiritually and personally, like a friend who truly cared about me and my family. Each week, I had a to-do list that kept me on track. The weekly meetings made all the difference because tackling finances can feel overwhelming. Knowing I had that support gave me confidence.

Today, the Davis family's finances are organized and optimized for long-term success. Their business entities are structured to minimize taxes while protecting family assets in a scalable way. They're saving about $45,000 per year in taxes, a 19 percent reduction in their tax bill, equivalent to three percentage points of their adjusted gross income. They corrected past tax returns and received refunds. Their cash now moves strategically into passive investments that will generate millions in long-term wealth. Their tax payments are predictable, eliminating financial surprises. They have a strong advisory team in place and now know how to manage and interact with their advisors effectively.

Their documented financial system ensures a smooth estate transition, reducing complexity for their children if something happens to them. Their business expenses are managed efficiently, maximizing deductions and compliance. Their passive income investments provide financial security for when they eventually step back from the business. Their giving is now intentional, with a structured approach to charitable contributions.

They're even thinking about finally writing a book on marriage and dedicating more time to church ministry! I'll close this section with a quote from our conversation-turned-case-study together, from which all of the quotes from this section come.

> I have confidence in both today and our future. Before working with Firmstride, I felt like I wasn't doing enough. Now, I understand our financial system and can explain it to others. Without a vision, the people perish. Everyone needs a vision for their financial future—covering taxes, cash flow, investments, estate planning, and advisors. Firmstride brings that bird's-eye view to ensure every aspect is in place for success. I've never seen a firm like this. Most advisors only focus on their niche. Firmstride

helps you lead your financial team and keep everything in order . . . We've already recommended Firmstride to many other business owners. Every entrepreneur needs Firmstride to achieve financial well-roundedness. Now that our finances are in place, we can finally pursue our personal goals.

God bless the Davis family.

Where Firmstride Helps Here (And Everywhere Else)

Business makes money.

You may have started your business to get extra money to feed your family, or you saw an opportunity and took it. You saw early success, and for once, you didn't have to choose what to spend your money on and go without. In fact, you could do a whole lot more now! Small things at first—some nicer clothes, an upgraded car. Then sending your kids to private school. Then taking vacations. You've got money now, and you can do more than merely survive. Your head is not just above water, it's on a yacht.

But the honeymoon soon ends.

Perhaps you weren't earning as much as you thought. Or for years you've felt like you are overpaying your taxes. Several entities are suing you over dubious claims. You thought you had good knowledge, all the little 'tricks' that would give you a leg up, but it wasn't the case—small things were overlooked, and they led to big problems. You thought you could do it on your own, but it ended up costing you and your family a lot of money and energy.

But there's a way out. As you know, I, Nick Warren, run Firmstride. It's through this business that this book was birthed. What I teach our clients directly, I've now taught you indirectly—via this book.

What is Firmstride again?

Firmstride empowers family business owners earning between $200,000 to $2 million a year to save on taxes and get their money under control. We make sure you not only spend less on taxes - we show you where you can spend for maximum positive impact on your family wealth. You'll manage your passive income, head off risk, and have enough left over to give to causes you care about.

Do not wait—request a free forty-five minute consultation with me personally at firmstride.us/meet.

And if you're not ready for that, that's just fine. Because we're not done yet anyway, with the book portion of our time together.

I've written a **Bonus Chapter** for you on an advanced yet essential topic for the shrewd business owner. It covers anonymity as a business owner so you can protect yourself, your family, and your assets from "bad actors" (and I don't mean Hollywood).

Your financial future is too important to leave to chance—or the bad luck of a bad review or bad vibes from people out to get you. Such people are real. Let me help you hide from them.

Get the free chapter by simply going to **firmstride.us/bonus-chapter** right now. It's entitled **"The Secret Chapter: Anonymity in Business and How to Hide in Plain Sight . . . Like a Movie Star."** Go to that Bonus Chapter link, and I'll send it to you right away.

Thank you for reading all the chapters in this book—so far. See you in your inbox!

ACKNOWLEDGMENTS

I would like to thank Monica, my wife and better half, who has put up with me being an entrepreneur despite my best attempts to stop. A very special thank-you goes to my dad, who taught me about money and self control. I'd also like to acknowledge Evan Pageler, our first financial advisor, who spoke truth to me and my wife and got us on the right path, and Ark Financial Group, who opened my eyes to the ministry of financial coaching.

ABOUT THE AUTHOR

Nick grew up in Ohio in a conservative home located between Columbus and Amish Country. His father was a successful mid-level manager at the local telephone company, while his mother stayed home to raise the children. Nick earned a bachelor's degree in Electrical Engineering from The Ohio State University with a focus on system integration.

He later moved to Austin, Texas, where he spent nearly twenty years as a mid-level manager at one of Fortune's Top 100 Places to Work. During this time, he gained expertise in finance, management, and leadership under the guidance of talented mentors.

In 2015, Nick left corporate America to pursue his entrepreneurial ambitions. After several failed attempts, he returned to Dell, where he gained valuable experience as a business leader. However, the entrepreneurial lifestyle continued to call him, leading him to a small financial services company where he honed his coaching skills and deepened his knowledge of advanced wealth management and tax strategies.

Nick now lives in Austin, Texas, with his wife, creating training and coaching materials for clients looking to save money on taxes and build wealth.